Mending Minds

Healing the Damage of Psychological Trauma

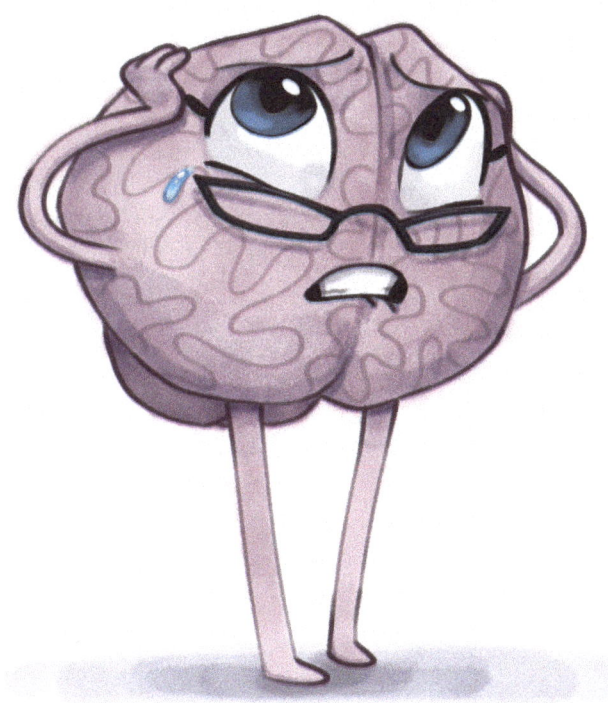

By Robyn Semple
Illustrated by Rachel Vella

Copyright © 2025 (Robyn Semple)
All rights reserved worldwide.

No part of the book may be copied or changed in any format, sold, or used in a way other than what is outlined in this book, under any circumstances, without the prior written permission of the publisher.

Inspiring Publishers
P.O. Box 159, Calwell, ACT Australia 2905
Email: publishaspg@gmail.com
http://www.inspiringpublishers.com

 A catalogue record for this book is available from the National Library of Australia

National Library of Australia The Prepublication Data Service

Author: Robyn Semple
Title: Mending Minds
Genre: Non-fiction, Inspirational

Paperback ISBN: 978-1-923449-81-7
ePub2 ISBN: 978-1-923449-82-4

My voice took years to find.
I'm keeping it.

Dedication

For survivors of grief and trauma,
those who have lost what cannot be replaced
and carry invisible scars,
know that being here is a quiet defiance.
You are not defined by what happened,
but by your strength to endure.
To feel deeply and persist is a form of courage.
To those who bear pain in silence, laugh with others,
and cry alone—
this book is for you.

Introduction

When I was 16 years old, my mother took me to an appointment with our family doctor to seek help for insomnia. I would lie awake for many hours most nights, and it was affecting my health. This was in 1979. General practitioners didn't talk much about psychological stress back then, so I was sent home with a prescription for Rohypnol. I was to take a quarter of a tablet before bed.

Rohypnol is a benzodiazepine used to treat severe insomnia and has also been utilised to induce anaesthesia. It is commonly referred to as the 'date rape' drug due to its powerful sedative properties. There was no follow-up for me, nor was there any discussion about why an otherwise healthy and active 16-year-old from a loving family struggled to sleep. This was the start of my experience with anxiety, depression, and eventually, post-traumatic stress disorder (PTSD).

When I was diagnosed with depression and anxiety 13 years later, I received vague information suggesting that chemical imbalances in my brain were responsible for what I saw as every flawed part of myself. Receiving these diagnoses brought mixed emotions; while it was relieving to know I was not 'mad,' it was equally shaming to be unwell without a clear, socially accepted cause. This led to feelings of shame, embarrassment, and perceived weakness.

I had never suffered a catastrophic, life-changing event and had never been a victim of, nor witnessed, severe violence or sexual assault (although I nursed many who had). For the longest time, I couldn't fathom how or why a privileged white woman from a caring family living in a first-world country could develop severe mental illness and suicidal ideation.

Antidepressant medication eased many of my symptoms. Until then, I had accepted frequent nausea, diarrhoea, abdominal pain, and anxiety as simply part of my life. Therapy offered further support. Yet despite these improvements, I was left wondering why I felt such deep sadness and anxiety when, outwardly, there seemed to be no clear reason for it.

Twenty-seven years later, at age 56, I finally felt well and emotionally strong enough to begin a five-year investigation into why I had been unwell for so many years. I read extensively, taking detailed notes from peer-reviewed papers, medical textbooks, and self-help books. My notes turned into this book—the one I wished I had read 40 years ago when I was a young woman dealing with undiagnosed major depressive disorder (MDD) and severe anxiety. Many years later, I was also diagnosed with post-traumatic stress disorder (PTSD) due to ongoing psychological trauma. My illnesses seemed to define my essence until I discovered that healing is possible, resilience is empowering, and life can be wonderful.

If you or someone you know is facing mental health challenges, I recommend reading this book. It explores why mental illness occurs, emphasising that there is no single cause. Since each of us has a unique genetic makeup and life experiences, our causes will be individual and genetic. The primary cause is trauma. *Mending Minds* focuses on psychological trauma, which is often imperceptible but can profoundly affect our health.

Psychological trauma results in damage to specific regions within the brain, serving as a precursor to numerous mental health disorders. The trauma doesn't need to be severe to cause harm; even mild trauma can lead to depression and anxiety if it is persistent or unavoidable. Consequently, conditions such as anxiety, depression, and PTSD are of biological origin. The pain, distress, and physical symptoms, such as headaches or diarrhoea, are tangible and scientifically validated, not merely imagined.

Psychological trauma induces stress responses within the body. When trauma is severe or persistent, the stress responses may fail to deactivate, leading to brain damage. The harm caused by psychological trauma originates internally, specifically from our stress responses; thus, healing must also be an internal process. Although this may seem challenging initially, this is good news.

Mending Minds is a book about hope and healing. It explores the development of mental illnesses and the factors contributing to individual vulnerability. It also elaborates on the available therapies and treatments, emphasises the importance of seeking professional assistance during acute episodes, and discusses strategies to develop and enhance resilience. Understanding the mind-body connection highlights the inextricable link between mental and physical health.

We can begin to heal when we understand how and why mental illnesses develop. Education empowers us to develop resilience, reduce symptoms, and regain health. This matter is of utmost importance because mental health problems are escalating rapidly worldwide, particularly in the aftermath of the COVID-19 pandemic. This pandemic created a surge in mental health issues, with many people around the world suffering from severe mental illnesses as a direct result. And unfortunately, our mental health support services and hospitals are struggling to cope with the overwhelming number of people afflicted with conditions such as depression and anxiety.

Depression, anxiety, and PTSD are the primary mental health issues addressed by *Mending Minds*, as they are the most prevalent. These conditions are all classified as disorders in The Diagnostic and Statistical Manual of Mental Disorders (DSM-5-TR). Dr. Robert Sapolsky, a professor of biology, neurology, and neurosurgery at Stanford University, considers depression to be among the most severe afflictions one can endure and refers to these conditions as diseases.

Labelling mental illnesses as diseases reinforces the understanding that psychological conditions have biological roots. While anxiety, depression, and PTSD might not be the absolute worst illnesses, they rank among the most serious. They are widespread and complex, with no simple cure available. Additionally, a significant moral judgement and social stigma still surround depression and anxiety, further compounding the deep shame already felt by sufferers.

Some people face severe hardships. They endure extreme tragedy or deep grief with remarkable resilience. While they may suffer intensely, their experiences don't always lead to long-term depression or anxiety. They cope, or at least they appear to. Conversely, some people develop severe mental illnesses from relatively minor or mild trauma. Why are some people resilient while others are more vulnerable?

Evidence suggests that genetics and the environment significantly determine susceptibility to these illnesses. A genetic predisposition supports the idea that mental health issues tend to run in families. So, if your mother, aunt, or brother has depression, for instance, you might also be at risk of developing it. Additionally, experiencing many adverse events during childhood can influence how well your brain develops and whether it forms healthy neural connections, which is essential for building a healthy adult brain.

A healthy brain is vital for developing resilience to trauma and stress. If your resilience is low, you become more susceptible to mental health issues. The nature and severity of your traumas can also influence your ability to cope. Sometimes, what seems like a 'mild' trauma is chronic or unavoidable, such as living with an abusive partner or working in a toxic environment.

My focus in this book is on psychological (emotional) trauma; it is based on my own experiences. I acknowledge that sexual assault and physical violence are among the worst traumas a person can face, especially during childhood when the brain is developing quickly. These traumas can evoke intense terror and rage, and I recognise that those who experience them often need trauma-informed professional support. Deep grief, such as losing a child, is agonising and usually needs specialised care to assist with healing.

Maintaining wellness is essential for reducing ill health, so I have included chapters on well-being. Every system in our bodies is interconnected, and growing evidence indicates that stress impacts the immune system and inflammatory processes that lead to diseases such as cancer, multiple sclerosis, and heart disease. Good physical health supports all bodily functions, including a healthy brain.

Two remarkable women allowed me to share their experiences with psychological trauma and profound grief. I am deeply grateful to Andrea and Bonnie for their trust in permitting me to include heartbreaking chapters of their lives in this book. Rachel Vella, a talented and insightful artist, created the illustrations. She captured the emotions I wished to convey with exceptional care and artistry.

Once I understood how and why I had been unwell for so many years, I wanted to share what I had learned. I experienced deep, ongoing psychological trauma that went unaddressed for years. I lacked the understanding and emotional resilience to confront the trauma; therefore, I adapted to it instead. Writing this book has been a healing experience for me on multiple levels. I am no longer a people pleaser. I recognise manipulation and toxic behaviour, and I have discovered my voice.

I hope this book might be the start of a healing journey for you and I hope it provides insight, encouragement, and hope. Healing is possible, and knowledge is power.

Let's begin.

Robyn

Trigger Warning:
This book contains sensitive content that may be distressing to some readers, including references to suicide, sexual abuse, psychological abuse, and domestic violence. Please take care of yourself while reading and proceed at your own pace. Support is available if you need it.

If you need immediate help with mental illnesses, a list of support services and phone numbers is included at the end of the book.

Healing

Step softly, restore to your former You
For the truth that was You is raw
And to stand before what was once broken and blue
And smile in awe and your soul
Sees through the lies that once tethered the pain and the rage
To the shadow of who
You could and should have been had depression not lied
Yes, depression—it lies
And so, slowly step backwards
Away from the edge
From the void, inky blackness
And hold yourself closely and gently reveal
The You—dipping a toe in the ocean called Life
And shine, oh please shine as you lift your head high
For your pain, scraped raw cleanly
Can softly recede, and quietly, list kindly
Step forward to You.

Contents

Introduction 5
Chapter 1 Unravelling the Mystery of Mental Illness 17
    Historical Beliefs 18
    General Information 18
    Why Are Mental Illnesses Linked with Emotions? 19
    What's Wrong with Me? 19
    Interconnectedness 19
    More Unfortunate Facts 20
    Hope 21
    Summary: 23
Chapter 2 Post-Traumatic Stress Disorder: The Battle Scars of Survival 24
    What is PTSD? 24
    Symptoms of PTSD 25
    The Biology of PTSD 25
    Who Is Vulnerable to Developing PTSD? 27
    How PTSD May Develop 28
    What We Know About PTSD? 29
    Living with PTSD 31
    Coping Methods 33
    Treatments 34
    Summary: 37
Chapter 3 Anxiety: Mind Over Mayhem 38
    What Is Anxiety? 38
    Types of Anxiety 39
    A Bit About the Brain 41
    General Symptoms 41
    Fear vs Anxiety 41
    Identifying Sources of Anxiety 42
    The Effects of Anxiety 42

    The Stigma of Anxiety 44
    Alleviating Anxiety 45
    Summary: 46
Chapter 4 Shining a Light on Depression 47
    What is Depression? 48
    Symptoms of Depression 48
    The Impact of Depression 51
    Causes of Depression 52
    What We Know About Depression? 52
    Who Is Vulnerable? 53
        Genetic Predisposition 53
        Experiencing Trauma 53
        Medical Conditions 54
        High Cortisol Levels 55
        Low BDNF Levels 55
    Treatments 57
    Understanding Antidepressants 57
    Summary: 60
Chapter 5 Broken Minds, Unseen Wounds:
Understanding Psychological Trauma 63
    Summary 67
Chapter 6 The Stress Response: Your Body's
Survival System 68
    The Nervous System: An Information Highway 70
        The SAM (sympathetic-adrenal-medulla) System 73
    The Endocrine System: Battling Hormonal Storms 73
        The HPA (hypothalamic-pituitary-adrenal) Axis 74
    Summary: 75
Chapter 7 The Brain: Your Personal Supercomputer 77
    Brain Regions and Their Functions 82
        Cerebrum 82
        Cerebral Cortex 83
        Glial Cells 84
        Frontal Cortex 84
        Brainstem 84
    The Limbic System: Our Emotional Epicentre 85

    Thalamus 86
    Hypothalamus 86
    Pituitary Gland 86
    Hippocampus 86
    Amygdalae 87
  Under Pressure: How Stress Affects the Brain 87
  Inundated and Overloaded 88
  Chronic Stress and the Brain 89
  Cognitive Resilience and Brain Health 91
  Summary: 92
Chapter 8 It's (Not) All in Your Head: The Gut-Brain Axis 95
  Miraculous Microbiomes 97
    What Influences Our Microbiome? 98
    Microbiome Meltdown: How Stress Impacts the Gut 99
    Improving Microbiome Health 101
    Psychobiotics: Healing Through the Gut 103
    Food for Thought 104
  Summary: 105
Chapter 9 Healing from Within: Transcending Invalidation
and Shame 108
  Repression vs Suppression 110
    Why We Repress or Suppress Emotions? 110
  Shame and Invalidation 111
    The Silent Suffering of Invalidation 111
    The Burden of Shame 113
  Emotional Intelligence and Recognising Emotional Abuse ... 117
  Healing 119
  Empowered by Resilience: Unveiling Your Inner Warrior 120
  Summary: 124
Chapter 10 Adverse Childhood Experiences:
Breaking the Cycle, From Survival to Thriving 126
  What are ACEs? 127
  Experiencing ACEs 127
  How ACEs Shape Adulthood 131
  Relevant Studies 131
  The Pitfalls of Unresolved Stress 133

Why Childhood Trauma Impacts the Brain 135
It's Not Your Fault—But It's Time to Heal...........................136
Summary:..137

Chapter 11 From Awareness to Empowerment: Navigating Toxic Personalities 138

Toxic Tactics and Traits 140
 Sabotaging Special Events...140
 Deception 142
 Tackling Workplace Toxicity 143
 Total Control and Manipulation..................................143
 Gaslighting...144
 Projection 144
 Dependent Personality Disorder 146
 Acknowledging Abuse 147
 Avoiding Conflict..147
 Setting Boundaries: Your Shield Against Toxicity...........148
 When Abuse is Hidden..149
 Understanding Personality 150
 Navigating Family Dynamics 153
From Adversity to Empowerment.......................................155
Summary:..158

Chapter 12 From Despair to Repair: Stories of Healing........161
Andrea's Story 161
Bonnie's Story..171

Chapter 13 The Healing Power of Nature.............................178
Forest Bathing...179
Key Studies 180
Nature and Mental Health 181
The Benefits of Nature 182
The Modern Disconnect...183
Where To From Here—and Why? 185
Summary:..186

Chapter 14 Movement Matters 188
A Few Interesting Facts Regarding Exercise 189
Why Movement Matters 189
Mental Health Benefits 190

The Science Behind It 194
Overcoming Barriers to Exercise 194
Don't Delay—Start Today 196
Summary: 199
Chapter 15 Namaste 201
The Origins and Philosophy of Yoga 201
Yoga for Trauma and Mental Illness 202
Trauma-Informed Yoga: Creating Safe Spaces 205
Yoga in Schools and for Children 207
Research on Yoga's Impact 208
Choosing the Right Type of Yoga 209
Summary: 210
Chapter 16 The Power of the Pet 212
Introduction to Animal-Assisted Therapy 212
   Canine-Assisted Therapy 213
   Equine Therapy: Healing Through Horses 215
   Other Animal Therapies: Cats, Dolphins, and More 219
AAT and Trauma Recovery 220
Summary: 222
Chapter 17 From Pain to Purpose: Transforming
Suffering into Strength 224
Making Good Choices 224
The Power of Tiny Changes 225
Breaking Cultural and Family Beliefs 226
Understanding Belief Systems 227
Building Resilience Through Self-Care 228
Insights from Experts 230
Healing Trauma, Breaking Cycles 233
Summary 235
A Final Word 237
Where to Seek Help (Australia) 242
For more services and information: 🔗 Healthdirect –
Australian Mental Health Services 242
Suggested Reading 243
Glossary 246
References 249
Index 262

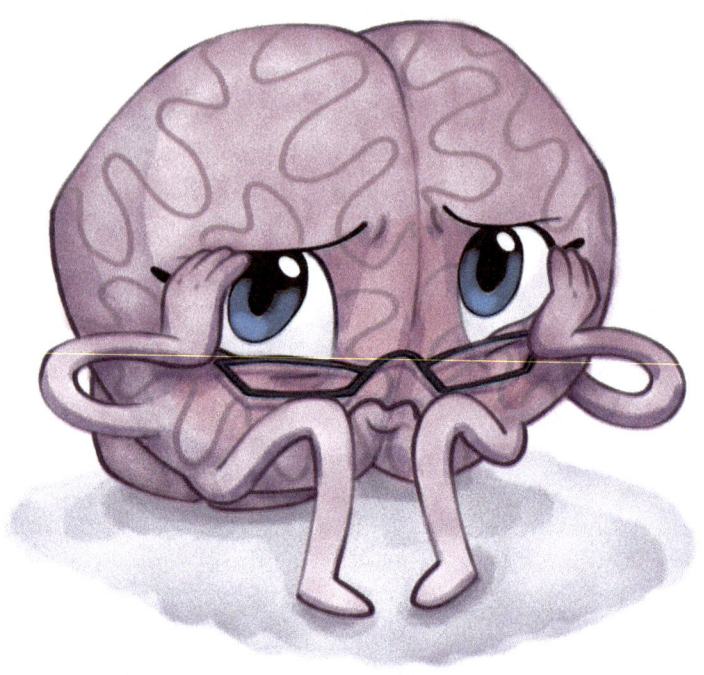

My Beast

*On my worst days, I build
high walls around my pain
to keep you safe.
I curl into my armoured shell
And fight the yearning to let you in.
On my very darkest days, the beast within me would
Flay you alive.*

Chapter 1

Unravelling the Mystery of Mental Illness

'The world breaks everyone and afterward many are strong at the broken places.'
— Ernest Hemingway, A Farewell to Arms, 1929, p. 249

Living with acute anxiety, severe depression, or post-traumatic stress disorder (PTSD) can make daily life feel like a relentless battle against sadness, fatigue, intrusive memories, a sense of impending doom, overwhelming fear, or profound emptiness. These conditions are isolating, distressing, and painful. They impact relationships and can impair your ability to work. Often invisible to others, they may go unnoticed, leaving the suffering hidden. Additionally, due to the stigma surrounding mental health, many people find it difficult to discuss their struggles openly.

If you view yourself as weak because you live with one of these illnesses, please remember this is not true. Mental health conditions are not a sign of weakness. However, living with them can be an immense challenge. The path to healing often resembles an uphill struggle marked by numerous setbacks.

Mental illness encompasses various disorders, including anxiety, depression, post-traumatic stress disorder, bipolar disorder, and schizophrenia. This chapter provides a general overview. In the following three chapters, we will explore PTSD, anxiety, and depression in greater depth. These are among the most common mental illnesses, and many individuals will experience at least one of them during their lifetime.

The Australian Institute of Health and Welfare estimates that since 2021, more than two in five Australians (44%) aged 16 to 85 have experienced a mental illness. These illnesses and other brain disorders account for over 40% of the disease burden in Australia. The World Health Organization reports that one in eight people globally lives with some form of mental illness. In 2019, it was estimated that 301 million people worldwide were living with an anxiety disorder, and 208 million with depression. While the individual suffering is often immense, the collective financial burden on healthcare systems, due to treatment costs and reduced productivity, demands urgent and coordinated responses.

Historical Beliefs

Mental illness is not a modern affliction. Writings dating back to Hippocratic times describe psychological suffering. In the past, conditions like insanity or delirium were often attributed to demonic possession or evil spirits. 'Treatments' were brutal and inhumane, ranging from toxic herbs and starvation to flogging and other vile interventions. We may never know how prevalent mental illness was in ancient times, but today it is affecting people at unprecedented rates.

> Mental illnesses are as biological in origin as diabetes, cancer, or heart disease.

General Information

The Diagnostic and Statistical Manual of Mental Disorders (DSM-5-TR), published by the American Psychiatric Association, is used worldwide to diagnose psychiatric disorders and guide treatment. It describes depression and anxiety as disorders.

A disorder refers to an impairment of normal functioning. A disease, on the other hand, has distinct, measurable signs and symptoms. While the terms are sometimes used interchangeably, they represent different medical concepts.

Why Are Mental Illnesses Linked with Emotions?

The areas of our brains most affected by mental diseases fall within the limbic system, the brain's emotional centre. This is why the signs and symptoms of mental illness often manifest in our moods and behaviours.

The limbic system includes several critical structures such as the hippocampus, amygdala, hypothalamus, and prefrontal cortex, each with specialised functions. These regions work together to regulate emotions and process complex information. (We will examine these structures in more detail in Chapter 7.)

What's Wrong with Me?

Psychological trauma induces stress, and severe or prolonged stress is one of the leading causes of mental illness. Other contributing factors include genetics, brain injuries, and substance abuse. Trauma can arise from sudden catastrophic events, such as witnessing violence or losing a loved one, or from chronic exposure to adversity, such as an emotionally abusive relationship or a toxic work environment. Regardless of the source, anxiety, depression, or PTSD may result.

This trauma damages specific regions in the brain, particularly within the limbic system. When trauma affects these areas, they may become dysfunctional. The damage is biologically real. Brain scans, such as magnetic resonance imaging (MRI), can reveal this damage, either through shrinkage or enlargement of key brain structures.

Interconnectedness

All parts of the brain are interconnected. Constant communication flows between regions. A brain cannot function efficiently when even one component is compromised. Consider a fuel-powered car with a broken fuel pump; the engine won't run. Or consider a blocked artery to the heart, which can lead to heart failure and affect blood flow throughout the body. Similarly, damage to a key region of the brain disrupts overall function.

For example, damage to the hippocampus, which can lead to cell death, impacts memory formation and learning. An enlarged amygdala, which processes fear, can lead to heightened anxiety, hypervigilance, an exaggerated startle reflex, and even aggression.

When one brain region is impaired, other areas attempt to compensate. This can lead to cognitive overload, resulting in fatigue, difficulty making decisions, and emotional distress. Symptoms such as feeling overwhelmed or unable to cope are not just emotional responses, but also biological.

If trauma-related stress is not addressed or resolved, it may evolve into a full-blown mental illness. In Chapter 6, we will examine the body's stress responses and how ongoing stress disrupts the nervous and endocrine systems. Chapter 7 will explore the specific effects on various brain regions.

When we understand how and why this damage occurs, we begin to recognise that mental illness is physical in origin. It is a biological condition, like asthma, cystic fibrosis, multiple sclerosis, cardiovascular disease, or cancer. Mental illness may present as psychological distress, but that doesn't make it less real or less severe. You can't 'snap out of' depression any more than you can 'walk off' a broken leg (well—you can, but it's dreadfully painful and not recommended).

Once we begin to understand how mental illness affects us—and why—we can finally start to unshackle ourselves from the shame and stigma we've often been taught to carry.

More Unfortunate Facts

In addition to causing changes in the brain, depression and anxiety can increase the risk of developing other physical illnesses, such as high blood pressure, heart disease, asthma, and gastrointestinal conditions. For example, depression can double your risk of developing heart disease, as dysfunctional stress hormones impact the heart's function. Furthermore, depression disrupts insulin regulation, which can lead to type 2 diabetes.

There are direct links between psychological disorders and physical diseases. Our brains are part of our bodies, so it should come as no surprise that what affects one affects the other. Anxiety and depression not only impact emotional and brain health, but they can also lead to illnesses throughout the body. This is yet another reason why mental illnesses must be treated seriously and addressed as early as possible.

Eliminating stigma and shame and normalising conditions such as anxiety and depression invite open conversation and encourage those who are unwell to seek treatment.

Hope

As grim as the previous section was (sorry about that), there is hope. Treatments and therapies for these conditions are constantly evolving. Doctors and scientists continue to explore the mysteries of the brain, uncovering new insights into genetic, biochemical, and environmental factors. Tailored treatments such as trauma-focused therapy, genetic testing, medications, and other innovative approaches are becoming more widely available to address the debilitating effects of mental illness.

Understanding how and why psychological trauma harms the brain is both empowering and healing. Knowledge is power. When we educate ourselves, we can take control of our lives, make informed decisions, and confront our challenges head-on. Every challenge we overcome builds resilience, reducing our vulnerability to psychological trauma in the future.

We may also become desensitised to people or situations that once triggered us, but this takes time. Mental illnesses usually develop over months or years, and healing is rarely immediate. Understanding why our brains are damaged begins with appreciating normal brain function, the processes of disease, and how the body's systems respond to stress.

The following chapters on anxiety, depression, and PTSD contain substantial information, especially the section on depression, which may feel overwhelming at times. Depression is a complex and emotionally exhausting illness. Understanding how it manifests and affects us is crucial to comprehending the symptoms, biological effects, and available treatments. When we know how and why depression begins, we can take meaningful steps to repair the damage.

The table below outlines the symptoms and common treatments of PTSD, anxiety, and depression.

Disorder	Symptoms	Common treatments
Post-traumatic stress disorder (PTSD)	An increased startle reflex Intense anxiety Hypervigilance Agitation/irritability Difficulty concentrating Insomnia Intrusive memories/flashbacks Emotional detachment Rage Avoidance behaviours	Trauma-focused therapy: Cognitive behavioural therapy (CBT); Eye Movement Desensitisation & Restructuring (EMDR); Prolonged Exposure Therapy (PE). Animal-assisted therapy Yoga Exercise Medications: fluoxetine, venlafaxine, paroxetine, sertraline.
Anxiety	Headaches Heart palpitations Agitation Inability to focus Insomnia Negative thoughts Overthinking Anger	Cognitive behavioural therapy (CBT) Prolonged Exposure Therapy (PE). Exercise Yoga Animal-assisted therapy Medications: sertraline, venlafaxine, escitalopram, fluoxetine, fluvoxamine
Depression	Sadness Guilt Anhedonia (loss of pleasure) Psychomotor agitation (restlessness, pacing, fidgeting) Psychomotor retardation (slowed thinking or movement) Insomnia Hypersomnia Suicidal ideation	Cognitive behavioural therapy Electroconvulsive therapy Transcranial magnetic stimulation Exercise Yoga Animal-assisted therapy Deep brain stimulation Medications: fluoxetine, venlafaxine, sertraline, citalopram, ketamine

We examine PTSD in the next chapter.

Summary:
- Mental illness includes disorders such as depression, anxiety, post-traumatic stress disorder, bipolar disorder, and schizophrenia.
- These illnesses primarily affect the limbic system, the brain's emotional centre, which explains why symptoms often relate to mood and behaviour.
- Mental illnesses are biological in origin, just like diabetes, cancer, or heart disease.
- Mental illnesses can lead to other physical illnesses, including high blood pressure, heart disease, asthma, and gastrointestinal issues.
- Understanding how and why mental illnesses develop can help us overcome them.

Chapter 2

Post-Traumatic Stress Disorder: The Battle Scars of Survival

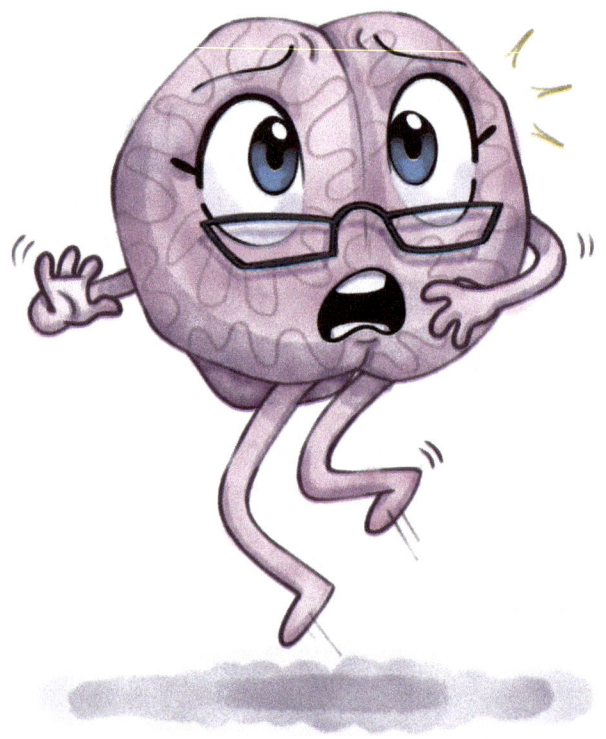

What is PTSD?

Post-traumatic stress disorder (PTSD) is a psychiatric disorder that can develop after experiencing (including witnessing) trauma that causes severe horror, terror, or powerlessness. It can occur at any age. There are two main categories of trauma: those that are 'human-made', such as war, terrorism, violent behaviour, and the like, and those that are natural, including earthquakes, major flooding, or bushfires, for example.

Not everyone exposed to deeply distressing traumas develops PTSD; some individuals are more prone to acquiring this illness than others. If you have been diagnosed with PTSD, you will be part of approximately 15% of those exposed to trauma who will develop it. You may also experience depression, as major depression accompanies PTSD in over 40% of cases. As with anxiety and depression, genetic, biological, and social risk factors are involved.

Symptoms of PTSD

PTSD is often chronic and disabling, causing intense fear and panic. If you have PTSD, you may experience intrusive and involuntary memories, dreams, or flashbacks. You may avoid situations, people, places, or objects that trigger fearful memories.

PTSD often evokes feelings of humiliation and shame, hyperarousal, including trouble falling or staying asleep, irritability, or anger. You may have difficulty concentrating, increased startle reflex, or display apparent physical distress or emotional damage—stress-induced changes to the brain cause these symptoms.

The Biology of PTSD

Witnessing or experiencing severe trauma, or living with ongoing trauma, activates our stress response systems—the nervous and endocrine systems. These systems are essential for survival, as they serve as natural defence mechanisms that respond to danger. When we perceive a threat, our bodies activate the fight, flight, freeze, or fawn reactions. Adrenaline, noradrenaline, and cortisol (our primary stress hormone) are released into the bloodstream, preparing our bodies to respond to the threat. This is a normal process, but in PTSD, the stress responses can become overactive or dysfunctional and remain 'turned on', flooding our brains with stress hormones. Each stress hormone connects and binds with specific receptors in the brain, many of which are located in the limbic system, where our emotions reside.

Regions of the brain, such as the amygdala and the hippocampus, have specific functions and are affected differently when these hormones flood the area. The table below briefly outlines the main regions and illustrates how PTSD influences each part.

Brain region	Acts like	Normal stress response	PTSD-related stress response
Amygdala	A guard dog	The guard dog barks to protect its owner from danger. Once the threat has passed, the dog stops barking.	The dog barks nonstop, even when no danger is present. The owner is constantly on edge and vigilant.
Hippocampus	A filing cabinet	Memories are stored chronologically to represent control and a sense of order.	Files are mislabelled and scattered amongst the many drawers, creating confusion and chaos. Memories are wildly dispersed with no sense of order.
The prefrontal cortex (PFC)	A negotiator	The PFC calms the amygdala and reassures the brain that everything is controlled.	The negotiator becomes overwhelmed and unable to remain calm, and the amygdala assumes control, generating fear and panic.
Thalamus	A switchboard operator	The operator transmits messages from one brain area to its required destination.	The operator feels overwhelmed, leading to messages being sent randomly to incorrect recipients.

Who Is Vulnerable to Developing PTSD?

There is no single cause of PTSD, but all cases involve the presence of trauma. If you have experienced significant life adversities, such as childhood abuse, neglect, or poverty, you may be more vulnerable to future traumas. Adverse childhood experiences (ACEs) are one of the most significant risk factors for developing PTSD later in life. Childhood maltreatment, institutionalisation, and poor living environments all contribute to chronic psychological stress, which can disrupt healthy brain development.

During childhood, the brain undergoes rapid development. Trauma during these formative years can interrupt normal development and lead to long-term changes in brain structure and function. Early exposure to trauma increases vulnerability to further trauma later in life, compounding the risk of developing anxiety, depression, or PTSD. This does not mean that everyone who experiences trauma in childhood will develop a mental illness, but the risk is significantly higher.

As with depression and anxiety, PTSD may have a genetic component. A genetic predisposition could increase your likelihood of developing the disorder. Ongoing research is investigating whether inherited changes to certain genes make some individuals more susceptible to PTSD.

Women are more than twice as likely as men to suffer from PTSD during their lifetime. Sexual assault is strongly associated with PTSD, more so than many other forms of trauma. Recent studies show that 36% of women who have been sexually assaulted meet the criteria for a lifetime diagnosis of PTSD. Women are also more likely than men to develop PTSD following physical assaults (excluding sexual assault), with the risk estimated at 32.3% for females compared to 6.0% for males. These figures are significant.

Age is another factor. Both young males and the elderly appear more vulnerable. The severity of trauma and prior exposure to trauma also influence the likelihood of developing PTSD.

Experiencing ongoing or recurrent trauma, along with suffering from major depressive disorder or other mood disorders, increases our risk of developing PTSD. Additional risk factors include the unexpected death of a loved one, severe physical assault, kidnapping, involvement in a serious car accident, and military combat.

It is increasingly understood that the development of PTSD may depend not only on the type or severity of trauma but also on the level of support available afterwards. The presence of professional care (from a psychiatrist or psychologist), community or social support, or meaningful assistance from family and friends can influence whether a person recovers—or suffers long-term consequences. Crucially, the validation of one's trauma also plays a role. If what you have experienced is acknowledged and recognised as traumatic, this fosters healing. If it is minimised or denied, the pain may worsen. We explore this idea further in Chapter 11, which examines invalidation, gaslighting, and toxic personalities closely.

How PTSD May Develop

It is normal to experience fear reactions along with feelings of helplessness and horror in response to severe trauma. The initial shock can be overwhelming, and processing what you have experienced or witnessed may take time. Hopefully, your immediate emotions will subside in intensity once your trauma has ended, and you no longer feel threatened.

If your fear remains severe after one month and includes symptoms in four categories (invasive thoughts or re-experiencing thoughts, numbing or avoidance, negative emotions, being on high alert—hyper-arousal), this may indicate a disorder.

If your symptoms are accompanied by severe distress, a diagnosis of PTSD can be made. This does not indicate a weakness on your part. It means that part of your brain has suffered physical damage as your body reacted to the horror to which you were exposed. Doctors and scientists can observe this damage through brain imaging. These are physical changes. Our feelings have biological causes, and the health of our brains influences our thoughts.

Thankfully, the brain can heal. However, from my own experience, I know that recovery from PTSD is not always complete. Despite countless therapies, I sometimes feel as if I am just one trauma away from relapse. This is why self-care is not just important—it is essential. Mental and physical well-being are both critical in building resilience.

> **Self-care is important and must be ongoing for good physical and mental health.**

What We Know About PTSD?

PTSD is often defined as an inability to regulate or suppress the ongoing recollection of trauma. Even years after the traumatic event, individuals may re-experience the same intensity of distress. The memories feel fresh, intrusive, and uncontrollable. This reactivation of traumatic memories can create the sensation that the trauma is occurring all over again.

These persistent memories reinforce the negative emotional state associated with the trauma. This hinders recovery and extends suffering. Replaying the trauma in your mind may heighten anxiety, amplify feelings of shame or fear, and lead to emotional dysregulation—the difficulty in managing emotional responses effectively.

In the acute phase following trauma, when emotions are still raw, you may find it difficult to move forward with your life. Personal and professional goals may seem unattainable. You might experience dissociation, feeling emotionally disconnected from yourself or your surroundings. Memory loss or gaps are common, and therapy is often necessary to help you recall, process, and integrate the experience.

A frequent feature of PTSD is alexithymia—a condition in which people have difficulty recognising and expressing their emotions. After trauma, it can be challenging to articulate what has happened, even to oneself. When the trauma is not verbally processed, the associated emotions remain unprocessed, trapped in the body and nervous system.

Behaviour may also become either inhibited or exaggerated as a means of coping. You might employ distraction, denial, or even humour to avoid confronting painful internal states such as fear, guilt, or shame.

Memories may sometimes be disjointed or disorganised, with eccentric thought processes attaching disproportionate justifications for how and why the trauma occurred—*I deserved it; I am a weak person; I will never recover from this. If only I had done it differently. Everyone hates me.* How we feel about ourselves before a traumatic event also plays a part. If we have poor self-esteem or have suffered through many traumas, we may have inadequate coping skills.

You might feel unsafe in a safe environment and continue to be hypervigilant, associating non-threatening signals with fear responses. This phenomenon is known as fear conditioning. Having a reduced ability to manage fear in non-threatening situations is a common symptom of PTSD. For example, a Vietnam War veteran may be triggered by the sound of a helicopter. It may take a long time to unlearn these triggers, even when knowing that the sounds no longer signify danger. Safety signal learning is a process that helps differentiate between threatening and safe situations. Psychologists who specialise in this field may be able to lessen your severe trigger responses.

Experiencing intrusive, negative thoughts that replay repeatedly in the mind can reinforce beliefs that your life is dangerous. Like anxiety, these feelings may induce agoraphobia, which can, in turn, affect your work and social interactions. Withdrawing from normal daily activities can limit social support from family and friends, potentially leading to increased feelings of detachment and avoidance. Heightened sensitivity to perceived potential dangers can inhibit your ability to process normal responses to everyday occurrences; instead, you might succumb to even minor stress by breaking down or shutting down. This phenomenon is sometimes referred to as mental defeat, with shutting down becoming a coping mechanism.

Another coping mechanism for victims of trauma is uncontrolled aggression or rage. This seems more common in men than in women because men are less likely to verbalise their distress and process their feelings. Anger and irritability are frequent symptoms of PTSD.

However, it may not always lead to aggression. You might turn your anger inward—becoming frustrated with yourself for what you may see as weakness in your inability to cope with life.

Insomnia is a well-documented issue for people living with PTSD. It may also hinder the process of unlearning fear triggers. Research indicates that 70–91% of individuals with PTSD experience sleep disruption, which can further contribute to emotional dysregulation and, at times, aggression. While insomnia is not known to cause aggression directly, sleep deprivation may lead to impulsive behaviour and difficulty concentrating. Addressing sleep issues can significantly ease PTSD symptoms.

Associated difficulties may include mood disorders, anxiety, anger management problems, depression, and even profound personality changes, especially in children exposed to prolonged trauma. Children may emotionally shut down and detach from relationships, particularly when the trauma is ongoing or unavoidable.

Living with PTSD

You may eventually learn from your trauma, process it, and move beyond it. However, for some, the experience remains etched in the brain, frequently relived in vivid and distressing ways. When this occurs, reversing the emotional impact can be challenging. Painful memories may overshadow new experiences, making learning and concentration more difficult. Hypervigilance and anxiety become the norm. You may struggle with attention, avoid certain places or people, and experience a distorted sense of reality.

You may ruminate endlessly on how you could have prevented the trauma or handled things differently. These intrusive thoughts can deeply undermine your self-belief. Self-blame—or blame directed at you by others—can amplify the pain.

Mental illnesses may not appear immediately after a traumatic event. They can emerge insidiously, sometimes years later, even when the trauma is no longer at the forefront of your mind. If the trauma hasn't been fully recognised or processed, your brain and body may revisit it without warning.

PTSD can increase vulnerability to future trauma, particularly when feelings of despair or hopelessness are present. Survivors often demonstrate reduced resilience and confidence. A classic example is a child who is bullied at school. Bullying induces shame, fear, humiliation, and powerlessness. A child who undergoes this type of trauma may avoid eye contact, seem self-conscious, and project vulnerability, which could attract further harm, even in a new environment.

Living with PTSD may cause you to restructure your life to avoid anything that could trigger distress. This often leads to withdrawal from people and activities you once enjoyed. Over time, this can increase emotional numbness, sometimes progressing from intermittent detachment to total disconnection.

Intense negative emotions distort how information is processed. You may start believing you are helpless, broken, or incapable of leading an autonomous life. Some turn to drugs or alcohol to dissociate or numb distressing emotions. While these substances may temporarily alleviate suffering, they almost always worsen symptoms in the long run.

A common emotional burden for trauma survivors is shame, not only because of what was endured but also due to feelings of being unable to cope. You may feel humiliated, helpless, threatened, and ashamed, which can alter your perception of your identity. Every area of your life—your lifestyle and relationships—can be affected.

However, social support can help lessen the impact of trauma. The first step in healing is creating a sense of safety and stability so that recalling traumatic memories doesn't re-traumatise you. Verbalising what happened is beneficial for some people in regaining psychological health. Once trauma is verbalised, the memory can be contextualised—placed in the past where it belongs. The memory may still hurt, but recognition and validation of the trauma are essential for healing. If you cannot speak about your trauma, engaging in self-care and having supportive people in your life will also facilitate your healing process.

If trauma remains unrecognised or invalidated, feelings of helplessness, anger, withdrawal, or disruptive behaviours may emerge. These are not signs of failure; they are common responses to unresolved trauma.

Coping Methods

Grounding is a therapeutic approach that helps manage flashbacks, dissociation, and emotional overwhelm. It involves using physical, sensory, or mental techniques to reconnect with the present moment.

Physical grounding may include techniques such as the 5–4–3–2–1 technique, where you identify five things you can see, four that you can touch, three that you can hear, two that you can smell, and one that you can taste. Deep breathing or splashing your face with cold water may also provide benefits.

Mental grounding helps shift attention away from intrusive thoughts and includes techniques such as counting backward from 100, listing all the cities you've visited, or describing your surroundings.

Sensory grounding includes touch (holding an object like a smooth stone or a fluffy blanket), smell (essential oils, candles, etc.), taste (eating something with a strong flavour, such as peppermint), sound (listening to nature or white noise), and sight (looking at something appealing, such as art).

Each of these grounding techniques helps calm brain activity and stimulate our parasympathetic nervous system, which is our 'rest and digest' system. They also encourage rational thoughts and break the cycle of intrusive thoughts.

Treatments

There are many treatments available for PTSD, including medications and therapy led by mental health professionals. Equine-facilitated therapy, or working with horses, is a valuable adjunct therapy (explored further in Chapter 16). Another widely used treatment is Cognitive Behavioural Therapy (CBT).

CBT is a type of psychotherapy provided by professionals such as psychologists, psychiatrists, mental health nurses, or counsellors. It helps patients understand the relationships among their thoughts, emotions, and behaviours. Therapy sessions focus on building self-awareness and developing cognitive and behavioural strategies tailored to the individual's needs.

CBT helps patients understand how to address their negative thoughts and behaviours. Therapists assess patients' symptoms, determine their mood scores through questionnaires, and develop plans to achieve specific goals. They use empathy and effective communication skills to build trust, reduce resistance to discussing the trauma, and assist their patients in confronting the negative thoughts they are experiencing.

The number of sessions required varies depending on the severity of symptoms and the patient's openness and readiness. Trust is crucial and may be difficult to establish, especially if the trauma is severe. Recalling distressing memories can be triggering, so a safe and confidential space is essential for therapy to be effective.

Psychiatrist Francine Shapiro developed Eye Movement Desensitisation and Reprocessing Therapy (EMDR) in the late 1980s. It employs guided eye movements or tapping techniques to assist in processing distressing memories. While the exact mechanisms are not fully understood, EMDR seems to aid in reprocessing trauma by gradually reducing its emotional intensity over time.

Group-based Cognitive Processing Therapy is an effective treatment that helps individuals process and recover from PTSD in a supportive group environment. Participants learn how trauma can influence their thoughts and behaviours and are encouraged to confront harmful beliefs—such as shame, guilt, or self-blame. Sharing within a group diminishes feelings of isolation and fosters a sense of community. It also provides validation by recognising that everyone's thoughts, emotions, and behaviours are legitimate. Participants are guided to understand that their distorted beliefs stem directly from their trauma and support their journey towards healing. Additionally, it empowers those who struggle to share their experiences.

Virtual reality (VR) is emerging as an effective treatment for PTSD, anxiety, and depression. Used in professional training, gaming, and fitness, VR is now integrated into the mental health sector. Computer-generated simulations enhance rehabilitation for neurological conditions such as strokes, Parkinson's disease, and brain injuries. Users are immersed in 3D virtual scenarios that can replicate real or imaginary environments.

VR is also becoming a valuable addition to traditional psychotherapies that treat mental illnesses. It establishes a safe environment for those undergoing exposure therapy, which addresses fearful situations and phobias that induce fear. Participants can engage in real-life simulations within a secure space.

Centres focusing on VR for treating mental illnesses and addressing behavioural challenges, particularly for adolescents, are opening across Australia. One such centre, called Vitalhub, has opened in Ipswich, Queensland.

VITAL stands for

Values

Integrated

Through

Action-based

Learning

VitalHub is an early intervention service that addresses the effects of trauma and mental health concerns for youth and young adults, with support from regional universities. It is a non-profit organisation founded by Russ Wright, who has over four decades of experience as a youth worker. He and his VITAL ProJex team assist disengaged young people in realising their potential by exploring their developing morals, values, and ethics through simulated scenarios, an alternative to talk therapy, thereby minimising potential re-traumatisation in troubled youth. The programmes focus on emotional and social intelligence, helping young people reintegrate into their lives and communities. These values-based immersive sessions assess character strengths and assist users:

- understand feelings
- reduce stress and anxiety
- take responsibility
- become optimistic
- develop self-control
- change attitudes and behaviour
- become more confident and engaged
- increase employability
- increase work performance.

An external evaluation conducted by Professor Peta Stapleton (Bond University, Robina) found that:

The Vital Hub program had a significant positive impact on participants' mental health and self-confidence. They appreciated the nonjudgmental and supportive environment, which differed from traditional talk therapy.

Virtual reality therapy offers a promising, innovative complement to traditional approaches. With more research, funding, and development, the future of mental health treatment appears increasingly hopeful.

As with all mental illnesses, treatments and therapies for PTSD are continually studied. Trauma is the leading cause of PTSD. Chapter 6 addresses how our bodies respond to stress. If you are enduring the intense pain of PTSD, know that there are remedies to alleviate your suffering and help you develop resilience.

Summary:

- Post-traumatic stress disorder (PTSD) arises from experiencing or witnessing trauma involving intense horror, terror, or helplessness.
- There are two broad trauma types: man-made (e.g., war, terrorism, violence) and natural disasters (e.g., bushfires, floods, earthquakes).
- Symptoms of PTSD include experiencing intrusive and involuntary memories, dreams, or flashbacks; avoidance of situations, people, places, or objects that may trigger intrusive memories; feelings of humiliation and shame; trouble falling or staying asleep; irritability or anger; difficulty concentrating, an increased startle reflex, and apparent physical distress or emotional damage.
- Stress-induced changes to the brain cause symptoms.
- There may be a genetic predisposition to developing PTSD.
- Ongoing or recurring trauma or suffering from major depressive disorder increases the risk of developing PTSD.
- People living with PTSD can feel unsafe even in safe environments—fear conditioning
- Treatments for PTSD include equine-facilitated therapy, cognitive behavioural therapy, Eye Movement Desensitisation and Reprocessing Therapy, Group-based Cognitive Processing Therapy, and virtual reality.

Chapter 3
Anxiety: Mind Over Mayhem

'...anxiety is one of the most troubling and pervasive emotions, and large numbers of people are distressed by inappropriate or excessive stress.'
— Rachman (2020)

What Is Anxiety?

Anxiety is a natural response to the anticipation of situations or events we perceive as necessary, unpleasant, or fearful, functioning like an alert system. It can help us prepare for important events by stimulating us to create agendas, establish strategies, and cultivate ideas to plan for the best possible outcome. Most of us experience anxiety regularly, worrying about upcoming tests, job interviews, or difficult conversations. This is a normal and often appropriate reaction.

Usually, once the event passes, anxiety eases—until the next challenge arises. For many people, anxiety is a manageable and even motivating force. But for others, it becomes debilitating—an overwhelming, crippling condition that infiltrates every aspect of life. It can create restlessness, difficulty concentrating, insomnia, persistent rumination, shortness of breath, and even dread.

Anxiety and depression are frequently comorbid, meaning they occur together. Anxiety is the most prevalent mental illness in Australia, with 75% of all mental health conditions involving anxiety, either alone or as part of another disorder.

You are not alone if you struggle with anxiety. Like depression, it is believed to arise from a combination of genetic, environmental, and biological factors. Physical illness, hormonal imbalances, vitamin and mineral deficiencies, and irregularities in brain chemistry can all contribute.

Types of Anxiety

The most common types of anxiety include generalised anxiety disorder, social anxiety disorder, panic disorder, agoraphobia, and obsessive-compulsive disorder.

Type of Anxiety	*Defining Features*	*Symptoms and Presentation*
Generalised Anxiety Disorder (GAD)	Persistent worry about everyday things	Feeling 'on edge' Fatigue Insomnia Racing thoughts Difficulty concentrating Muscle tension

Type of Anxiety	Defining Features	Symptoms and Presentation
Social Anxiety Disorder	Fear of social situations and being judged by others. Avoidance of social situations	Blushing, sweating, or trembling. Avoidance of meeting people, public speaking, or eating in public. Feelings of embarrassment or rejection. Difficulty participating in conversations with others
Separation Anxiety Disorder	Excessive fear of being separated from loved ones or home	Fear of a loved one being hurt. Nightmares about separation. Refusal to leave home to go to work or school
Agoraphobia	Fear of being in places that might cause panic	Fear of being alone outside the home. Fear of crowds. Fear of public transport. Fear of elevators or being in other enclosed spaces. Physical symptoms such as shaking, nausea, racing heart, chest pain
Phobias	Intense fear of specific items, situations, or activities that exceed actual danger, e.g., spiders, snakes, heights, flying, needles	Avoidance of the phobia. Acute fear when faced with a phobia
Obsessive-Compulsive Disorder	Fear of illness or contamination. Fear of being unsafe	Intrusive, unwanted thoughts or compulsions, obsessions, e.g., excessive handwashing, checking appliances have been switched off repeatedly
High-Functioning Anxiety	An anxiety that doesn't hinder productivity but still causes inner unrest, turmoil	Perfectionism. Chronic overthinking. Insomnia. Difficulty relaxing

A Bit About the Brain

In anxiety disorders, the amygdala—the brain's alarm system—becomes hyperactive and may overreact to even minor threats. The prefrontal cortex, which regulates decision-making, planning, and rational thought, may struggle to manage this heightened response, leading to persistent anxiety or lingering dread.

The hippocampus, which is responsible for processing and storing memories (especially those involving fear), works in tandem with the amygdala, prefrontal cortex, and hypothalamus. When anxiety becomes chronic, nerve cells in the hippocampus may shrink or die, impairing memory and learning.

General Symptoms

If you are experiencing anxiety, you might have symptoms such as:

- headaches
- heart palpitations
- stomach discomfort
- insomnia
- agitation, which includes hypervigilance and shaking
- psychomotor agitation, a type of restlessness characterised by behaviours like toe-tapping and pacing
- overthinking and negative thoughts
- anger.

What can begin as mild apprehension with no apparent source may be accompanied by physical symptoms such as abdominal discomfort, diarrhoea, nausea, headaches, uncontrollable shaking, or changes in breathing patterns. These bodily sensations can reinforce the belief that something is indeed very wrong, thereby intensifying anxiety. Breaking this cycle can become quite complex.

Fear vs Anxiety

Fear and anxiety are often confused. Fear usually involves a clear and specific threat, such as a venomous snake or a confined space. It can also generate irrational phobias, in which the response far exceeds the danger.

Anxiety, in contrast, is more diffuse. It may manifest as an overwhelming sense that something is wrong, even in the absence of an identifiable threat. It is often harder to articulate, resulting in hypervigilance and a vague but persistent sense of dread.

Identifying Sources of Anxiety

Anxiety becomes easier to manage when its source is identifiable. For example, anxiety during a severe storm is understandable—there is a real risk involved. However, when anxiety arises without any clear cause, it becomes more challenging to process.

You may fear new environments, disruptions to routine, or the possibility of panic attacks. This uncertainty can lead to isolation, which may evolve into agoraphobia—a fear of public or unfamiliar spaces. In extreme cases, sufferers may feel unable to leave their homes, negatively impacting work, study, and social life.

The Effects of Anxiety

Persistent fear and panic profoundly impact your ability to cope. Remaining on high alert can be exhausting, especially when there is no evident threat. Anxiety disorders drain significant amounts of energy, both physically and emotionally.

The shame of not being able to control or explain your anxiety can be just as distressing as the anxiety itself. Even when you know the fear is irrational, you may feel powerless to stop it. The Greek playwright Sophocles (497–405 BC) captured this perfectly in one line:

'To a man who is afraid, everything rustles.'

The effects of anxiety are often destabilising. As the condition worsens, it can feed off itself, creating a self-perpetuating loop of dysfunction and fear. Even mild anxiety attacks may lead to irritability and intrusive ruminations. The fear of what might occur during these episodes can destabilise your sense of safety, causing you to live in a constant state of defensiveness. This hypervigilance can result in social withdrawal and the pushing away of others as a form of self-preservation.

Fear of judgement or disapproval may also lead to frustration. You might feel compelled to justify your feelings or behaviours, even when unsure of their origin.

Anxiety can sometimes feel like the flip side of depression. It exists on a continuum, ranging from mild apprehension to full-blown panic attacks.

Mild anxiety is generally manageable. It may be irritating but can often be eased through relaxation techniques such as deep breathing, walking, listening to music, or engaging in creative activities like art therapy.

Moderate anxiety may involve increased physical symptoms such as trembling, sweating, or being easily startled. You may find yourself frozen with fear. Although you may recognise the need to manage the symptoms, engaging in calming techniques can feel significantly more challenging.

Severe anxiety is overwhelming. If you have experienced a panic attack, you will know it can feel as though you are dying. Your heart may race uncontrollably; your breath becomes shallow and rapid, and you may feel numbness or tingling in your face, lips, hands, and fingers. A cold sweat might break out across your body. In these moments, your sense of self and connection to the world around you disappears. You fear that control may never return.

I had my first panic attack in an unfamiliar shopping centre parking lot. I could not find the exit and needed to pick up my children from school. I knew the feeling was irrational. I told myself to calm down and think clearly. However, rational thinking and panic attacks exist in different realms. Despite years of treatment and medication for mental illness, I couldn't control my symptoms in that moment.

In hindsight, I now understand that I continued to suffer because I hadn't addressed the psychological trauma I was experiencing. I did not recognise the devastating impact of narcissistic personalities and manipulative behaviour in my life. Medication and therapy helped alleviate the symptoms, but the underlying cause persisted. When trauma is unprocessed, the body can remind you of it at any time. That panic attack was my body doing just that.

Panic attacks may feel unpredictable, but they often stem from past traumas and fear conditioning. Some triggers are obvious: if you have been in a car accident, for instance, driving under similar conditions may bring back the same fear. While distressing, this type of trigger is understandable—your body reacts to a memory of danger.

Other triggers are harder to identify. We sometimes bury painful memories, and our bodies later react with panic, seemingly out of nowhere. Most triggers are linked, either directly or indirectly, to trauma.

Discussing these fears with a trusted friend or psychologist can be valuable—if it is safe to do so. However, this strategy is most effective outside acute episodes. In the grip of intense anxiety, the prefrontal cortex (our rational brain) struggles to regulate the limbic system (our emotional brain). We'll explore this further in Chapter 7, which focuses on stress responses and the body's survival mechanisms.

The Stigma of Anxiety

In his book Anxiety, psychiatrist Dr. Mark Cross states that at least 11% of Australians live with anxiety-related conditions. That's approximately 2.6 million people—one in eight women and one in ten men. He differentiates between internal causes (such as genetics and inherited traits) and external factors (such as upbringing and exposure to stress).

Despite how common anxiety is, stigma and misunderstanding persist. Some people still believe it's 'not a big deal' and that we should 'pull ourselves together'. This kind of thinking is unhelpful and harmful.

Trauma alters brain function, making the fear response system overly vigilant even in safe situations. The amygdala, our brain's alarm system, becomes hyperactive, detecting threats where none exist.

The prefrontal cortex, which is responsible for rational thought, may be less effective at calming the amygdala, resulting in heightened fear responses.

The hippocampus, which plays a crucial role in processing memory, may struggle to distinguish between past and present experiences, leading to heightened confusion and fear.

Continuous trauma sensitises this fear circuitry, making the brain more reactive to triggers and slower to return to calm.

The brain also begins to associate certain sounds, smells, or sights with danger, activating the fight-or-flight response unnecessarily.

Excessive stress hormones can amplify the brain's response to even minor challenges, making daily life feel overwhelming and threatening.

Alleviating Anxiety

Some techniques and therapies can alleviate anxiety. They are simple; however, if you have been feeling agitated for some time, even straightforward remedies may be challenging. Similar to PTSD, grounding exercises may help reduce symptoms.

Breathing slowly for four seconds, holding the breath for four seconds, exhaling for four seconds, and then holding again for four seconds can be beneficial. This technique is known as square breathing. Repeating this exercise ten times can help calm the nervous system. Other remedies include medication, deep breathing, mindfulness, yoga, animal-assisted therapy, leisure time, and emotional processing therapies. These will be examined in Chapters 13–16.

If you're struggling to manage acute anxiety symptoms, allow yourself time and seek support. Sharing your feelings with trusted family and friends is a good first step. Unfortunately, it's not a quick fix. Anxiety typically develops over many years and is often a gradual, insidious process. It cannot be 'cured' quickly, so recognise the small steps you take to alleviate it.

Summary:
- Anxiety and depression are often comorbid—they occur together.
- Anxiety is the most common mental illness in Australia.
- Anxiety disorder is destabilising and debilitating.
- The fear centres in the brain become overactive during anxiety.
- Anxiety can range from mild, moderate, or severe.
- Anxiety is caused by genetic makeup, damage to regions within the brain, changes in hormone levels, deficiencies in some vitamins and minerals, trauma, and other physical illnesses.
- Symptoms of anxiety include headaches, heart palpitations, agitation, inability to focus, insomnia, negative thoughts, overthinking, and anger.
- Anxiety can be managed with medication and therapies.

Causes of anxiety:
- genetic make-up
- abnormalities in the brain
- chemical imbalances
- variations in hormone levels
- deficiencies in some vitamins and minerals
- other physical illnesses

Symptoms of anxiety:
- headache
- heart palpitations
- abdominal discomfort
- agitation—shaking, hypervigilance
- psychomotor agitation—anxiousness, restlessness, including pacing, toe-tapping
- inability to focus
- insomnia
- negative thoughts
- overthinking
- anger

Chapter 4
Shining a Light on Depression

'The defining symptom of depression is a biochemical, genetic, and environmental disorder where you can't appreciate sunsets, where you lose the capacity to feel pleasure. This is the core symptom, anhedonia.'
— *Sapolsky (2015b)*

What is Depression?

Depression is a severe medical disorder characterised by both physical and emotional symptoms—fatigue, sadness, loss of self-worth, and a diminished ability to function. It can present as mild, moderate, or severe, and symptoms vary greatly from person to person. It is complex, multi-faceted, and often deeply misunderstood.

If you are suffering from depression, know this: it lies. If your brain tells you that you are worthless, unlovable, loathsome, or that everyone would be better off without you, this is depression talking. Depression lies. You are not weak, nor are you mad.

Although the symptoms manifest emotionally, depression is a physical illness that affects the limbic system in the brain, the region responsible for emotions. This is why symptoms are expressed through mood.

Symptoms of Depression

Depression can erase your self-esteem, confidence, and even your will to live. It may leave you unable to get out of bed, or it may manifest through unexplained physical complaints—stomach pain, headaches, migraines, muscle tension, or loss of libido.

One of the most distressing symptoms is anhedonia—the inability to feel pleasure. Not only can you no longer experience joy, but you also can't recall what it felt like.

Even thinking becomes exhausting. This is known as psychomotor retardation. You struggle to move. Basic self-care becomes challenging. Tasks that once felt simple—choosing clothes, deciding what to eat, or understanding a conversation—can feel insurmountable. Motivation fades.

If left untreated, these symptoms may develop into major depressive disorder (MDD)—a potentially lifelong condition. It sounds grim because it is, but do not lose hope. Although there is no definitive cure yet, depression is largely treatable. Many people live fulfilling lives with treatment and support.

Depression is often accompanied by grief, guilt, and the crushing weight of stigma. Despite the well-established medical understanding that depression is a physical illness, a moralistic judgement still lingers. This adds another layer of suffering.

When I was first diagnosed with depression and anxiety, I felt a sudden wave of shame. I berated myself for what I perceived as weakness. I could not cope, even though others around me seemed to manage fine. Being prescribed antidepressants brought both relief and disappointment. The medication helped ease my suffering, but needing it felt like proof that I was somehow broken.

I had no understanding that what I was experiencing was a biological illness. In the early 1990s, knowledge about mental illness was still trickling into public discourse. Mental health was not something we spoke about—certainly not at social gatherings. It was taboo. If discussed at all, it was in whispers. I often heard people say, 'She has nerve troubles.' I became one of those people. I hid my condition, pretended I was fine, and spent what little energy I had trying to appear 'normal'.

One of my most visible symptoms was being on the verge of tears; therefore, I avoided conflict by people-pleasing and retreating from social contact. Covering up despair was exhausting. Many of my interactions with others remained superficial because I was too embarrassed to let anyone see the pain I felt. Humour became a shield—a curtain on my stage.

I did not know that the physical symptoms I was experiencing—muscle aches, tinnitus, blurred vision, sore throats, chest tightness, exhaustion, diarrhoea—were part of my illness. I was caring for a toddler and a new baby at the time. 'Self-care' was not a concept we discussed. As young mothers, we were expected to just carry on. Mental health was barely acknowledged, let alone supported.

Depression is a strange illness. It is often insidious—it slowly envelops you. It is frequently described as 'brain fog', which makes it harder to concentrate and make decisions. The debilitating symptoms can creep up on you, and you may be quite ill by the time you recognise you need treatment.

As it worsens, physical symptoms become more pronounced. Limbs begin to feel heavier, and movements become slower. Confidence wanes, making it nearly impossible to make once-easy choices.

Initially, the loss of joy is subtle. You may continue to smile, work, and engage in conversations. You seem present. However, depression is often invisible. It quietly erodes your well-being.

Our bodies often sense illness before we do. However, we misattribute the signs, blaming them on life stress, parenting fatigue, or work pressure. We continue to function, albeit with less energy, clarity, and emotional capacity.

We go through the motions—raising children, paying bills, maintaining friendships—but we do so in a disconnected, almost automated way. It becomes performance, not presence. Sometimes, we are so removed from ourselves that we no longer feel we are living—just existing.

In his book, *The Noonday Demon: An Atlas of Depression*, Andrew Solomon describes his experience with depression using the analogy of a vine that has wound itself around a massive oak tree and grown so immense that it is almost smothering the tree. *It was hard to say where the tree left off and the vine began.* Solomon felt that his depression was like the vine that had grown around him, sapping his energy and causing his very being to slowly disintegrate. *If my trunk was rotting, this thing that fed on it was now too strong to let it fall; it had become an alternative support to what it had destroyed.* Depression had depleted every semblance of his being, and he no longer had the energy to combat it. Even if he were to overcome the depression, his very essence had weakened so severely that there would be little left of him. His depression (the vine) was all that supported him. He speaks of the agony of suffering depression, the treatments available, along with side effects and his fear of experiencing another debilitating major depressive attack. This vine analogy illustrates how powerful the symptoms of depression can be and how challenging they are to manage.

The *Diagnostic and Statistical Manual of Mental Disorders* (DSM-5-TR) classifies major depressive disorder (including major depressive episodes), persistent depressive disorder (dysthymia), depressive disorder due to another medical condition, and other specified and unspecified depressive disorders under the umbrella term of depressive disorders. It states that standard features of these disorders include sad, irritable, or empty moods, which are accompanied by physical and emotional changes in the body.

Major depressive disorder (MDD) is the most common of these disorders. If you have been diagnosed with MDD, this diagnosis is based on your experiencing at least two weeks of depressive symptoms. If you have experienced MDD for at least two years as an adult or one year as a child, it is considered persistent depressive disorder, which is a chronic form of MDD.

The Impact of Depression

Depression is the leading cause of disability and lost productivity worldwide, surpassing even cancers, coronary artery disease, and strokes. Consequently, extensive research is being conducted to develop more effective treatments and, ideally, a cure.

In 2020, an additional 53.2 million cases of depression worldwide were linked to the COVID-19 pandemic. Because depression is such a complex illness with many diverse symptoms and varying degrees of distress, diagnosing its causes remains challenging despite extensive research.

The brains of people who are depressed are generally less active than usual. This has been confirmed by magnetic resonance imaging (MRI) and supports the symptoms of lethargy, lack of joy, and excitement experienced in depression. It's important to remember that the effects of depression can be seen—it's a physical, biological illness. You are not mad. You are not imagining your symptoms. Doctors can see the damage to brain regions using brain imaging studies. By examining brain activity and other biological markers (molecules that indicate normal or abnormal processes), along with determining individual symptoms, doctors can formulate the most effective treatments for each patient.

> Depression lies.

Causes of Depression

The causes of depression vary. Genetic susceptibility is one cause; this is an inherited factor that may increase your likelihood of developing depression. Environmental influences also play a part. If you suffer a loss or encounter a stressful event without a safe outlet to process what has happened, or if you feel a lack of control or predictability, you may struggle to manage these stressors well. When you perceive your situation as worsening or have little social support, continued exposure to stress in these circumstances can lead to depression.

If a situation is ongoing and inescapable (consider domestic abuse), stress levels remain heightened, resulting in hypervigilance, an exaggerated startle reflex, and anxiety. Melancholia or extremes of psychological stress can lead to depression, which can, in turn, create a pathological intensity of your feelings.

Once we understand that general health, genetic makeup, and circumstances influence how we react to trauma, we can appreciate how one person can experience intense trauma and recover from it relatively unscathed. Conversely, another individual who has had the same experience (or even milder circumstances) may develop severe depressive symptoms.

> *'A major depression is amongst the worst diseases anyone could suffer.'*
>
> *— Sapolsky, 2015b.*

What We Know About Depression?

The individual causes of depression are uncertain as they can vary from person to person. It is believed that there is no single cause of depression; instead, it arises from a combination of biological, psychological, neurochemical, hormonal, and genetic factors. Stress plays a significant role, yet it does not explain why some individuals respond differently to the same stress, why some appear resilient, and why others may break. It is a complex issue.

There are two primary types of depression: unipolar and bipolar. Unipolar depression does not include episodes of unusual euphoria or mania, while bipolar depression is characterised by fluctuating highs and lows. Women are twice as likely as men to experience unipolar depression, whereas bipolar depression affects men and women equally.

Who Is Vulnerable?

Genetic Predisposition

Research estimates that up to 40% of the risk for major depressive disorder is inherited. This may explain why depression runs in families and why two people experiencing the same trauma may react differently.

Just as specific gene mutations (like BRCA1 and BRCA2) can increase the risk of cancers, researchers believe that genetic variations can also raise the risk of depression and other mental illnesses. However, possessing these genes does not guarantee illness—it merely elevates the odds, especially when combined with environmental stressors.

Professor Avshalom Caspi from Duke University identified variations in the serotonin transporter gene (SERT) as a potential risk factor. Individuals with altered versions of this gene are more susceptible to depression after experiencing trauma or prolonged stress.

In a large-scale study involving 135,458 individuals with depression and a control group of 344,901 persons, researchers identified at least 44 gene variants associated with an increased risk. These findings are assisting scientists in uncovering the biological basis of mental illness and moving closer to more targeted treatments.

Experiencing Trauma

Trauma experienced in adulthood—whether physical, psychological, or sexual—increases the risk of developing mental illness. Often, a combination of genetic predisposition and environmental exposure contributes to conditions like depression.

Importantly, trauma does not have to be extreme to create an impact. Even mild but persistent stress can trigger the body's stress responses. A toxic work environment, for example, can lead to daily anticipatory anxiety. If you wake up with a sense of dread each day, your stress systems may activate before you even leave the house.

Anticipating a distressing event—a difficult conversation, an upcoming appointment, or an unresolved conflict—can be as emotionally damaging as the event itself. Living in a sustained state of dread or helplessness offers little time for recovery, allowing depression to build silently, layer by layer.

Adverse Childhood Experiences (ACEs) are strongly associated with lifetime mental health disorders, including mood disorders, conduct disorders, psychoses, and personality disorders (see Chapter 10). Childhood trauma and family dysfunction are linked to dysregulation, cognitive distortion, and in some cases, violent behaviours.

Childhood traumas include neglect, abuse, bullying, or witnessing violence. Family dysfunction can lead to cognitive distortion (exaggerated or irrational thought patterns) and an inability to accurately process what is happening around you.

Natural disasters, including flooding, earthquakes, and bushfires, can generate emotional instability, panic, a sense of loss, and grief. The devastation wrought by these events can be overwhelming and disorienting. War zones and communities exposed to violence, terrorism, pandemics, and even extreme weather abnormalities may experience ongoing trauma responses that contribute to mental illnesses.

Medical Conditions

There are medical conditions that can induce depression and anxiety. For example, untreated hypothyroidism, characterised by decreased production of thyroid hormones, is associated with anxiety and depression, while untreated hyperthyroidism, characterised by increased production of thyroid hormones, is associated with depression. It is essential to test these levels to rule out hormonal abnormalities.

Living with chronic pain may increase your risk of developing depression, as can suffering from medical conditions such as diabetes, arthritis, and multiple sclerosis. Heart and kidney diseases, cancer, and inflammatory bowel diseases, such as Crohn's disease, may also increase your vulnerability to developing depression.

High Cortisol Levels

Cortisol is the body's primary stress hormone, released from the adrenal cortex, which is the outer layer of the adrenal glands located above the kidneys. It plays a central role in activating our fight, flight, freeze, or fawn responses (see Chapter 6). In healthy individuals, cortisol levels should return to baseline after the stressor has passed.

However, chronic or severe stress can lead to consistently elevated cortisol levels. This prolonged exposure may harm areas of the brain—especially those involved in regulating emotions and memory—increasing the risk of depression and anxiety.

Steroid medications (e.g., prednisone), often prescribed for asthma, eczema, arthritis, or autoimmune conditions, can also elevate cortisol levels. Long-term use must be closely monitored, as it can trigger or exacerbate depression. If steroid therapy is necessary, it is essential to monitor mental health alongside physical health.

> There are many causes of depression. Some are genetic, some are environmental.

Low BDNF Levels

Brain-derived neurotrophic factor (BDNF) is a neurotrophin, a protein that aids in the development, function, and survival of neurons. Neurons are nerve cells that transmit messages throughout the body. BDNF is an essential neurotrophin during foetal brain development and continues to be produced by the adult brain. It is vital for the growth and survival of new brain cells, and it aids in learning and memory.

Neurons receive and relay information throughout our bodies. Neurotrophins support neurons and ensure they survive and function correctly. Different types of neurotrophins exist, each with unique properties and purposes. BDNF is one of the primary neurotrophins. If our neurons are not healthy, our brains cannot function properly; therefore, maintaining their health is essential.

Whether there is a direct association between low levels of BDNF in the body and major depressive disorder is being investigated. Low levels of BDNF have been observed in individuals who suffer from chronic stress, depression, major depressive disorder, bipolar disorder, anxiety disorders, schizophrenia, and those who exhibit suicidal tendencies. Additionally, reduced BDNF levels have been linked to Alzheimer's disease, Huntington's disease, Parkinson's disease, multiple sclerosis, obesity, and accelerated aging.

BDNF levels can be measured through blood testing. Low levels in the blood may aid in diagnosing mental illnesses; therefore, BDNF levels may serve as beneficial markers, indicators that may reveal the presence of diseases. BDNF levels increase after certain antidepressant treatments, which may suggest a connection between BDNF and mood disorders.

BDNF levels also increase with exercise, which helps maintain brain health. Activities such as yoga, walking, mindfulness, and psychotherapy can help reduce stress and raise BDNF levels. This will be explored in more detail in Chapter 14.

> Low levels of brain-derived neurotrophic factor (BDNF) are associated with depression. Exercise can increase BDNF levels.

Treatments

Treatments for depression continue to evolve. Advances in diagnostic imaging, medication, and digital health tools are improving clinicians' understanding and management of mental health illnesses.

From smartphone apps that support self-care to cutting-edge interventions like deep brain stimulation, treatments are becoming increasingly tailored to individual needs. Genetic studies are aiding in the identification of predispositions, and newer medications strive to minimise side effects while enhancing efficacy.

If your current treatment isn't effective, or if you feel hopeless, know that research is ongoing. Often, a combination of therapies produces the best results. Healing takes time, and your journey may require adjustments along the way. Collaborating with empathetic, skilled professionals can lower relapse risk and support long-term recovery.

Understanding Antidepressants

Antidepressants have been used to treat depression since the 1950s, when a drug called iproniazid (synthesised from isoniazid) was administered to treat tuberculosis and was found to enhance mood. This was the first of the monoamine oxidase inhibitors (MAOIs), which slow the breakdown of the neurotransmitters dopamine (DA), noradrenaline (NA), and serotonin (5-HT). These are our 'feel good' chemical messengers, so slowing their degradation in our brains improves our moods. New MAOIs were subsequently developed and used clinically to treat depression about a decade later. Two types of MAOIS are available in Australia (phenelzine or Nardil and tranylcypromine or Parnate). They are not used as the first drugs of choice for depression, as they can cause serious side effects; however, they may be prescribed to patients with treatment-resistant depression where other drugs are ineffective.

Next came the tricyclic antidepressants (TCAs). These block the reuptake of dopamine, noradrenaline, and serotonin, preventing their reabsorption. This increases their ability to transmit signals across nerve pathways, improving emotional regulation.

Neurons do not physically touch; there is a tiny space between each one called a synapse. (We examine synapses and nerves more closely in Chapter 6.) When a drug blocks reuptake, it allows neurotransmitters—chemical messengers such as dopamine, noradrenaline, and serotonin—to remain in the synapse longer, increasing their uptake by the next neuron. The more of these 'feel-good' messengers transmitted, the more our moods can improve.

Imipramine (Tofranil), amitriptyline (Endep), clomipramine (Placil), and nortriptyline (Allegron) are still used in Australia; however, they are not the first choice for treating depression due to the potential for various side effects.

By the 1970s, selective serotonin reuptake inhibitors (SSRIs) were being developed. These drugs solely block the reuptake of serotonin, increasing serotonin levels in the body. They have minimal effect on noradrenaline or dopamine. Compared to earlier medications, they have fewer side effects and are safer to use. Examples of SSRIs available in Australia include citalopram (Celepram), escitalopram (Lexapro), fluoxetine (Prozac), fluvoxamine (Luvox), paroxetine (Aropax), and sertraline (Zoloft). Although these drugs can cause side effects, they tend to be milder and of shorter duration.

Serotonin and noradrenaline reuptake inhibitors (SNRIs) were developed in the 1990s. These drugs inhibit the reuptake of serotonin and noradrenaline and have fewer side effects than tricyclic antidepressants (TCAs). Available SNRIs in Australia include venlafaxine (Effexor-XR), desvenlafaxine (Pristiq), and duloxetine (Depreta).

There is a growing interest in the use of ketamine and esketamine (a derivative of ketamine) for treating depression. Ketamine works differently from traditional antidepressants—it targets glutamate, a neurotransmitter involved in learning and memory and affects the glutamatergic system.

Originally used as an anaesthetic, ketamine has been found to produce rapid antidepressant effects, sometimes within a single day. It also significantly reduces suicidal ideation, making it a promising option for treatment-resistant depression; in some cases, it is as effective as electroconvulsive therapy (ECT).

However, ketamine is classified as a Schedule 8 controlled drug in Australia due to its addictive potential, and its use must be carefully monitored. The Therapeutic Goods Administration (TGA) has recently approved esketamine as a nasal spray; however, at the time of writing, it is not yet licensed for the treatment of depression. Doctors must follow strict guidelines when prescribing esketamine for treatment-resistant depression or patients at high risk of suicide.

Antidepressants can be lifesaving and life-changing. Some individuals may need them only for the short term, while others require lifelong treatment. Despite the lingering societal stigma, antidepressants are no different from medications for pneumonia, diabetes, or heart disease.

Refusing antidepressants for a legitimate illness based solely on stigma is like refusing antibiotics for an infection. If your doctor recommends antidepressants, it deserves serious consideration, particularly when combined with psychological therapy, which further enhances outcomes.

In later chapters, we explore adjunct therapies (e.g., exercise, mindfulness, nutrition, and animal-assisted therapy).

The table below summarises the most common types of antidepressant medications.

Type of Antidepressant	*Process*	*Medications*
Monoamine oxidase inhibitors (MAOIs)	Slows down the breakdown of the neurotransmitters dopamine (DA), noradrenaline (NA), and serotonin (5-HT)	phenelzine or Nardil and tranylcypromine or Pirate

Type of Antidepressant	Process	Medications
Tricyclic antidepressants (TCAs)	Blocks the reuptake of DA, NA, and 5-HT	Imipramine (Tofranil), amitriptyline (Endep), clomipramine (Placil), and nortriptyline (Allegron)
Selective serotonin reuptake inhibitors (SSRIs)	Blocks the reuptake of serotonin	citalopram (Celepram), escitalopram (Lexapro), fluoxetine (Prozac), fluvoxamine (Luvox), paroxetine (Aropax), and sertraline (Zoloft)
Serotonin and noradrenaline reuptake inhibitors (SNRIs)	Inhibits the reuptake of serotonin and noradrenaline	venlafaxine (Effexor-XR), desvenlafaxine (Pristiq), and duloxetine (Depreta)
Ketamine	Targets glutamate and glutamatergic system	esketamine

Summary:

- Depression is a severe disorder that is characterised by emotional and physical symptoms, including fatigue, sadness, intense guilt, self-injury, loss of libido, anhedonia (the inability to feel pleasure) and feelings of worthlessness.
- Doctors can see changes in the brains of depressed people.
- Depression is a severe disease and the main contributor to disability and lost productivity worldwide.
- Causes of depression vary and include genetic, epigenetic, and environmental influences. Epigenetics is environmental and behavioural influences that can change how much information our genes express; our DNA does not change, but positive or negative experiences can affect how genetic information is passed to the next generation.
- There is a 40% heritability for developing major depressive disorder.
- People who experience trauma, including physical, sexual, or psychological, are at risk of developing depression.

- Childhood trauma and family dysfunction are linked to depressive disorders, inappropriate emotion regulation, and violent behaviours.
- Natural disasters and violence can generate depression.
- There are medical conditions that can induce depression and anxiety.
- Hormone deficiencies and low levels of serotonin, noradrenaline, and dopamine can generate depression.
- Depression can be managed with medications and therapies.
- High levels of our primary stress hormone, cortisol, can lead to depression and anxiety. This can include taking steroid medications.
- Low levels of brain-derived neurotrophic factor (BDNF) are linked to those who suffer chronic stress, depression, major depressive disorder, bipolar disorder, anxiety disorders, schizophrenia, and those who display suicidal tendencies.
- Depression causes changes in communication between the limbic system and the brain's frontal cortex.
- There is increased activity in the hypothalamic-adrenal-pituitary (HPA) axis, which controls how we react to stress.
- Above all: depression lies. It distorts your sense of self and reality—but it is treatable.

What happens in the body?

- Changes in the levels of neurotransmitters such as serotonin, dopamine, and noradrenaline.
- Changes in communication between the limbic system (where emotions reside) and the pre-frontal cortex in the brain (responsible for decision-making, planning, and behaviour).
- A reduction in neuroplasticity—the ability of nerve cells within the brain to adapt and change connections and behaviour.

- Increased activity in the hypothalamic-adrenal-pituitary axis (HPA axis) causes high levels of the main stress hormone, cortisol, to flood the brain and body. The HPA axis controls how we respond to stress. Sustained activation prevents cortisol levels from returning to normal, causing damage to regions in the brain.
- Increased levels of inflammation throughout the body, which may be chronic and may cause Alzheimer's Disease, asthma, heart diseases, arthritis, Type 2 diabetes, and other autoimmune conditions.

What emotions and symptoms do these changes create?

- Sadness
- Guilt
- Anhedonia—the loss of the ability to feel pleasure
- Psychomotor agitation—anxiousness, restlessness, including pacing and toe-tapping.
- Psychomotor retardation—slow thinking, slow body movements.
- Insomnia
- Sleeping too much
- Suicidal thoughts or ideation

Chapter 5

Broken Minds, Unseen Wounds: Understanding Psychological Trauma

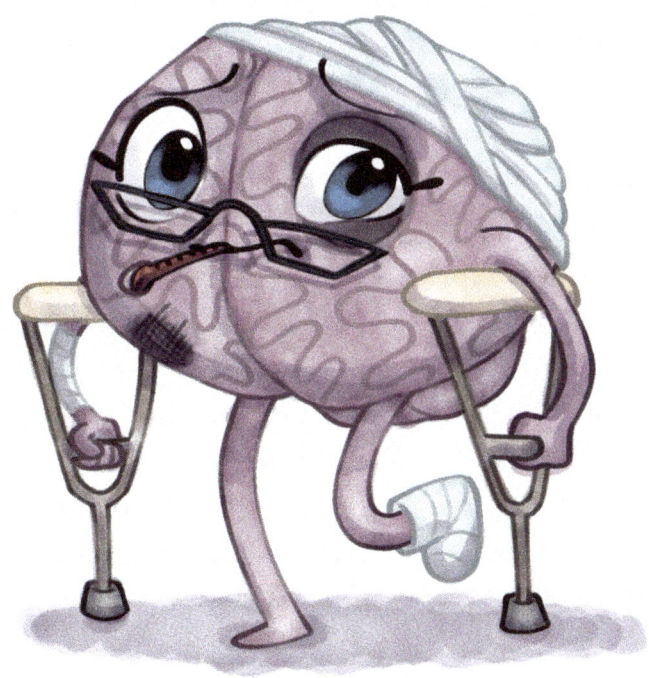

In the medical world, trauma often refers to physical injuries—broken bones, blood loss, or damage to vital organs. This is physical trauma, and it is easy to understand because we can see or imagine the harm done. In contrast, psychological trauma is a less visible form of injury—emotional damage arising from within the body in response to distressing or frightening situations.

You are not mad. This trauma can cause biological changes within the body, which may be as damaging as physical trauma.

Some may be caused by a single incident, such as witnessing violence, or the trauma may be inescapable or chronic situations, such as domestic abuse or a toxic workplace environment. It is important to note that the trauma does not have to be significant, such as being involved in armed conflict, suffering sexual or physical abuse, or experiencing a natural disaster. Bullying, humiliation, shame, or invalidation can all generate psychological distress, as can bereavement, neglect, relationship breakdowns, and other conflicts.

Trauma activates stress responses from our bodies' stress response systems. These responses are normal. They are protective networks to shield us from harm and promote survival. The body is designed to respond to stressful situations by increasing heart rate and improving blood flow to muscles, such as when we need to outrun danger or fight for survival. It then returns to a state of normality, or homeostasis, once the stress has passed. Problems can arise if the stress is ongoing, severe, or inescapable, and these stress responses do not 'turn off'. The body is bombarded by stress hormones, that circulate through our bloodstream and flood specific regions of the brain.

Excessive stress hormone saturation can damage these brain regions, affecting normal brain functioning, including how the brain processes the information it receives. This can continue long after the stress has passed. It's as if the brain's filters become distorted, leading to the ongoing activation of survival responses. It can create irrational thoughts and hypervigilance. It can also lead to suppressing or an inability to discern your feelings.

If stress is left untreated, brain cell death or changes in cell function can occur in specific brain structures. Our brains comprise different regions, each with a distinct function. All areas are connected; therefore, damage to one region disrupts its normal functioning and affects the rest of the brain. For example, damage to our fear centres (amygdala) can make them hyperactive, resulting in magnified fear responses. Our fear centres become more effective in doing what they are meant to do if they are constantly being activated. It is like exercising a muscle, and it becomes stronger.

This results in difficulties making rational decisions, as our thinking brain regions are affected by damage to our fear-based structures. A heightened startle reflex is a typical example: leaping in fright at the slightest touch or responding to sudden, loud noises. We react disproportionately because we've not processed a situation correctly or constantly feel agitated or on high alert. These stress reactions can be managed with a combination of therapies, but may not ever be entirely resolved. Treatment will vary for each individual and may be ongoing. Fortunately, scientists are slowly unravelling the mysteries of the brain and how it functions, with treatments and therapies expanding and adapting to this evolving knowledge.

What generates intense stress in one individual may not have the same effect on another. What creates such differences in resilience and vulnerability? Does our genetic makeup or personality determine how well we manage adversity? Are we influenced by our life experiences—the challenges we've faced or the suffering we've endured? Research suggests that all play a role.

Human beings have fundamental emotional needs. These include the need to be acknowledged, understood, loved, appreciated, accepted, respected, valued, trusted, and supported. When these needs are not met, we can experience psychological stress. The impact of stress on individuals is complicated and varies from person to person. We will be affected differently because we are unique in our genetic make-up and lived experiences.

> **Problems occur when our stress response systems don't turn off.**

Challenges such as altered sleep patterns (as experienced in those who do shift work), death of a loved one, financial worries, childhood adversities (childhood sexual abuse, poor parenting, death of a parent), dealing with a person with a personality disorder (particularly a family member, or a person in a senior position where there is an unequal power balance), suffering physical trauma (e.g. car accident), emotional abuse, or distress caused by chronic or acute illnesses can all cause anguish, horror, and helplessness.

> **Mental illnesses can be treated. Don't lose hope.**

Each of us will experience trauma. Trauma can destabilise our resilience and vulnerabilities. How we cope with trauma depends not only on our personalities and genetic makeup but also on our resilience. Our genetic makeup and life experiences shape our resilience, how well we can adapt to changes in our circumstances, how much support we have during difficult times, and our vulnerability. How vulnerable we are is influenced by our ability to recognise our emotions, accept why we are experiencing them, and learn how to validate our thoughts.

> **Trauma causes stress;**
> **how our bodies respond to stress can make us sick.**

Developing or improving resilience can be life-changing and empowering. Understanding how psychological trauma can cause biological damage to our brains is essential for planning therapeutic and restorative remedies. Once we appreciate that the damage to our brains is biological, we can forgive ourselves for what we may have thought was a weakness of character. Once healing begins, wellness can follow.

Healthy Brain	Adverse childhood experiences
Conflict resolution	Past traumas
Being believed	Exposure to abusers
A sense of justice	Invalidity
Developing good coping skills	Being disbelieved
Support from family and friends	Humiliation
	Shaming

Summary

- Psychological trauma is internal hurt generated from within the body in response to frightening or distressing situations.
- Trauma causes a stress response.
- The leading causes of trauma are physical, sexual, and psychological. They include violence, serious accidents, natural disasters, the death of a loved one, and man-made disasters.
- Stress responses are normal.
- The stress response causes physical changes in the body.
- Severe or ongoing stress can cause damage to the brain if our stress response systems don't 'turn off'.
- Managing stress responses depends on our genetic makeup, our vulnerability to past exposures to adverse life experiences, and our resilience.
- Each of us can develop resilience.
- When we understand how psychological trauma can damage our brains, we can forgive ourselves for what we may perceive as weakness.

Chapter 6

The Stress Response: Your Body's Survival System

In this chapter, you will learn how the human body and brain respond to stress, and how this can generate depression, anxiety, and PTSD in some people. While the information may seem dense, the core message is empowering: our brains can heal. Our brains can often repair and rewire themselves even when injuries or illnesses have caused damage. This knowledge encourages us to take ownership of our healing and to maintain our overall well-being.

The brain is a complex network of interconnected structures, each with its vital functions. These parts work in harmony, and a disturbance in one can send ripples through the others. This chapter introduces the systems involved in stress responses, explains how they can become stuck in the 'on' position even after danger has passed, and describes what we can do to support the restoration of normal, healthy functioning.

Stress is a normal part of life, and our bodies are equipped to respond to it. Trauma that leads to severe or chronic stress activates our usual stress responses, which may contribute to mental illnesses. Our understanding of this process is still evolving. Most of us didn't learn how our bodies react to stress because, until recently, science had not fully grasped it. Gaining insight into how the human body and brain respond to stress and how depression, anxiety, and PTSD might arise is empowering.

The human body has built-in threat detection systems that protect us and those around us. You've likely heard of the "fight, flight, or freeze" response. Today, we also acknowledge a fourth response: fawn—a trauma response where individuals appease others or become submissive to avoid conflict. This often emerges as a coping mechanism in situations of chronic stress or unsafe relationships.

For example, if you were raised in a household with a parent prone to volatile outbursts, you may have learned to 'walk on eggshells' to stay safe. Over time, this survival strategy may become ingrained, leading to people-pleasing, difficulty in setting boundaries, or an over-prioritisation of others' needs at the cost of your own. While it might have protected you in the past, this fawning response can erode your sense of self and cause lingering stress—unless it is recognised and healed.

Stress can be physical or psychological. Our brains trigger stress responses in seconds and are not consciously controlled. Understanding how your body responds to stress—and recognising the undeniable connection between mind and body—reinforces the idea that what affects your mind also impacts your body.

As we know, psychological stress can originate from trauma, memories of trauma, lack of emotional support, physical or mental illnesses, previous life experiences, genetics, and environmental factors. Coping strategies include support from family, friends, and medical professionals, positive interactions with animals, exercise, a healthy diet, medication, meditation, therapies, and time.

Two systems in the body are responsible for the stress response: the autonomic nervous system and the endocrine system. Both are controlled by a structure in the brain called the hypothalamus (the Master Gland). The hypothalamus is located deep in the brain, below the thalamus (hypo means below), and near the pituitary gland. It is part of the limbic system within the brain. (We will address the limbic system shortly.) Despite its small size (the size of an almond), it has many essential functions. Its main functions are to connect the autonomic nervous system and the endocrine system and control the functions of each system.

The hypothalamus links and coordinates the autonomic nervous and endocrine systems, maintaining homeostasis. Homeostasis refers to the body's ability to maintain a stable internal environment despite external influences. When the hypothalamus receives information from the body, it can 'switch on' or 'switch off' the required responses. The information is known as feedback. This feedback encompasses chemical messages transmitted by the brain and nerve cells throughout the body. These nerve cells are part of the peripheral nervous system, transmitting information between the brain and the rest of the body.

The peripheral nervous system responds to signals from both external environments, such as temperature and touch, as well as internal environments, including blood pressure and digestion. There is constant communication within the body to manage all the processes required to keep all systems functioning and stable. This occurs outside of awareness. Understanding a little about the nervous and endocrine systems helps demystify what happens when exposed to stressful situations.

> The hypothalamus in the brain links our two stress response systems—the nervous system and the endocrine system.

The Nervous System: An Information Highway

The nervous system consists of the brain, spinal cord, and all nerves throughout the body. It enables all parts of our bodies to communicate with each other through electrical and chemical messaging. Nerve cells (neurons) create pathways throughout our bodies, linking our brains and spinal cords (central nervous systems) to all other parts (peripheral nervous systems).

The Stress Response: Your Body's Survival System

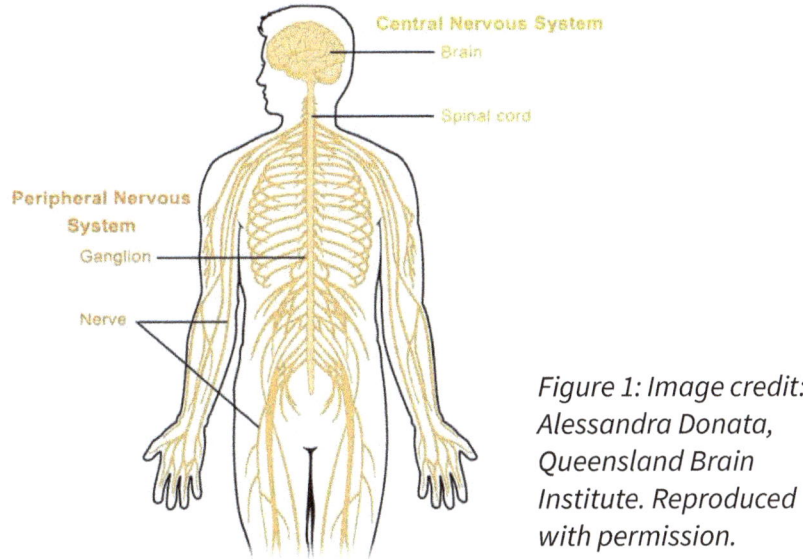

Figure 1: Image credit: Alessandra Donata, Queensland Brain Institute. Reproduced with permission.

The nervous system is easier to understand when organised by function, as shown in the diagram below. Some parts of our nervous system are voluntary, meaning we can control functions such as moving our limbs; others are involuntary, meaning they occur automatically, often outside our conscious awareness. This includes processes like digestion, for example.

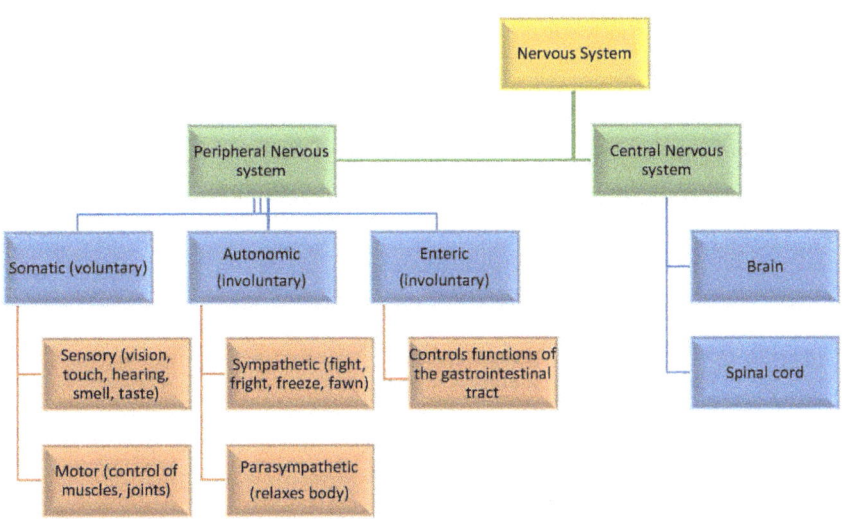

Figure 2: Organisation of the Nervous System

Communication between neurons regulates everything our body does. Electrical impulses transmit signals along the nerves from one part of the body to another at high speeds. Some communication is under our control, such as movement (controlled by the somatic nervous system), while much occurs outside our control (controlled by the autonomic nervous system).

Stress responses are regulated by our autonomic nervous system (ANS). The autonomic (automatic) nervous system controls and coordinates the functions of organs, including digestion, excretion, heart rate, pupil dilation, and constriction. We have no control over this system; it operates outside of our awareness as intended. It is divided into the sympathetic nervous system, the 'fight, flight, freeze, or fawn system', and the parasympathetic nervous system, the 'rest, digest, and relax system'.

The sympathetic and parasympathetic nervous systems have opposing functions and work together to maintain normal bodily function. The sympathetic nervous system stimulates, while the parasympathetic nervous system relaxes.

When a threat is perceived, such as encountering an aggressive person or nearly stepping on a snake, signals travel to the brain's fear centre (the amygdala). The amygdala alerts the hypothalamus, which then initiates the stress response. These responses are designed to prepare our bodies and keep us safe from threats. They begin with increased adrenaline and noradrenaline. Adrenaline and noradrenaline are released into the bloodstream by our adrenal glands, providing our bodies with extra energy to manage stress while elevating our heart rates and blood pressure.

You may recognise this as an adrenaline rush—that intense moment when your heart pounds, palms sweat, and your body tenses. Once the threat has passed, these hormone levels return to normal if the stress response system is functioning properly.

This system is often referred to as the SAM system: Sympathetic–Adrenal–Medulla system—our body's first line of defence against perceived threats. The diagram below illustrates the cascade of reactions in our body.

The SAM (sympathetic-adrenal-medulla) System

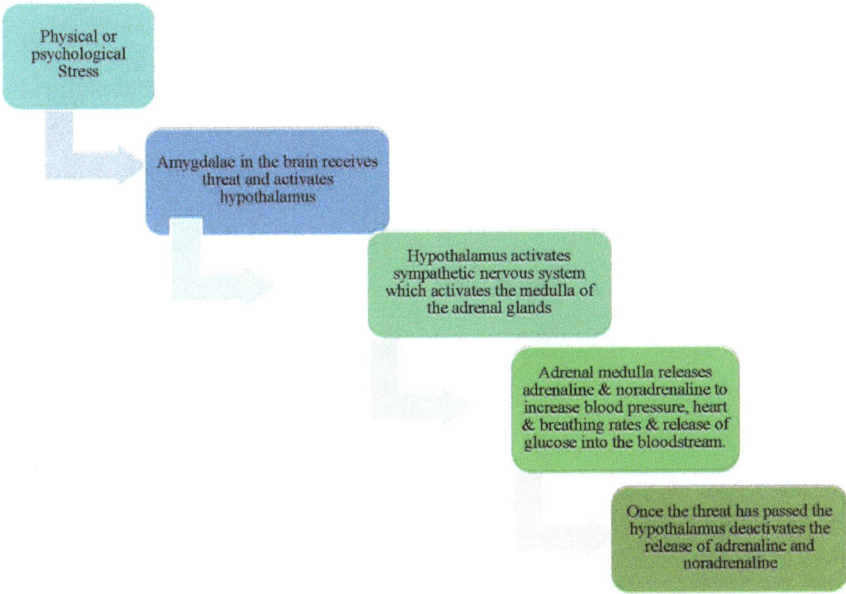

> The amygdalae in the brain are our fear response centres.

The Endocrine System: Battling Hormonal Storms

The endocrine system is our second line of defence against stress. It consists of a network of glands that produce hormones—chemical messengers that help regulate growth, metabolism, puberty, appetite, fertility, and mood. These hormones are typically released in small amounts and travel through the bloodstream to target areas.

When we experience stress, our bodies quickly activate this system to produce the main stress hormone: cortisol.

Within microseconds of activating the SAM system, the hypothalamus signals the endocrine system to release cortisol via the hypothalamic–pituitary–adrenal (HPA) axis. This system, along with the SAM system, responds to various types of stress, including climbing stairs, navigating traffic, preparing for a job interview, or fleeing danger.

These systems are essential for survival. The hypothalamus, though only the size of an almond, plays a critical role by regulating adrenaline, noradrenaline, and cortisol levels in the bloodstream. It enables us to respond to daily challenges and return to balance once the threat has passed.

This diagram illustrates how our second stress response operates.

The HPA (hypothalamic-pituitary-adrenal) Axis

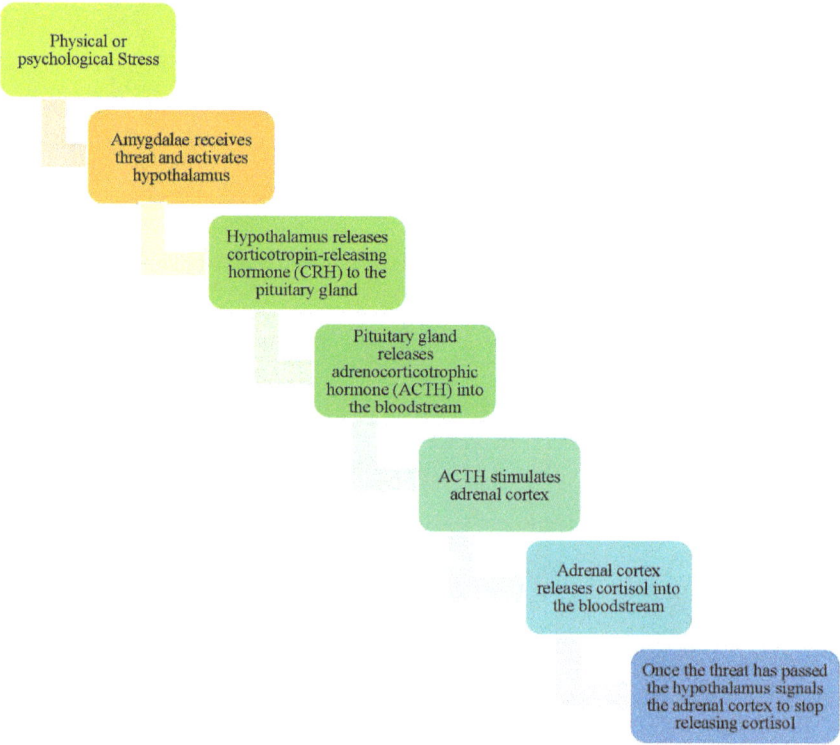

Every new challenge, whether large or small, generates stress. Stress, in itself, is not bad—it's normal, and our bodies are designed to respond to it. Our stress response systems are regularly activated, shaped by thousands of years of evolution.

In prehistoric times, the fight-or-flight response helped humans evade predators or react to physical danger. Today, stressors may include looming deadlines, toxic relationships, or overwhelming social media exposure, but the physiological responses remain largely the same.

When our bodies function properly, our stress-response systems work in perfect harmony, enabling us to rest and digest while facing challenges in our daily lives. However, when the body's systems are overwhelmed by stress, they become unbalanced, leading to the manifestation of mental illness. Chronic or severe stress ultimately harms the brain, disrupting the delicate systems' ability to function effectively.

To understand how stress affects the brain, it is essential to have a basic understanding of the brain, including how it functions, how the limbic system regulates emotions, where memories are stored, and the processes involved in responding to stimuli. We will study the limbic system and the brain in the next chapter. By understanding how trauma damages the brain, we can learn how mental illnesses develop.

Summary:
- Our bodies have two main stress response systems—the nervous and endocrine. These built-in detection and response systems protect us and help us survive.
- The nervous and endocrine systems are linked and controlled by a brain structure called the hypothalamus.
- The hypothalamus maintains homeostasis (internal balance) by switching on or off responses from the nervous and endocrine systems.
- The nervous system comprises the brain, the spinal cord, and all nerves throughout the body.
- Messages are sent throughout the body by electrical impulses along nerves.
- The first stress response is through the sympathetic nervous system (fight, flight, freeze, or fawn).

- Messages are sent to the hypothalamus from our fear centres in the brain—the amygdalae.
- The hypothalamus signals our adrenal glands (medulla region) to release adrenaline and noradrenaline into the bloodstream to respond to stress. Once the stress has passed, the blood levels of adrenaline and noradrenaline return to normal. This is called the sympathetic-adrenal-medulla (SAM) system and is our first stress response.
- The second stress response system is the endocrine system, the network of glands that release hormones. The hypothalamus signals the endocrine system very soon after activating our SAM response.
- The hypothalamus signals the pituitary gland by releasing corticotropin-releasing hormone (CRH). The pituitary gland responds by releasing adrenocorticotropic hormone into the bloodstream, which travels to the cortex of the adrenal glands. The adrenal cortex releases our primary stress hormone, cortisol, into the bloodstream. Once the threat has passed, cortisol levels return to normal.
- Stress is normal, and our bodies are designed to respond to it.

Chapter 7

The Brain: Your Personal Supercomputer

The brain is immensely complex. Despite the advent of advanced technologies such as magnetic resonance imaging (MRI), computed tomography (CT), and positron emission tomography (PET) scans, much of its inner workings remain mysterious. It is the most intricate organ in the body, composed of over 100 billion neurons—specialised cells that receive and transmit information at incredible speeds.

Neurons communicate with the rest of the body and with one another. Each brain region has its own distinct population of neurons, which work together to support thought, emotion, behaviour, and function.

Our brains grow and develop rapidly in the first few years of life. In infancy, nerve connections, or synapses (links between individual neurons), can form at rates of millions per second. How well the brain develops depends not only on genetic influences but also on environmental conditions. Nerve connections are stimulated in positive and happy environments, but some critical structures can shrink if stress hormone levels are high in a developing brain. What we experience in our early childhood shapes our brains.

An easy way to understand how the brain works is to imagine it as having three separate regions: bottom, middle, and top. Dr. Paul Maclean, an American physician and neuroscientist, explained his theories on how the brain evolved using what he called the Triune Brain (tri = 3). This model is helpful for gaining a basic understanding of how the brain functions.

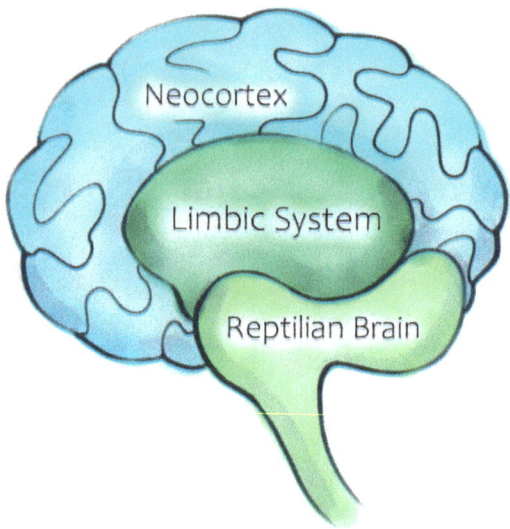

Figure 3: The Triune Brain

The base of the brain is what Dr. MacLean called the Reptilian Brain. This part of the brain is our instinctive and reflexive area—it runs on autopilot and is where information from parts of our bodies enters the brain via the spinal cord, nerve pathways, and blood vessels. This area is responsible for survival and controls functions such as consciousness, heart rate, blood pressure, breathing, and digestion. It is also responsible for maintaining homeostasis, or normality, within the body. Additionally, it regulates reflexes such as coughing, vomiting, and swallowing. It includes the brainstem, cerebellum, and spinal cord.

Sitting atop the reptilian brain is what Dr. MacLean termed the Paleomammalian Brain/Mammalian Brain. This area is now known as the limbic system and is responsible for emotions (a simple explanation). It is where habits and memories reside, decisions and judgements are made, and a sense of purpose and duty exists. Relationships and feelings are centred here and can be communicated into thoughts when sent to the upper part of the brain, called the neocortex.

The neocortex is the thinking brain. It is responsible for rational thought, imagination, abstract thinking, logic, problem-solving, and language. This part of the brain enables us to plan, weigh options, and navigate complex social situations.

When information enters the brain through the brainstem, it travels to a region in the limbic system known as the thalamus, functioning like a complex switchboard or major relay station. The thalamus processes the information and forwards it to the neocortex, where it can be processed and addressed accordingly.

The thalamus in the brain is like a switchboard, sending information where it needs to go.

The information travelling through nerve pathways in the brain relies on chemical messengers known as neurotransmitters. These allow all areas of the brain to communicate with one another. Neurons send signals through these electrical delivery systems. Neurons consist of three major parts: a cell body, dendrites, and axons. Dendrites receive messages from other cells, like an inbox, while axons transmit messages, acting as an outbox.

Neurons are not physically connected; instead, there is a microscopic gap between each one known as a synapse. Neurons 'speak' to each other by sending and receiving neurotransmitters across the synapses that separate them. This process occurs continually and at great speed. Neural pathways crisscross and connect various brain areas, allowing the billions of neurons to function simultaneously. This interplay enables us to feel, think, and process many things at once.

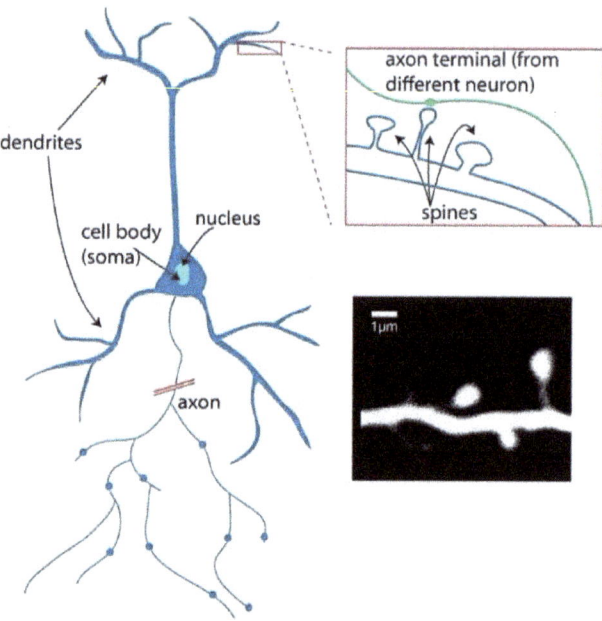

Figure 4: A neuron. Dr Alan Woodruff, Queensland Brain Institute. Image reproduced with permission.

Different types of neurons utilise specific neurotransmitters. Examples of these neurotransmitters include glutamate, dopamine, noradrenaline, serotonin, and histamine. Each neurotransmitter has corresponding receptors to which it binds, akin to a round peg fitting into a round hole. Receptors receive and transmit signals to cells.

Considering that a healthy brain contains approximately 100 billion neurons of various types, which send messages, create memories, and generate actions, it's unsurprising that much of the brain remains a mystery. This also clarifies why mental illness is so challenging to treat. It is important to recognise that while different parts of the brain have specific roles, they do not operate independently of one another; rather, they communicate and function collectively, often simultaneously.

Although most neurons are formed before birth, some parts of the brain, including the hippocampus, can generate new neurons (neurogenesis)—a function once thought impossible in an adult brain. These stem cells were discovered in parts of the adult brain only in the 1990s. They can form different types of neurons, and this neurogenesis occurs during periods of new brain cell growth when the brain is healthy and functioning properly. Therefore, we are aiming for healthy brains.

Understanding that the brain can regenerate damaged areas encourages us to manage and maintain our wellness. Regular exercise, adequate sleep, a balanced diet, staying mentally active, and learning to cope with stress all contribute to brain health.

Another fantastic feature of our brains is their ability to form new pathways and grow new connections by reorganising structures within them in response to trauma, such as damage from a head injury or a stroke. This phenomenon is called neuroplasticity. Neuroplasticity refers to the brain's capacity to modify or adapt to changes occurring either intrinsically (within the body) or extrinsically (in the environment). It's adaptable.

It was once believed that an adult brain could not change, but it is now recognised that our brains can form new pathways or reorganise to shift functions from a damaged part to an undamaged area. This enables some individuals who have suffered brain injuries to recover over time. The brain can also change due to learning or experiences. When we learn or encounter new things, we create new connections within our brains. Our brains are in a constant state of change and adaptation.

Neuroplasticity demonstrates that the brain is not static but a dynamic and adaptable organ. This remarkable adaptability enables the brain to rewire itself, even after facing trauma or injury, enabling the recovery of lost functions. For example, stroke survivors can regain mobility through consistent physical therapy exercises, illustrating how new neural pathways can compensate for damaged ones.

The brain undergoes similar physical changes as we develop resilience and emotional regulation. This gives us hope that the harm from psychological trauma does not have to be lasting—we can heal from past traumas and build resilience, effectively preparing ourselves for future challenges.

We can enhance neuroplasticity by continuously learning new things, exercising regularly, practising meditation and mindfulness, ensuring adequate sleep, eating a healthy diet, and surrounding ourselves with kind and supportive people.

Understanding that our brains can heal themselves can motivate and inspire us when we feel discouraged that good mental health is beyond our reach. The brain is a remarkable organ. We will examine some of its regions to gain a better understanding of their anatomy and how they work together.

Brain Regions and Their Functions

Cerebrum

The cerebrum is the largest region of the brain, comprising over 75% of its volume. It is divided into two hemispheres: left and right. These hemispheres communicate via the corpus callosum, a thick band of more than two million nerve fibres.

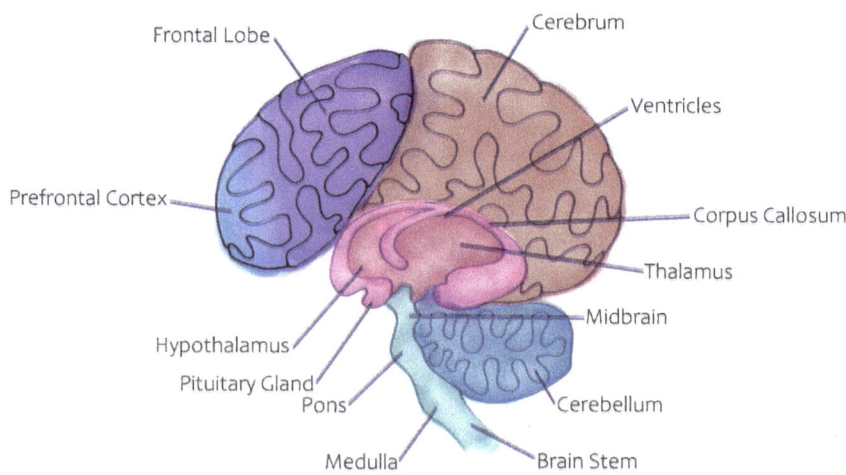

Cerebral Cortex

A thin, grey layer covers each hemisphere of the cerebrum, called the cerebral cortex. This layer is responsible for higher brain functions, including conscious sensations (awareness of something), abstract thought processes (creativity, organising thoughts, storytelling, etc.), reasoning, planning, working memory, voluntary muscle movement, and other similar higher mental processes.

The cerebral cortex contains 14–16 billion neurons and sends and receives messages to and from other areas of the brain. Some of these messages are sensory, such as what we have seen or heard and how we are feeling, while others are motor messages that instruct our bodies on how to move (voluntary movements) and provide awareness of those movements.

The grey colour comes from the nerve cell bodies (also known as grey matter). Beneath this layer lie structures of white matter—nerve fibres called axons coated in myelin, a fatty substance that insulates them and facilitates rapid signal transmission.

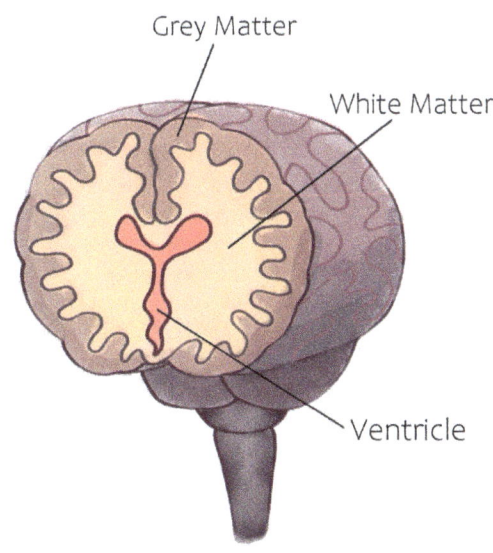

Glial Cells

Myelin is produced by a specific type of brain cell known as oligodendrocytes, which are one of the four main types of glial cells in our brains. Glial cells are a type of nerve cell in the nervous system that do not generate electrical impulses. Their primary functions include:

- providing structural support to neurons
- insulating neurons with myelin
- supplying nutrients and oxygen
- removing pathogens (disease-causing organisms)
- assisting in neuron repair and maintenance.

Frontal Cortex

The frontal cortex is one of the four lobes of the cerebrum and is the last part of the brain to develop fully. It is located at the front of the brain, just behind the forehead. Since this region of the brain continues to develop until around the age of 25, any trauma experienced before it has fully matured can influence its overall health. Consequently, adverse childhood experiences can impact brain health.

The front region of the frontal cortex is referred to as the prefrontal cortex (PFC) and is generally viewed as part of the limbic system. The PFC is responsible for thought processing, decision-making, personality, behaviour, differentiating between good and evil, self-control, planning, and problem-solving. This has been partially determined through brain imaging techniques, such as MRI scans.

The cortex is believed to receive information from other areas within the brain and use it to plan actions, communicating with different brain regions to execute a response. Brain imaging studies of individuals suffering from depression show a significant decrease in activity in the prefrontal cortex.

Brainstem

The brainstem is located at the back of the brain and connects the brain to the spinal cord. It consists of three main sections: the mesencephalon, pons, and medulla oblongata. The brainstem serves as a conduit for information passing between the brain and the spinal cord. It regulates movement, pain modulation, autonomic reflexes, consciousness, and arousal.

The neurotransmitters serotonin, noradrenaline, and dopamine are produced in specific areas of the brainstem. Together with the cerebellum, the brainstem forms the hindbrain. This region coordinates vital functions such as heartbeat and breathing and acts as the gateway to the brain.

The Limbic System: Our Emotional Epicentre

The limbic system in the brain is responsible for automatic behaviours (innate behaviours that do not require learning, such as survival instincts and maternal instincts), deep-seated emotions, basic impulses, motivations, relationships, memories, and behaviours. This system includes the thalamus, hypothalamus, pituitary gland, hippocampus, and amygdala. These areas, along with the prefrontal cortex, play a significant role and are impacted by mental illnesses such as anxiety and depression.

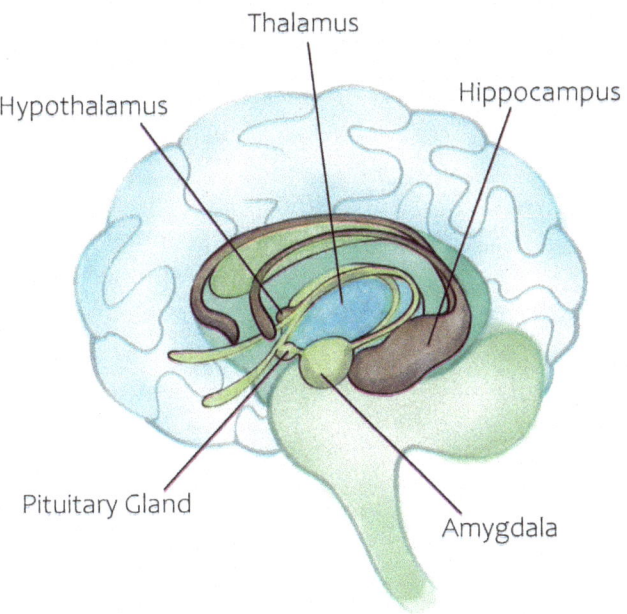

Figure 5: Structures of the Limbic System

Understanding each structure in the limbic system allows us to comprehend how trauma leads to mental illness.

Thalamus

The thalamus consists of two symmetrical, oval-shaped clusters of grey matter located centrally in the brain—one in each hemisphere. It functions as a hub, processing and transmitting sensory input (except smell) from the spinal cord and brainstem to higher cortical areas. The thalamus regulates consciousness, sleep, and alertness and helps coordinate, plan, and initiate movement. Specific cells in the thalamus connect it to other structures in the limbic system.

Hypothalamus

The hypothalamus is located below the thalamus and plays many varied roles in conscious behaviour, emotions, instincts, attention, learning, mood stability, and emotional control. We have learned that it regulates and connects the autonomic, nervous, and endocrine systems. The hypothalamus receives signals from various brain areas, including the cerebral cortex and the peripheral nervous system. It contains cells that produce and secrete hormones.

Pituitary Gland

The pituitary gland hangs from the hypothalamus by a stalk. When the body needs hormones released, the hypothalamus signals the pituitary gland, which in turn releases the necessary chemical message to the relevant gland. Once hormone levels in the bloodstream are optimal, the pituitary gland ceases its signalling to the gland.

Hippocampus

Memories are formed and stored in the hippocampus. The word "hippocampus" comes from the Greek word for "seahorse," which describes its shape. Two lobes, one in each hemisphere, sit deep in the brain. This is one of the brain regions where adult neurogenesis occurs. Neurogenesis is the process by which new neurons are formed in the brain. Learning and memory tasks help stimulate neurogenesis. Cells in the hippocampus exhibit a high degree of plasticity, meaning their experiences can shape them and strengthen their connections with repeated use.

Amygdalae

The amygdalae (singular amygdala) are almond-shaped clusters of neurons located next to the hippocampus. They play a significant role in our emotional responses, including feelings such as pleasure, fear, anxiety, and anger/aggression. The amygdalae attach emotional content to our memories and are crucial in forming new memories. It is believed that the amygdalae are responsible for anxiety disorders, functioning as a relay station for fear-related behaviours.

Our brains are unique and complex. They serve as the command centres for our bodies. Our skulls protect our brains from external injuries. Learning how psychological trauma can damage them internally helps us consider the most effective treatments and therapies. Understanding why we struggle with memory loss, chronic hypervigilance, sadness, and anxiety facilitates our healing.

Under Pressure: How Stress Affects the Brain

Any traumatic experience triggers the release of high levels of adrenaline, noradrenaline, and cortisol from the adrenal glands. If the trauma is severe, ongoing, or inescapable, our stress responses react accordingly, and the releases may be continuous.

Consider a person subjected to psychological trauma, such as bullying or humiliation at work, or who is a victim of domestic abuse. The stress keeps recurring and is likely to persist. This can result in ongoing releases of cortisol, adrenaline, and noradrenaline without respite; the brain never gets a chance to rest and recover.

Trauma leading to stress inundates the brainstem with a barrage of information, causing survival instincts to kick in. We enter the fight, flight, freeze, or fawn state. This also occurs when those suffering from acute anxiety or post-traumatic stress disorder recall unpleasant memories and perceive the trauma as still being present. If stress levels don't return to normal, regions within the brain can be damaged by the constant presence of stress hormones, as can other areas of the body.

Prolonged exposure to high levels of adrenaline can increase the risk of heart issues, while noradrenaline imbalances are linked to depression and PTSD. Interestingly, those living with chronic PTSD may sometimes show lower cortisol levels—a paradox that remains under investigation.

Inundated and Overloaded

Remember that the brain has nerve pathways that quickly relay information to all its parts. During stress, the brainstem sends continuous messages to the limbic system, which activates our emotions, such as fear, anger, humiliation, and shame. The thalamus contacts the neocortex to report on the stress, and this thinking and rationalising part of our brain tries to process what is happening and how we should best respond.

It then instructs the limbic and survival systems on the most suitable actions. This sounds reasonable and controlled, but when the information is sent to the thalamus (the switchboard), it takes a shortcut straight to the amygdala (our fear centre) before reaching the thinking brain.

The amygdala can react and make snap decisions before the neocortex can make an informed or rational judgement. Consider how quickly we recoil when we are about to step on a snake! Then, our brain suddenly tells us it's just a garden hose. This all happens at incredible speeds, of course. Our amygdalae instruct us to react to what we initially think is a snake, and then logic (aka our neocortex) kicks in, allowing us to realise it's just a hose.

Whenever we witness an overreaction, it is because someone's amygdalae have jumped in to protect them from a threat before their neocortex can reassure them that everything is okay. Road rage is an example. Minor incidents with another driver can be amplified if our amygdalae react before the neocortex determines that the incident is insignificant. Family conflicts can also explode out of control in the same way. Our brains are designed to protect us from harm, but when our fear centres are constantly triggered, this can lead to stress and anxiety.

Trauma exposure leads to continual information overload from the brainstem that can overwhelm the limbic system. The barrage of messages regarding potential threats disrupts the limbic system's capacity to receive coherent and rational thoughts from the neocortex.

This explains why we may become speechless, unable to process information, or struggle to make decisions when under stress. Our limbic systems become flooded with stress hormones, and the information pathways between the neocortex and limbic areas become congested, resembling a traffic jam.

If the stress subsides, we can think more clearly and process what happened. This is often when we reflect on things we should have said or done but didn't. Severe, ongoing, or inescapable trauma can trap our brains in this state; over time, it can develop into physical illnesses, including depression, anxiety, and/or PTSD.

Normal brain functioning becomes impossible when stress hormone levels do not return to normal. The survival systems protecting the body remain activated. This can result in living in a state of learned helplessness.

> Structures in the brain can be damaged when our stress response systems don't 'turn off'.

Chronic Stress and the Brain

Persistently high levels of cortisol—the body's main stress hormone—can cause the frontal cortex to atrophy (shrink), making it harder to make decisions, reason, or regulate behaviour.

Meanwhile, the amygdalae, which detect threats and generate fear responses, are hyper-efficient—so skilled at sensing fear that they may overreact to minor threats. This overactivity increases anxiety and emotional reactivity.

The hippocampus is affected in different ways. It plays a significant role in responding to stress, and scanning techniques show hippocampal involvement in diseases such as anxiety and depression. The formation of new cells (neurogenesis) either decreases or does not occur, and cells can shrink (atrophy). This, in turn, affects our ability to process and remember new information.

When the hippocampus functions properly, we can learn new things and establish neural pathways that help solidify what we have learned into implicit memory—where we subconsciously recall how to perform tasks. For example, when learning to drive a car, we eventually integrate various components of driving (such as checking rear vision mirrors, signalling, and changing gears) without conscious thought. We have formed an implicit memory.

New connections enable us to learn more information and enhance our recall. If we are not stressed when acquiring new facts or procedures, these connections can become strengthened through repeated stimulation of the pathways. This phenomenon, known as long-term potentiation, remains in our memories. We can complete familiar tasks with little or no conscious effort.

Try brushing your teeth with your non-dominant hand and observe how well you perform. If you don't do this regularly, your brain won't have formed a pathway to accomplish it, and you may be surprised at how challenging such a simple task can be. It will become easier with practice, as practice creates new neural pathways.

When stressed, the formation of new memories and memory recall are affected, but memories from before the stress remain intact. Therefore, we can recall older memories while having difficulty remembering what we did last week. Chronic stress also leads to the loss of glial cells, including oligodendrocytes, which are responsible for producing myelin.

Recent studies have revealed that oligodendrocytes are involved in learning, as well as in both long-term and short-term memory, and memory consolidation. They secrete and regulate brain-derived neurotrophic factor (BDNF), which is essential for the survival and protection of neurons.

Addressing chronic stress may protect against the development of diseases such as multiple sclerosis, where the protective myelin sheaths covering nerve fibres in the brain and spinal cord are damaged. High cortisol levels can reduce myelin thickness and impair its production. Studies support a relationship between stress and multiple sclerosis, and those who suffer from this condition endorse the premise that psychological stress triggers relapses of this debilitating disease.

Cognitive Resilience and Brain Health

Reduced stress helps the brain function at optimal levels and enhances brain health. This supports normal brain functioning, aiding developmental delays in children and impairments in adults, particularly the elderly. Of course, we can't always eliminate stress in our lives but understanding how it affects us can help mitigate its impact. Knowing what happens and why we feel the way we do can empower us to change our responses.

We can reduce our vulnerability to stress by improving and maintaining our overall health and adjusting our coping strategies. You may find it difficult to accept that you can develop resilience, but knowing that our brains can repair the damage they have suffered is encouraging and positive. There are therapies and techniques we can learn, and repeating these can create new and beneficial neural pathways. The brain is believed to have emotional circuits that link many areas and respond to emotional stimuli based on the type of emotion and the situation experienced.

Scientists still have much to learn before thoroughly plotting an entire 'emotional map' of all these brain circuits. Repeating healthy habits remains the most effective approach. Our lives are unpredictable, and trauma is largely unavoidable, but understanding how stress affects us and engaging in activities and treatments to address our stress responses can lessen their impact.

Summary:
- The brain is the most complex organ in the body, consisting of over 100 billion nerve cells.
- It's essential to understand the brain and how it works to understand how stress affects it.
- The Triune Brain model helps us understand the brain by imagining it as having a bottom (reptilian brain), a middle (limbic system), and a top (neocortex).
- The thalamus is like a switchboard, sending information where it needs to go.
- Fear messages take a shortcut route from the thalamus to the amygdala (fear centres) before they reach the neocortex (our rational and thinking brain). This explains why we can overreact before logic kicks in.
- Glial cells are nerve cells in the nervous system that don't produce electrical impulses. They provide structural support, insulation of neurons, supply nutrients and oxygen to neurons, destroy pathogens (organisms that cause disease), and repair neurons.
- The limbic system is the primary system involved in stress responses.
- The limbic system consists of the thalamus, the hypothalamus, the pituitary gland, the hippocampus, the amygdala, and the pre frontal cortex. These can be damaged when stress-response systems don't 'turn off'.
- Amygdalae are our fear centres—they can become more prominent if stressed and work much better to make us more fearful.
- The hippocampus stores memories, and new brain cells can be made.
- The thalamus is like a switchboard, sending messages to specific regions in the brain.
- The pituitary gland produces many hormones and is controlled by the hypothalamus.

- The frontal cortex does not finish developing until the age of 25 years.
- Our brains can repair some damage they have suffered.
- We can reduce our vulnerability to stress by improving and maintaining our general health and changing how we cope.

Restoration

If you could prise open my skull
You would see
The white-hot tangle of nerves arcing and firing
And the red, raw flesh beneath
The acid comments dripping upon it.
Vulnerable, exposed,
Shame, derision.
If you could be the balm of kindness
Soothing, smoothing, balm repair
If you could neutralise
The toxic disdain
Why wouldn't you?

Chapter 8

It's (Not) All in Your Head: The Gut-Brain Axis

'The human gut is one of the most diverse and rich ecosystems on Earth.'
— *Spohn and Young (2018)*

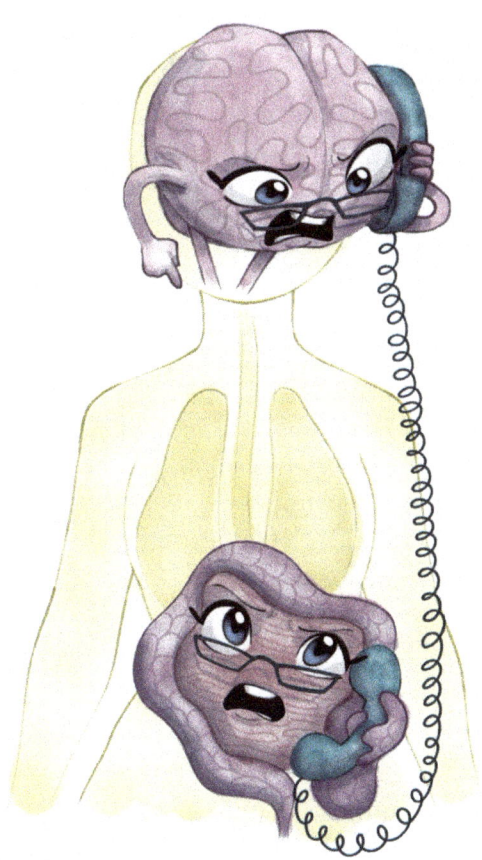

We have learned that our brains and bodies don't function independently. All bodily systems are interconnected and interrelated, performing essential functions to maintain our bodily balance. Each biological system performs specific functions to maintain homeostasis, working together for our overall health. If one system is not functioning correctly, it will impact all others. It has been discovered that even the tiniest microorganisms living within us play critical roles in maintaining our health. These organisms reside in our guts and are linked to our brain cells.

It may be hard to imagine, but our brains and guts are closely linked and constantly communicate. This communication is bidirectional, meaning it flows in both directions. The brain 'speaks' to the gut, and the gut can 'speak' to the brain; this communication between them regulates each other's health and affects their overall function.

When we feel butterflies in our stomachs or develop nervous diarrhoea, these reactions result directly from our brains communicating with our guts. We aren't conscious of it, but there's a complex interaction between the micro-organisms (microbiota) in the gut and neurons in the brain. It's called the gut-brain axis, and scientific studies prove the remarkable communication between these two vital organs.

It is not yet known exactly how the interactions between the two influence each other's health. Still, there is a growing body of evidence suggesting that changes to the microbiota in our gut (these changes are called dysbiosis) might be responsible for causing mental illnesses such as depression and anxiety. Dysbiosis primarily occurs due to dietary changes, but is also influenced by medications and certain diseases.

Dysbiosis is an imbalance in which 'bad' bacteria outnumber 'good' bacteria. Further studies are needed to clarify the effects on brain function. Still, research in this field supports the idea that our brains and guts are closely linked, and that 'following your gut instincts' is more than simply relying on intuition or experience. Our microbiota may play a far more significant role in supporting our health and preventing diseases than previously thought. The microbiota and the environment in which they live are referred to as a microbiome.

Our microbiomes function as vast, hidden, living metabolic 'organs'. They play crucial roles in our nutrition, metabolism, immune functions, and responses, as well as in the efficiency of all bodily systems and their interactions. Various types and amounts of gut microbiota contribute uniquely to maintaining health, preventing diseases, digesting food, absorbing nutrients, and facilitating elimination functions.

The gut has its own nervous system, the enteric nervous system, which is one of the main branches of the autonomic nervous system. This system is akin to a web of nerve fibres embedded in the linings of our intestines and comprises approximately 500 million neurons. It influences our immune, autonomic, and endocrine systems.

Our enteric nervous systems are linked to our central nervous systems via the gut-brain axes. Despite this connection between the two systems, the enteric nervous system can act independently of the brain. It has a 'mind of its own'. This is why it is often called our 'second brain' or 'brain in the gut'. It controls both the external and internal environments of our digestive system, i.e., what happens within and around it. It's yet another immensely complex system within our amazing bodies.

Miraculous Microbiomes

It's estimated that our bodies contain over 100 trillion microorganisms, with approximately 80% living in our gut. New research has determined that there are over 15,000 species in the human gut. It's a bustling ecosystem of bacteria, viruses, archaea, algae, and fungi. These tiny organisms are only visible under a microscope, but they are vital to our health.

Each gut function—digestion, absorption, elimination—depends on specific microbiota in the right proportions. Any imbalance or deficiency can impact the overall functioning of the system.

> **Microbiota are micro-organisms that are vital to our health. A microbiome is the microbiota plus the environment in which they live.**

What Influences Our Microbiome?

Each person has a unique and diverse microbiome influenced by genetic and lifestyle factors. Microbiota begin colonising the digestive system at birth, and their diversity is shaped by:

- birth method (vaginal delivery vs. caesarean section)
- duration and exclusivity of breastfeeding
- the health of the mother during pregnancy and delivery
- environmental exposures during childhood.

Although each person has a unique microbiome, there are commonalities among people with healthy microbiomes, i.e., all with healthy guts will have more 'good' microbiota than 'bad'.

External factors such as medications, particularly antibiotics that treat harmful bacteria while also killing beneficial bacteria, will affect the diversity of our microbiomes. Additionally, diet, body mass index, age, and sex are also contributing factors.

These variances make it difficult for scientists to determine 'normal' levels and whether an abundance or depletion of specific microbiota may be due to illnesses or life experiences. What's normal for you is not the same for others. This poses perplexing puzzles for scientists attempting to understand the relationship between dysbiosis and various diseases.

Further studies are needed to determine which changes in the microbiome are relevant to certain illnesses, including insulin resistance, Type 2 diabetes, high blood pressure, and fatty liver disease. Research suggests that our gut-brain axis also influences our susceptibility to developing certain brain disorders, such as Alzheimer's disease, Parkinson's disease, schizophrenia, multiple sclerosis (MS), and neurodevelopmental disorders like autism.

Dysbiosis also appears to be associated with autoimmune diseases and psychiatric illnesses. Studies reveal that individuals suffering from MS, for instance, show a decrease in a particular type of bacteria in their microbiota. Different illnesses exhibit varying compositions of the microbiota in the guts of affected individuals.

> **There's a growing body of evidence that suggests changes to the microbiota in our gut might be responsible for causing mental illnesses such as depression and anxiety.**

Microbiome Meltdown: How Stress Impacts the Gut

Remember, the HPA axis response is a normal reaction to the daily stresses we encounter. However, severe or chronic stress can negatively impact this system, leading to HPA axis dysregulation. When this occurs, individuals may feel constantly overwhelmed, irritable, have difficulty concentrating or sleeping, and experience chronic pain or illness.

A dysregulated HPA axis affects not only the brain but also the body. Elevated cortisol levels over an extended period influence how we feel. Chronic inflammation throughout the body results from persistently high cortisol levels and a dysregulated hypothalamic-pituitary-adrenal (HPA) axis. This inflammation impacts our intestinal health by causing dysbiosis. Thus, our microbiota affects our HPA axis stress responses, and our stress responses can lead to dysbiosis in our guts. The communication is bidirectional, meaning that what impacts one will impact the other.

Dysbiosis can affect the permeability (leakiness) of our intestinal linings. When we have a healthy microbiome, our gut linings are also healthy. An unhealthy microbiome can alter our gut lining, allowing harmful bacteria to pass through the intestinal wall. Leaky gut syndrome refers to our gut linings becoming more permeable. Bacteria entering the bloodstream leads to increased inflammation within our bodies. This rise in inflammation, in turn, causes dysbiosis, creating a vicious cycle. This inflammation can heighten the risk of not only chronic diseases such as depression and anxiety but also heart conditions, Type 2 diabetes, obesity, non-alcoholic fatty liver disease, and aging.

Stress makes our gut linings more permeable. It influences our gut microbiota, triggering inflammation and potentially contributing to chronic conditions like anxiety and depression. These conditions increase our vulnerability to stress—continuing the cycle. Studies show that people with depression often have higher levels of pro-inflammatory microbiota and lower levels of anti-inflammatory strains, compared to those without depression.

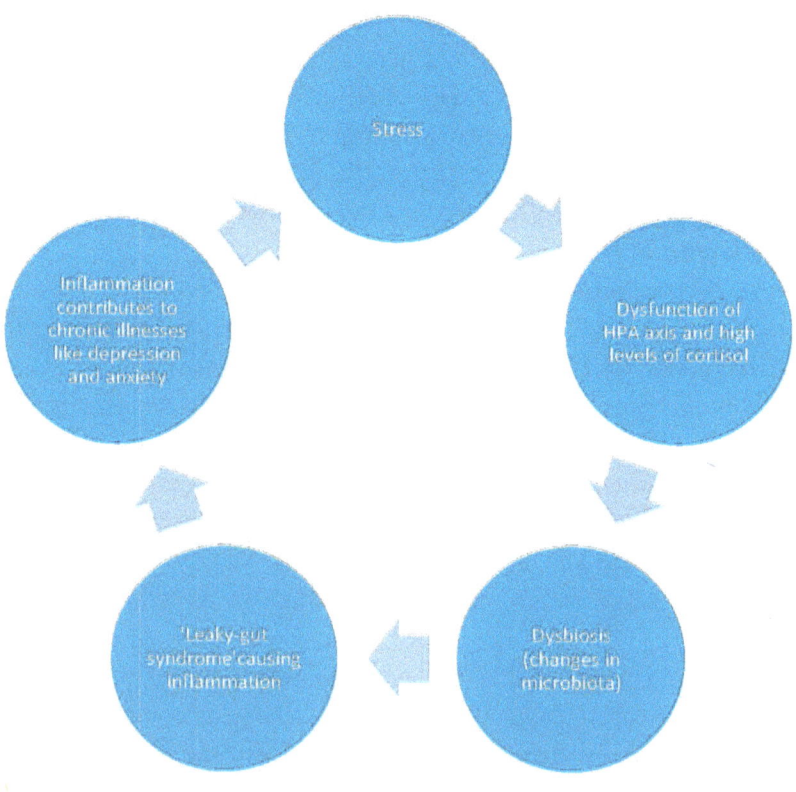

Improving Microbiome Health

Just as our microbiomes influence our health, we can support them—primarily through diet. The simplest and most effective way to improve gut microbiota is by consuming a diverse, nutrient-rich diet.

Of course, coping with severe mental illness can make it difficult to eat well. Depression, anxiety, or PTSD can cloud our ability to make nourishing choices. Nevertheless, small, positive changes—when and where they're possible—can make a real difference. Even incremental shifts can support both physical and mental health.

Once we feel better, even slightly, making healthy choices becomes easier. It won't always be simple. You may manage to eat well one week and then less well the next, depending on life stresses and the subsequent worsening of symptoms. There's no shame in experiencing these lapses. We do our best during times of grief and stress. However, small steps towards healthy choices are what we can return to when we feel ready. Improving our overall wellness strengthens our resilience and enhances our ability to cope. Enhancing our diet offers multiple benefits.

A good starting point is to reduce processed food intake and increase whole, fresh foods like fruits, nuts, and eggs. Eventually, you might consider adopting a Mediterranean-style way of eating—not a restrictive "diet" per se, but a lifestyle associated with anti-inflammatory benefits. It emphasises fibre-rich fruits and vegetables (skins included), fish, legumes, seeds, olive oil, dairy (yoghurt and cheese), poultry, and whole grains, while avoiding processed foods. When fresh vegetables are unavailable or costly, frozen ones are a great alternative.

Eating a diet high in fibre helps our guts process and digest the food we consume. When dietary fibre is consumed, a substance called butyrate is produced. Butyrate is a short-chain fatty acid (SCFA) that is vital for gastrointestinal health and serves as an essential energy source for the cells in the intestines. It helps maintain normal functions within the bowel. If we don't consume enough fibre, we won't produce sufficient butyrate to keep our guts healthy.

Butyrate helps prevent leaky gut syndrome, which contributes to inflammation throughout our bodies. Consuming foods rich in dietary fibre promotes the growth of bacteria that produce butyrate, thus reducing inflammation and alleviating symptoms. What we eat can impact the levels of inflammation within our bodies.

Complex carbohydrates such as unprocessed grains, nuts, and seeds serve as excellent sources of fibre, protein, healthy fats, and minerals. A high daily intake of vegetables provides essential nutrients for our gut health and, consequently, our overall well-being. Unprocessed 'real' food is best for your gut and your brain.

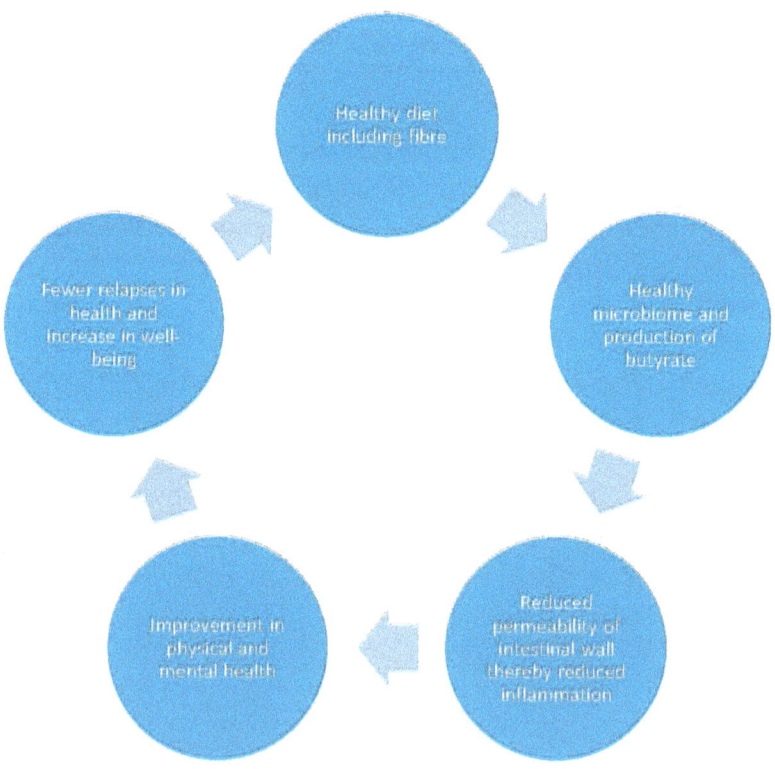

Another way to improve our gut health is by taking probiotics (live bacteria helpful to the gut) and prebiotics (non-digestible fibre that encourages good bacteria growth). Both are beneficial for enhancing our microbiomes and preventing dysbiosis, particularly when experiencing illness or when under intense physical or mental stress. They can also repair dysbiosis following long-term antibiotic therapy or during chronic diseases.

Antibiotics can kill the beneficial microbiota in our guts, and probiotics and prebiotics help replenish them. Eating foods like yoghurt supports the levels of good bacteria in the gut, which can aid in times of stress or during recovery from illness.

Synbiotics are a combination of probiotics and prebiotics that enhance the survival of live bacteria in supplements and promote the growth of healthy bacteria. They also offer benefits in lowering blood pressure, treating liver diseases, aiding weight loss, and improving the absorption of magnesium, calcium, and phosphorus. Research has demonstrated that they protect against neurological and mental illnesses, including depression, autism, Parkinson's disease, and Alzheimer's disease.

Psychobiotics: Healing Through the Gut

Support for the use of probiotics, prebiotics, and synbiotics in treating mental illness is increasing. These treatments are supplements known as psychobiotics. They are proving to be beneficial for alleviating psychiatric conditions. Evidence from both human and animal studies indicates that including them as treatments for mental illnesses can reduce symptoms of depression, anxiety, and stress.

Eating fermented foods is also highly beneficial, with studies suggesting that such foods positively influence gut microbiota. These foods include, but are not limited to, yoghurt, sauerkraut, kimchi, and kefir.

> *'The precise mechanisms underlying the pathophysiology of depression remain unknown, but evidence suggests that the gut-brain-microbiota axis is responsible for the pathophysiology of depression.'*
> — *Chang et al. (2022)*

Food for Thought

The increased prevalence of chronic diseases, such as depression and Type 2 diabetes, may, in part, be due to the rise in the consumption of simple carbohydrates. Carbohydrates can be a healthy inclusion in a diet but shouldn't be highly refined. We consume more highly refined carbohydrates than at the beginning of the 20th century when whole grains containing considerable fibre were eaten. Processing these grains into white flour has removed approximately 80% of the fibre and nearly 30% of the protein.

Unprocessed flours are made from all parts of the grain—the bran, which contains nutrients and fibre; the germ, which contains healthy fats, vitamins, and minerals; and the endosperm, which contains starch and sometimes oils and protein. Swapping white flour for unprocessed or wholemeal flour is worth considering. Choosing wholemeal bread over white bread is another good option.

High-fructose corn syrup (HFCS) production has played a significant role in the rise of chronic illnesses and is present in many processed foods, including fruit juices, soft drinks, and fast food. It is derived from corn starch, serves as a sweetener, is cheaper than sugar, and is sometimes labelled as fructose or corn syrup. It's banned in Australian products but may appear in imported goods.

HFCS continues to be used in food processing in the United States, including sweets, fruit juice drinks, soft drinks, fast foods, cereals, and condiments like sauces. HFCS is a major contributor to obesity, fatty liver diseases, heart disease, and Type 2 diabetes. It's prudent to read the ingredient labels on processed goods and limit the intake of foods high in sugar.

Consuming a diet high in sugar, including fructose, glucose, and sucrose, can increase inflammation in the body. Limiting soft drinks, fruit juice drinks (i.e., not 100% juice), and many packaged cereals can significantly improve health. Swapping 100% fruit juice for a single piece of fruit is also a healthier option. A glass of juice may contain up to six oranges, for example. A single orange not only contains far less fructose but also includes pulp, which is fibre. Fibre helps propel food through the gut more quickly, slowing fructose absorption.

Replacing processed foods with whole foods significantly reduces our risk of developing chronic illnesses and ensures our microbiomes contain the beneficial microbiota we need. Drinking water instead of fruit juices and soft drinks is extremely beneficial. It lowers our risk of heart disease and diabetes, decreases blood pressure, aids in weight loss, and reduces tooth decay. Additionally, it keeps us hydrated, maintains healthy kidney function, and helps prevent constipation.

Eating well promotes well-being. For many of us, this is not always financially or otherwise feasible. However, if we can access and afford fresh, nutritious food, it will benefit us greatly. Remember that psychological trauma causes internal damage to our bodies. Healthy eating aids in restoring and repairing our bodies from the inside out.

Summary:
- The gut and the brain are closely linked and communicate almost constantly with each other. The communication is bidirectional, or two-way, called the gut-brain axis.
- Our bodies are estimated to contain over 100 trillion microorganisms, of which approximately 80% live in our gut. There are over 15,000 different species in the human gut, including bacteria, viruses, archaea, algae, and fungi. Collectively, they are called microbiota, and the environment in which they live is called the microbiome.
- There is growing evidence that changes in our microbiota (dysbiosis) might be responsible for causing mental illnesses such as depression and anxiety. These changes occur primarily through diet, medications, or diseases.
- The gut has its own nervous system—the enteric nervous system. This system is like a cobweb of nerve fibres embedded in the linings of our gut and comprises approximately 500 million neurons.

- Our enteric nervous system is linked to our central nervous system via the gut-brain axis.
- The enteric nervous system can sometimes act independently of the brain, often called our 'second brain' or 'brain in the gut'.
- Our brain influences the health of our gut, and our gut influences the health of our brain.
- Microbiomes vary between individuals. Genetic inheritance and lifestyle factors, including diet, body mass index, and age and sex, influence these differences.
- A healthy gut has more 'good' microbiota than 'bad'.
- Stress affects our HPA axis, and this may become dysregulated. Dysregulation of the HPA axis can cause increased inflammation in our bodies, which can influence our gut health by causing dysbiosis. Dysbiosis in our gut can affect the HPA axis and cause dysregulation. One involves the other.
- Dysbiosis can affect how permeable (leaky) the linings of our intestines are. When our guts are healthy, their linings are healthy too. Dysbiosis can result in harmful bacteria passing inside our intestines into the bloodstream. 'Leaky-gut syndrome' can result. This bacterium increases inflammation within the body. An increase in inflammation, in turn, causes dysbiosis. It becomes a vicious circle.
- Inflammation within the body increases our risk of developing chronic diseases such as anxiety, depression, heart conditions, Type 2 diabetes, non-alcoholic fatty liver disease, and aging.
- Our microbiome influences our health, and we influence the health of our microbiome, primarily through diet—both co-evolve over time.
- The easiest way to improve the gut microbiota is through diet. A healthy diet promotes diverse and healthy microbiota and helps reduce symptoms of depression.

- Adhering to a Mediterranean diet is showing beneficial results, possibly because it is an anti-inflammatory diet.
- Eating foods high in fibre helps our guts process and digest the foods we eat. Dietary fibre helps generate bacteria that produce a short-chain fatty acid called butyrate, vital for gut health. Butyrate helps prevent 'leaky-gut syndrome', thus decreasing inflammation within the body.
- Probiotics are live bacteria that are helpful to the gut. Prebiotics are non-digestible fibres that encourage good bacteria growth. Synbiotics are a mixture of probiotics and prebiotics. The use of all three in treating mental illnesses is showing promising results. They are being called psychobiotics and appear to reduce symptoms of depression, anxiety, and stress.
- Fermented foods create positive effects on the gut microbiota. These foods include yoghurt, sauerkraut, kimchi, and kefir.
- The increase in prevalence of some chronic diseases such as depression and Type 2 diabetes may be due in part to the increase in consumption of simple carbohydrates. Processing of complex carbohydrates removes approximately 80% of fibre.
- High-fructose corn syrup production has also contributed to the increase in chronic illnesses. It is found in many processed foods, including fruit, soft, and fast food.
- Eating well helps us be well.

Chapter 9

Healing from Within: Transcending Invalidation and Shame

This chapter discusses emotional health, the impact of trauma on your ability to recognise and understand your emotions, the pain caused by invalidation and shame, and how to build resilience.

Emotions are a normal part of life, and you are meant to experience them. They represent a physiological response to your perceptions of what is happening around you and are influenced by your thoughts. They facilitate communication with others and are often expressed as either positive or negative.

Basic emotions include anger, sadness, fear, enjoyment, love, surprise, shame, and disgust. Emotions can be triggered quickly and are often fleeting. If an emotion lasts for an extended period, it is generally considered a mood. Ongoing moods can reflect temperaments.

Good emotional health involves coping with everyday stress and managing your emotions effectively, rather than allowing them to control you. Positive emotional health acknowledges your feelings and those of others, supporting a sense of purpose in life.

When emotional health is strong, you feel invincible, approaching situations and challenges with confidence, feeling capable, empowered, and in control. If you have experienced severe or chronic trauma, your emotional health may be poor, making you feel helpless or incapable. Managing your emotions can be challenging when dealing with trauma and subsequent stress. Fortunately, emotional management is a skill that can be developed.

Many of us were not educated about managing our emotions as children, or about the normalcy of having them. It may also have been unsafe to express these feelings. If you were raised in an environment where showing emotions was dangerous, forbidden, or regarded as a weakness, you likely learned from an early age that it was safer to repress or suppress them.

What we experience as children shapes our perceptions as adults, and you may find it challenging to ensure that your emotional needs are met in adulthood. This includes attending to your fulfilment, caring for your emotional well-being, and protecting yourself from psychological abuse. Our upbringing can influence how we think and feel as adults, affecting our societal and cultural expectations.

Exposure to trauma, particularly in children, profoundly affects self-esteem. Feelings of powerlessness, defeat, anger, self-deprecation, and fear can lead to extreme self-criticism and self-contempt. Repetitive trauma alters the neural pathways in our brains due to the ongoing stress responses of the nervous and endocrine systems reacting to the abuse. The inability to process and reconcile emotions over time results in confusion and dissociation, destabilising one's sense of self and perception of the world.

Repeated trauma is linked to the development of PTSD, which, in turn, can lead to flashbacks, a state of high arousal, and feelings of fear. These emotions feed off one another. Alcohol and drugs are common, though counterproductive, coping tools. Remember that these feelings have arisen because you have experienced trauma. The trauma has affected parts of you, but you can address these negative emotions. We will explore how to manage and treat psychological trauma in later chapters.

As adults, we expect to handle difficult situations calmly and not react impulsively. As we discovered in Chapter 6, our stress responses can overreact before logic kicks in, especially if we have been exposed to chronic or severe trauma. Overreactions can be mortifying and shame-inducing, which may cause further distress. Remember: you are not weak or mad. Your brain has been damaged by trauma, and it can heal.

Repression vs Suppression

Repressing emotions differs from suppressing them. Repression involves unconsciously pushing down feelings, while suppression is the conscious avoidance of emotions to cope at any given moment. When emotions are uncomfortable or intrusive, we may repress them. Many of us do this daily. We set aside our feelings when we're busy with work or home schedules that demand our full attention, until we have the time or energy to address them. Alternatively, we might ignore situations that generate uncomfortable emotions to avoid conflict or apprehension.

Suppression is a protective mechanism that shields you from the despair of raw emotions. These feelings can be too painful to process and are pushed deep within you. Suppressed emotions can lead to illness and may resurface, causing intense pain at any moment. They might remind you of past hurts, like a raw wound that hasn't healed. However, suppressing emotions to avoid or deflect conflict does not resolve them; they persist until they are processed and understood.

Why We Repress or Suppress Emotions?

You may fear repercussions or ridicule if you express your feelings. This can stem from having your emotions quashed or dismissed as a child. It might have felt unsafe to show fear of a parent, or perhaps you were shamed for expressing emotions like crying when hurt or sad. Demonstrating feelings may also have been seen as a weakness. If your childhood home was not a safe space for expressing feelings, advocating for yourself as an adult can become challenging.

Being humiliated or shamed as a child for expressing viewpoints different from others can lead to a reluctance to voice opinions later in life. You may also have been conditioned as an adult to believe that your feelings are irrational or insignificant. This can make you feel unworthy, contributing to emotional repression or suppression.

Suppose you struggle to express your feelings or have trouble controlling them. In that case, you may have experienced unresolved psychological trauma or may still be in an unsafe environment, walking on eggshells to maintain the peace. Expressing normal emotions and having them accepted and validated is a fair expectation. It's okay to be angry or sad. It's also okay to communicate those feelings to others—or it should be.

Experiencing abuse or trauma, whether severe or chronic, can impact our ability to express normal emotions such as anger, sadness, frustration, or joy. Our perception of safety in the world becomes distorted when we feel uncomfortable expressing our feelings. Negative thoughts tend to fester and can become disproportionate, intensifying as we ruminate on what might have been said or done. This may lead to unexpected outbursts of rage.

Shame and Invalidation

Condemnation from abusive individuals often manifests as invalidation and shaming. Invalidation and shame are powerful emotions that can serve as tools of psychological trauma. Invalidation acts as a weapon for some to assert dominance and dismiss or belittle others' feelings. Invalidation is a form of manipulation.

Shame is a deeply painful emotion that may arise from feelings about yourself or be an act against you intended to humiliate and expose perceived weaknesses. Both can lead to extreme distress. Recognising tactics to induce these emotions is the first step in developing resilience against them. Understanding vulnerability and resilience will aid you in healing.

The Silent Suffering of Invalidation

R. D. Laing (MD, psychologist) said: '*When we invalidate people or deny their perceptions and personal experiences, we make mental invalids of them. When one's feelings are denied, a person can be made to feel crazy even when they are perfectly mentally healthy.*'

Emotional invalidation is one of the most damaging forms of psychological abuse. It is characterised by negating, ignoring, trivialising, rejecting, mocking, judging, or teasing another's feelings. This behaviour is linked to depression, anxiety, and social avoidance. At the same time, impulsivity, rule-breaking, and aggression can hinder the development of a healthy emotional attachment to yourself, others, and your feelings.

> **Invalidation is more than being contradicted. It implies that there is something fundamentally wrong with what we are feeling.**

If you have been invalidated, your emotional needs have not only remained unmet; they have also been weaponised against you. Invalidation differs from disagreement and suggests that there is something fundamentally wrong with your feelings. It leads to increased emotional distress and pain. Physical changes can occur—your blood pressure may rise, as can cortisol levels.

There is likely to be increased activity in the region of your brain called the dorsal anterior cingulate cortex (dACC), which is the same brain region stimulated during physical pain. This region is also believed to activate in response to social rejection or exclusion, such as when family or friends alienate someone. Losing a loved one stimulates the dACC, and the pain feels akin to physical pain.

Furthermore, this region can motivate us to take action to alleviate the pain, for example, seeking help from friends when we are upset. It can also help us understand why we experienced a painful situation and how to avoid similar ones in the future.

The pain you feel is real, and studies confirm this. Imaging techniques, including MRIs, reveal that the dACC activates when patients encounter emotional pain, similar to physical pain. Invalidation can lead to feelings of not belonging, a decreased sense of control, lowered self-esteem, and the belief that your existence lacks meaning.

Emotional invalidation during childhood is linked to chronic emotional inhibition in adulthood, which significantly predicts psychological distress, including depression and anxiety. This signifies psychological trauma. Narcissistic parents or caregivers excel at invalidation. They demonstrate little to no empathy while having an overinflated sense of entitlement, prioritising their needs over yours, even at the expense of your well-being. We will examine narcissists more closely in Chapter 11, 'From Awareness to Empowerment: Navigating Toxic Personalities'.

The Burden of Shame

The role of shame must not be underestimated when considering its damaging effects on the brain. Shame is described as a negative emotion that can range from shyness to self-loathing, with or without self-harm. It can be excessive, prolonged, and unbearable, and may be as damaging to the brain as trauma. Shame and guilt are negative feelings that can lead to vulnerability, difficulty focusing, acute embarrassment, and a tendency to withdraw from social contact. Both are moral emotions that govern our social behaviours and are painful to experience.

Shame differs from guilt in that guilt can usually be alleviated through acts of apology or reparation, whereas feelings of shame lead to profound anguish and self-deprecating thoughts. It is a more intense and unbearable emotion than guilt and involves an internally focused attention on your emotional pain. Guilt involves externally focused attention on the emotional pain of others. Shame may compel you to hide or deny a misdeed, while guilt encourages you to make amends for your wrongdoing.

Feelings of withdrawal often arise from self-loathing, humiliation, inadequacy, a sense of disappointing family and friends, feelings of undesirability and unworthiness, and disgust with oneself. If you struggle with shame, you may possess little sense of pride. This can exacerbate already acute feelings of unworthiness and exclusion from social behaviour.

Shame prompts disconnection: disconnection itself is experienced as shameful. To be humiliated, banished, objectified, or embarrassed can produce intense and painful feelings of shame. Self-worth and pride can disappear instantaneously. The loss of self-esteem, self-confidence, and dignity constitutes a complex set of feelings to navigate. Self-loathing, self-contempt, and self-castigation are not only emotionally damaging, but their presence also inhibits positive emotions. The constant barrage of negative self-talk leads to anhedonia and often culminates in depression.

> Shame is a more intense and unbearable emotion than guilt.

Shame may be external—a negative view of yourself as seen through the eyes of others (being condemned by others), or internal—seen through your own eyes (blaming yourself). The external component involves the thought that others view you negatively; for example: 'You all hate me.' 'You think I am ugly, unattractive, unlovable!' 'You are ashamed of me!' The internal component is how you see yourself as flawed, inadequate, a bad person— 'I am disgusting, dirty, despicable!'

Internal and external shame often coexist. You may feel as though the outside world has turned against you, creating overwhelming emotions that can lead you to shut down and withdraw from all social contact. Your sense of self can become warped and misguided, self-critical, and self-persecuting, with seemingly no safe place for you, either within yourself or outside. Feelings of despair can become unbearable. This may lead you to self-harm and/or contemplate suicide. Hang on. Remember, you can heal.

Anger and shame are commonly linked. Anger is often directed inward as self-loathing or self-contempt; however, hostility may be directed toward others. Outbreaks of intense rage may occur, potentially including physical aggression. Feelings of shame can unleash severe resentment or bitterness, which can suddenly erupt if one feels scorned or condemned.

You may feel a sense of addressing what has been done to you by attacking another. Aggression is sometimes used to avoid revealing and reliving painful memories; however, this can backfire quickly and induce more shame against yourself. Often, the emotional pain misrepresents the severity of a situation, as you may exaggerate the degree of disgrace in which you perceive yourself.

You may experience a 'flood' of shame brought on by certain stimuli that can cause sudden, acute emotional pain as you are transported back to a shameful period. Shame responses can include freezing, numbness, hypervigilance, the fight-or-flight stress response, and violence. If you experience acute shame, you may become vulnerable to further shame. Having low self-worth and self-esteem, coupled with submissive behaviour, increases vulnerability to additional trauma.

Shame is closely linked to depression. Parental neglect and abuse lead to issues in brain development. Shame, along with negative evaluations and criticism from others, triggers cortisol stress responses that, if the abuse continues, result in depression. If you experienced abuse or neglect as a child, it is not your fault.

> **Shame is strongly connected with depression.**

Brené Brown, an American professor, lecturer, author, and podcast host, wrote an article in 2006 titled "Shame Resilience Theory: A Grounded Theory Study on Women and Shame" to introduce new theories for understanding shame and its impact on women. It also describes how women can develop resilience against shame. The three main concerns expressed by the 215 women who participated in this study are that shame led them to feel trapped, powerless, and isolated.

Awareness that cultural and social expectations can shape our vulnerability is crucial to understanding whether our shame stems from societal conditioning. Once we become aware and engage with others to discuss feelings of shame, we can develop resilience against it. Shame is a complex emotion rooted in society's expectations of who we are, what we do, who we should be, and how we should behave.

Cultural, religious, racial, and sexual orientation are all examples of expectations that are required, demanded, or implied by individuals and groups and which are often reinforced by the media. Body image, aging, professions, motherhood, etc., are all areas that can induce feelings of shame in women.

The participants in Brené Brown's study reported that receiving empathy and understanding from others, as well as from themselves, helped diminish their shame. When they felt supported, they regained more power. Sharing their shameful feelings helped them recognise and normalise their understanding of shame. This contributed to their ability to change how they perceived the expectations placed upon them and to develop resilience.

Being aware of what makes them vulnerable helps them become more resilient, as does developing empathy and connecting with others. Brené Brown's work is good news for those of us who have experienced psychological trauma because it proves we can learn to heal ourselves. Understanding what may trigger your shame reactions, learning self-assertion, and rejecting the negative judgements of others may also help you recover from shame.

Self-reflection, self-awareness, and recognising that you are only responsible for your own behaviour, not for what has happened to you, are crucial in helping you overcome shame. For example, survivors of rape may need assistance in understanding that sexual arousal during their assault is a biological response and does not imply that they are in any way responsible or derived pleasure from the abuse they endured. Furthermore, if the rapist is known to them, there may be feelings of loyalty toward their perpetrator and a sense that they somehow enabled or encouraged the attack against them. Denial and refusal to disclose painful details contribute to the grief and self-persecution felt by these trauma survivors.

It can help to remember that what you perceive as shameful likely stems from what you learned as a child. These perceptions often include cultural, religious, or societal beliefs. An example of this is the many cultures and societies that still hold women accountable for the sexual, physical, or emotional violence committed against them. 'What were you wearing?' What did you say? Do? Think? These insinuations can generate feelings that we are damaged or flawed if we experience abuse, leading to feelings of intense shame.

The same applies if your sexual orientation differs from heterosexuality. Many of us were taught that homosexuality is a sin, and you could be criminally prosecuted for engaging in homosexual acts. Some religions and cultures still regard it as sinful. Although many countries now accept homosexuality, including same-sex marriage, religious and political attitudes vary significantly from country to country.

We must regularly examine our belief systems and adjust them when they no longer serve us, questioning why we continue to hold onto ideologies inherited from previous generations. The limiting beliefs we carry into adulthood can produce painful emotions (see Chapter 17).

Shame can be an overwhelming and debilitating emotion for many years. Even memories of what triggered your shame can lead to waves of distress. Addressing these feelings with trusted friends or professionals can help relieve this emotional burden through empathy and communication. If you struggle with the pain of abuse, please believe me: the shame is not yours to bear.

Emotional Intelligence and Recognising Emotional Abuse

Emotional self-awareness is often referred to as emotional intelligence. Individuals with healthy emotional intelligence can utilise their prefrontal cortex to evaluate their emotional responses to situations and skillfully manage their emotions and relationships. They have control over their impulses, make rational decisions, and are motivated. Those who have experienced trauma may lack these skills, but remember, these are learned abilities. We can all acquire them.

It's essential to recognise how psychological and emotional forms of abuse present themselves in our homes, workplaces, or public. They are not always obvious and can be hard to define, but once we can recognise the patterns of psychological abuse, we can protect ourselves from the impact. Once we understand that the behaviour of others is not our responsibility, nor a reflection of ourselves, we can become impervious to it.

This can be very difficult if you cannot set firm boundaries, especially with toxic parents or those in positions of power, such as a bullying boss. Such situations are challenging. Having manipulative or controlling people around you who evoke negative emotions, like guilt or frustration, is distressing and draining. You may lack the emotional intelligence to recognise and understand calculating and manipulative behaviour. We address toxic personalities further in Chapter 11.

Another person's behaviour and feelings, as well as their conduct, are their responsibility. We are not responsible for the behaviour or reactions of others. Each of us chooses our words and actions. Others may blame you for their behaviour, but know this is untrue.

This blame game is explained brilliantly in Jess Hill's book, *See What You Made Me Do,* where she addresses domestic abuse and the propensity of offenders to blame their victims for what the abuser has done. If you are (or have been) a victim of domestic abuse, you may have heard accusatory comments such as: *You made me so angry; If only you would do what I tell you, I wouldn't get mad; I had a bad day at work*; etc. Adults are accountable for their behaviour; if people can't manage how they respond to situations, they need to address this, seek therapy such as anger management therapy, and stop blaming others.

Once we recognise the mind games that are played to destabilise our sense of self, we can become resilient to them. We grow stronger and learn to let go of reacting to accusations. Strength involves developing resilience against the words and actions of others while remaining open and vulnerable to the goodness around us.

Healing

Once we heal, we can recognise the hurt in others. Being who we are with self-confidence and a willingness to be kind to others, even after facing trauma, reflects healing. We have the power to choose whether to let the actions of others define who we are. Understanding that we are only responsible for our behaviour empowers us to become immune to how others act. It can be a long journey to develop resilience and heal past traumas so that we can remain vulnerable and empathetic without being paralysed by shame or invalidation. Vulnerability is a strength. The ability to be vulnerable allows us to connect with ourselves and others.

Learning resilience is empowering. We can gain self-confidence and self-worth. We can develop the courage to dismiss others' unkind or abusive behaviour and speak our truth. It's challenging when the hurt runs deep, but courage and resilience become our security as we begin the healing process. If we are struggling to cope, we should seek help or treatment. Becoming an adult means accepting responsibility for our actions and behaviours. Resilience protects us from being hurt by others and helps us live fulfilling lives.

Allowing ourselves to feel emotions instead of suppressing them enables us to understand our feelings. We can give ourselves permission to express anger, rage, sadness, or fear if a situation requires it. There is no shame in being authentic with our emotions and having emotional awareness. We need self-compassion.

> **We are not responsible for the behaviour of others. We are responsible for our own behaviour.**

Developing self-compassion is beneficial for enhancing well-being and facilitating healing from trauma. Professor Paul Raymond Gilbert, a British clinical psychologist, developed Compassionate Mind Training (CMT). CMT was initially designed for individuals with high levels of shame and self-criticism, trauma survivors, and those at risk of developing depression and/or PTSD. It has become so successful as a treatment that CMT courses are now available to people in the general population and staff in organisations such as schools and healthcare facilities.

Self-compassion develops in a nonjudgmental, secure environment through kindness. It promotes empathy, understanding, sympathy, acceptance, and the ability to regulate behaviour. It helps establish a focus on self-soothing and compassion, reducing feelings of threat and hostility. Self-compassion fosters resilience.

Empowered by Resilience: Unveiling Your Inner Warrior

Resilience can be defined as the ability to achieve a successful outcome despite adversity. We can adapt to challenging situations, endure difficulties, and overcome tough times. Developing mental strength and flexibility to handle unexpected setbacks or tragedies decreases the likelihood of becoming overwhelmed by suffering. Mental wellness influences resilience.

Each of us faces stressful situations throughout our lives. Some are mild, others are moderate, and some are severe. Mild stress includes worrying about a job interview, for example. Moderate stress can involve family conflict, academic failure, or losing a loved one, particularly when sound support systems are available and the grieving process can be navigated. Severe or toxic stress refers to overwhelming stress—significant life events during which you lack any support or means to cope. As the brain is the organ that responds to challenges (stressors), it makes sense that a healthy brain copes better than an unhealthy one.

Many factors influence our ability to cope with stress. Various coping methods can depend on the severity of the stress and an individual's perception of it. Two people may experience similar trauma yet respond quite differently. This variability can occur even when the stress is intense.

Coping strategies include problem-solving to determine whether it is feasible to work through the issue and take steps to alleviate it. Another approach is to accept that the problem is too complex, distressing, or beyond your control and to seek help to manage it. How each of us copes may depend not only on past experiences but also on the nature of the stressor.

Our coping ability is shaped by our upbringing, social status, culture, exposure to previous traumas, and personality. Perception is influenced by well-being, the amount of available social support, and our belief in our own capabilities and confidence in managing stress. Mental wellness affects both our abilities and perceptions.

Poor mental health often prevents individuals from coping with even minor stressors. If you have experienced distressing trauma and feel grief-stricken and broken, it can be too painful to comprehend even a minor inconvenience, let alone a severe problem. When the brain is flooded with stress hormones, the limbic system cannot receive input from the prefrontal cortex, where our ability to rationalise and make decisions originates. Remember that when you are feeling despair and anguish, your limbic system is being bombarded by stress signals from your reptilian brain. As a result, your thinking brain cannot transmit rational and meaningful information to help you cope.

Suffering from psychological illnesses such as depression or anxiety hinders the brain's capacity to make sensible decisions and evaluate the severity or intensity of any given situation. Once your emotions are under control, you can make logical and clear judgements. Unfortunately, having mental illnesses diminishes the ability to cope with stress because your brain is too unwell at the time. Once healing begins, resilience can develop.

Resilience depends upon:

- the nature of the stressor (interestingly, whether the stressor is a natural disaster or a man-made one. Chronic exposure to stresses and traumas that are man-made tends to be associated with more severe and complex PTSD symptoms.)

- the resources available for coping (supportive families and friends, healthcare professionals, etc.)
- our self-esteem and sense of self-worth
- how susceptible we are to psychological problems due to past traumas
- other demands we have upon us at the time (it is far more challenging to cope with a demanding problem during busy or stressful times or when we are ill).

Healthy self-esteem enhances the ability to respond more productively when faced with trauma. Situations become more tolerable when your brain is healthy. If you have experienced chronic or severe stress and trauma, you may have fewer coping strategies. Childhood trauma restricts cognitive flexibility in the brain. If, as a child, you faced significant trauma, structures within your brain may not have developed as they should. The development of self-esteem and self-worth requires a healthy brain. The capacity to cope with stress relies on both internal support from the brain and external support, such as a healthy environment.

Growing up in a family characterised by conflict, neglect, violence, and inadequate parenting contributes to childhood trauma and hinders the development of healthy self-esteem and positive thoughts. Inadequate parenting may involve tactics such as withdrawing affection to manipulate a child's emotional and psychological well-being.

Risk factors include negative interpersonal relationships, such as experiencing humiliation, bullying, and early exposure to dysfunction or trauma. The fear of being scorned or humiliated can foster hopelessness, leading to feelings of entrapment, depression, and suicidal thoughts. You may find it extremely challenging to solve problems or set goals, and you may have limited resilience.

Trauma affects your ability to move forward in life, and you may constantly revisit past traumatic events. These painful memories and the replaying of overwhelming experiences etch trauma more deeply into your brain, resulting in intrusive thought processes, and revisiting the trauma becomes a vicious circle.

With so many negative memories taking up space in the brain, there is little capacity left for creating positive, happy memories.

We can also compulsively expose ourselves to situations that remind us of our traumas. Over time, this can lead to a generalised numbing of feelings, decreasing our capacity to deal with future stressors.

Fortunately, resilience can be developed with the support of both psychological and physical resources. Mental health can be maintained or regained despite experiencing childhood adversities. Resilience protects against the development of psychiatric symptoms; you can learn how to cultivate it. Resilience is supported by good physical health (see Chapter 17).

Getting enough sleep, exercising, and maintaining a balanced diet contribute to withstanding stressful times. Having faced similar past adversities prepares us to combat difficulties, as do strong personal values such as courage and bravery. Optimism plays a role. Positive life experiences help develop a healthy brain that can adapt to change.

Another factor is our perception of whether life is improving or worsening. The ability to maintain or generate positive emotions in response to adverse events, such as trauma, personal attacks, or witnessing cruelty, reduces our likelihood of developing depression and anxiety.

> **Resilience is supported by good physical health.**

Expressing gratitude for every positive experience, influence, and support can help cultivate effective and beneficial attitudes. We can seek the good and the beauty in the world around us, concentrating on what we can do to enhance our situations. We must acknowledge that resilience is like a muscle that can be strengthened through positivity and optimism. Self-care and reaching out for help when we can't manage what's happening to us or within us bolster our resilience.

Summary:
- Emotions are normal, and we are meant to feel them.
- Many of us have been raised in a culture where showing emotions was unsafe or forbidden.
- Normal emotions can become distorted if we have suffered abuse.
- Psychological trauma can be present in our homes, workplaces, or public.
- Repression: Pushing emotions down unconsciously.
- Suppression: Consciously avoiding emotions to cope temporarily.
- We have the power to choose whether we allow the actions of others to define who we are. We must recognise that each person is responsible for their behaviour. We are not responsible for the behaviour of others.
- Developing resilience is empowering. It is also hard work. Courage and resilience become our security.
- Vulnerability is a strength. Being vulnerable but resilient against hurt from others helps us live fulfilling lives.
- Invalidation is a weapon used to assert power and dismiss or diminish the feelings of others. It is one of the most damaging forms of psychological abuse.
- Invalidation is linked to depression, anxiety, social avoidance, impulsivity, rule-breaking, and aggression. It impedes the formation of a healthy personality attachment to others, self, and emotions.
- Invalidation is more than disagreement; it implies something fundamentally wrong with our feelings.
- Shame is a negative emotion that can range from shyness to self-loathing, with or without self-harm.
- Shame differs from guilt in that guilt can usually be alleviated by apologising or reparation, whereas shame is often experienced as one's entire being is fundamentally flawed. Shame is a more intense and unbearable emotion than guilt.

- Self-reflection, self-awareness, and understanding that you are only responsible for your own behaviour, not what has been done to you. They are vital in helping us overcome shame.
- Anger and shame are closely linked. Feelings of shame can unleash severe resentment or bitterness, which may erupt if we feel scorned or threatened. Aggression towards others can quickly lead to renewed shame.
- A 'flood' of shame can cause sudden, acute emotional pain.
- Shame is strongly connected with depression.
- Repeated trauma is linked to developing PTSD.
- Self-compassion is developed through kindness in a nonjudgemental, secure environment. It promotes empathy, understanding, sympathy, acceptance, and the ability to regulate behaviour.
- Brené Brown explains that women who received empathy and understanding from others had their shame diminished. This helped their perceptions of themselves, helping them develop resilience.
- What we perceive as shameful may have stemmed from what we learned as children, including cultural, societal, and religious beliefs.
- Addressing feelings of shame with trusted friends and/or professionals can help eliminate these emotional burdens.
- Resilience can be defined as the ability to achieve a successful outcome in the face of adversity and whether we can adapt to challenging situations, withstand troubles, and overcome hard times.
- Resilience depends upon the nature of the stressor, the resources we have for coping, our self-esteem and sense of worth, how susceptible we are to past traumas, and other demands we have upon us at the time.
- Resilience is supported by good physical health and can be strengthened by positive attitudes such as gratitude.

Chapter 10

Adverse Childhood Experiences: Breaking the Cycle, From Survival to Thriving

Imagine growing up in a home where silence is the norm; speaking up often leads to harsh criticism or physical violence. As an adult, you may avoid conflict at all costs, even to your detriment. If expressing your opinions invites cutting remarks or if you have witnessed or experienced violence, you may struggle to convey emotions or share your opinions. You might also find yourself becoming a people pleaser to keep those around you happy. Our upbringings can significantly influence the level of emotional intelligence we possess as adults.

Our childhoods shape us, and children who grow up in homes with emotionally unstable or abusive caregivers are often negatively affected both psychologically and physically. It may take many years to recognise that you carry the burden of trauma within you. It is now known that any trauma experienced in childhood profoundly affects our mental and physical health unless treated.

What are ACEs?

The term "Adverse Childhood Experiences (ACEs)" was created in 1998. It describes childhood exposure to physical, sexual, and emotional abuse, emotional maltreatment, and household dysfunction. It encompasses a wide range of traumas, from mild to severe. You may have had a caregiver or parent who was incarcerated, struggled with addiction to alcohol or drugs, attempted or committed suicide, engaged in domestic violence, or suffered from mental illnesses, including depression. All of these are considered traumas. Other examples include:

- living in a war zone
- living through natural disasters
- witnessing community violence
- experiencing peer victimisation
- living in poverty
- having a chronic illness.

These are all situations that impact health.

Harvard University's Center on the Developing Child describes toxic stress as *the excessive or prolonged activation of stress response systems in the body and brain*. Adverse childhood experiences affect normal brain development, particularly in the limbic system, which influences our behaviour, emotions, and memory. As we have learned from previous chapters, our genetic makeup and environments shape how well we cope with these complex challenges.

Experiencing ACEs

If you grew up tiptoeing around emotionally damaged parents or caregivers, you are likely to develop depression. The same is true if you witnessed parents or loved ones being abused. Your stress-response system as a child would have been on high alert multiple times a day, inundating your body with stress hormones. Experiencing high levels of stress at an early age can lead to:

- negative self-esteem
- poor coping skills
- difficulty adapting to change
- high levels of self-criticism
- avoidance and disengagement tendencies
- being overly vigilant
- an increased reactivity to threats
- be at greater risk for substance abuse
- mental illness
- poor physical health.

Physical, sexual, and emotional abuse during childhood increases the likelihood of binge eating and the pursuit of thinness. This is particularly evident in cases of sexual abuse, although obesity can also result from these experiences.

Childhood sexual abuse is associated with higher rates of generalised anxiety disorder, social anxiety disorder, panic disorder, and other conditions such as agoraphobia. Those who have experienced childhood abuse are twice as likely to experience psychotic symptoms and to develop borderline personality disorder, schizophrenia, and obsessive-compulsive disorder.

Child sexual abuse (CSA) is one of the most severe adverse childhood experiences (ACEs). It is highly toxic, affecting individuals both physically and psychologically. Experiencing CSA as a child is profoundly humiliating and shameful. While perpetrators are solely to blame, it is the victims who endure the suffering and guilt, often carrying these burdens well into adulthood.

Recent studies reveal that enduring both sexual and physical violence can make a person six times more likely to experience suicidal ideation. This suffering is not your fault. The stigma and shame of the abuse inflicted upon you do not reflect who you are; however, this, sadly, does not lessen the pain felt.

Chronic illnesses such as PTSD and the experience of revisiting abuse can be common torments. Trauma has a cumulative effect, and maltreatment during childhood can lead to heightened reactivity to new stressors in your life. This is not your fault. Trauma distorts self-perception. Healing is possible, although it may take time. Support from survivor groups and compassion from family and friends can help you recognise that you are worthy and deserving of living a happy life.

> Children who have suffered both sexual and physical violence are six times as likely to develop suicide ideation.

Just like traumas experienced in adulthood, childhood traumas don't have to be severe to be psychologically harmful. If you faced verbal abuse as a child, you are likely to experience 1.6 times more symptoms of depression and anxiety. You are also twice as likely to develop a mood disorder in your lifetime compared to a child who has not faced this kind of abuse. Your emotional skills may be underdeveloped, and feelings of low self-esteem and self-criticism are common. Additionally, this increases your risk of developing mental health disorders.

Epigenetics,

Epigenetics studies gene expressions that are 'turned on or off' due to our environmental experiences and lifestyles. It's a tricky scientific concept to understand but consider this scenario: identical twins are adopted at birth into two different families. Each has the same DNA. Twin A is welcomed into a home with loving parents, raised in a clean and healthy environment, and is not exposed to poverty or abuse. Twin B lives in a clean environment and is not exposed to poverty, but experiences household dysfunction through emotionally unstable parenting and witnesses verbal abuse.

If each child is examined at, say, age 8, Twins A and B will still share identical DNA; however, differences will arise in which genes have been 'switched on or off' due to their environments. This illustrates the concept of epigenetics. The twins began life with the same DNA, but their differing life experiences shaped epigenetic changes between them. Twin A would have fewer health issues and healthier brain development than Twin B because Twin B's stress response systems have been activated more frequently due to trauma.

These gene expressions can also be passed from one generation to the next (transgenerational epigenetic inheritance), as discovered in a 2015 study of Holocaust survivors and their families. Researchers found changes in the survivors' genes in their offspring, even though the children did not experience the trauma. These inherited changes increase the likelihood that children of survivors will develop anxiety, depression, and PTSD at a higher rate.

Similar changes have been observed in Indigenous communities worldwide. These support the argument that intergenerational trauma is real. The colonisation of Indigenous peoples, characterised by cultural suppression, forced displacement, residential schools, and violence, has negatively impacted successive generations through epigenetic changes. These inherited changes have affected psychological health and resulted in physical health disparities within these communities. It is as though the trauma of past generations has been etched into the biological makeup of their families.

It is also interesting to note that conditions such as schizophrenia and autism are linked to epigenetic dysregulation. It is believed that this may be due to 'switching on or off' the genes relating to brain functions and stress responses. PTSD, bipolar disorder, anxiety, and depression are also thought to be influenced by epigenetic inheritance.

Other factors such as diet, exercise, and pollution may also influence epigenetics. The good news is that these changes do not have to be permanent. They can be reversed through stress management, meditation, regular exercise, a balanced diet, and, in some cases, medication. Remember, our brains can heal.

How ACEs Shape Adulthood

The trauma suffered during childhood can impact our health well into adulthood. It not only affects brain development during childhood but also intensifies the risk of mental illnesses and directly influences the likelihood of developing physical diseases, including asthma, cancer, multiple sclerosis, or heart disease throughout our adult lives.

Children cannot manage the stress they feel when exposed to toxic behaviour. This emotional dysregulation can continue into adulthood. Consider working in a position where your boss is a bully or a sexual predator. If you have suffered ACEs, you may be too fearful to speak out. You may fear retaliation and ridicule. Or disbelief.

Studies confirm the link between experiencing trauma as a child and poor physical health in later years. Understanding how and why childhood trauma influences adult health empowers us to be proactive and resolute in managing our wellness. Once we comprehend why we are unwell, we can focus on remedies to minimise or possibly reverse physical ailments. Recognising that ACEs can lead to diseases later in life reminds us that what affects our brains also impacts our bodies, and healing from past traumas fosters overall wellness.

Relevant Studies

Dr. Nadine Burke Harris is a Canadian American paediatrician who realised the impact adverse childhood experiences had on the health, behaviour, and growth patterns of children she treated in her practice. She noticed high rates of asthma and other illnesses, including two children with autoimmune hepatitis (a rare disorder). She recognised that there was a direct link between the poor health of her patients and childhood adversity.

In 2015, she delivered a powerful TED Talk sharing information on how children who are exposed to severe trauma or adversities sustain damage to their brains and bodies. Each adverse experience (losing a parent, divorce, abuse, parental neglect, etc.) equates to one point on an ACE score. She explains that ACEs are very common, with at least 67% of the population having at least one ACE and one in eight people, or 12.6%, having four or more ACEs.

The higher a person's ACE score, the greater their risk of poor health in adulthood. Someone with a score of four or more ACEs is two and a half times more likely to have chronic obstructive pulmonary disease or hepatitis than someone with a score of zero. They face four and a half times the risk of developing depression and 12 times the risk of suicidality. A person with a score of seven or more has three times the risk of lung cancer and three and a half times the likelihood of developing coronary artery disease.

Other studies demonstrated that the presence of at least one ACE was linked to a two-to-five-fold increase in attempted suicides. With seven or more ACES, this rate rose to over 30 times the likelihood.

Dr. Burke Harris states that visible differences are observed on MRI scans of the brains between children with high ACE scores and those with low scores. She noted that children who are exposed to toxic stress experience ongoing activation of their stress response systems. This leads to health-damaging changes in children's bodies, impacting the immune system, brain structure and function, as well as the hormonal system, and can result in a significantly lower life expectancy—a 20-year difference.

However, this doesn't necessarily mean that if you have experienced many childhood adversities, you are doomed to live a life of poor health. It's important to remember that our brains and bodies can regenerate and heal from psychological maltreatment. What's crucial is that we recognise and address the traumas we have faced so we can heal.

Dr. Burke Harris' book, The Deepest Well: Healing the Long-term Effects of Childhood Adversity, explains in simple, easy-to-understand language how adversities faced in childhood change the biological systems within our bodies, leading to diseases and ill health later in life.

She discusses how these adversities affect our immune systems, levels of inflammation within the body, and genetic and epigenetic influences that are passed from one generation to the next. Furthermore, she emphasises that early detection of ACEs in childhood is imperative to minimise the damage done and reduce the likelihood of diseases developing in later life.

Dr Burke Harris explains how our stress-response systems are 'switched on' when we face danger. They are meant to turn off once the threat has passed. She uses the analogy of how being chased by a bear activates these systems, but will 'turn off' once we escape the bear. She then explains that for some of us, the 'bear' is someone we live with or have regular close contact with—someone who is abusive or neglectful, and there is no escape. Your stress-response systems don't turn off if your 'bear' is a constant threat.

Dr. Burke Harris believes that children should be screened for ACEs early and that support systems should be implemented if they are identified. She emphasises the importance of educating parents about the consequences of ACEs and toxic stress, just as parents are taught about the dangers of lead-based paint, for example.

When we understand how the traumas we face as children or adults can impact the lives of the children we raise, we gain insight into intergenerational trauma. Healing ourselves benefits our children. Even a reduction of just 10–25% in child abuse and neglect could potentially prevent 31.4–80.3 million cases of depression and anxiety worldwide.

The Pitfalls of Unresolved Stress

Unfortunately, unresolved stress can lead to impaired immune responses and increased inflammation. It is now recognised that this may contribute to the development of autoimmune diseases such as rheumatoid arthritis, inflammatory bowel disease, and multiple sclerosis. Chronic stress exposure causes changes to the structure and function of the nervous and endocrine systems (our stress response systems).

> Adverse childhood experiences can lead to coronary artery disease, chronic obstructive pulmonary disorder, cancer, Type 2 diabetes, hepatitis, and more, in adulthood.

Our bodies reflect our experiences, putting us at an increased risk of developing Type 2 diabetes, heart disease, lung and liver disease, and cancer later in life. This underscores the importance of addressing the adversities and traumas we have suffered. Our brains and bodies can heal by confronting the damage we have endured, ultimately reducing our susceptibility to future illnesses.

We may also be at risk for neurodevelopmental disorders if we are exposed to toxic childhood stress. Neurodevelopmental disorders are disabilities resulting from impairments of the brain and/or central nervous system, affecting brain function. These disorders may arise from genetic defects, medical conditions, or delays in normal development.

According to the *Diagnostic and Statistical Manual of Mental Disorders: DSM-5-TR*/American Psychiatric Association, neurodevelopmental disorders are ...*a group of conditions with onset in the developmental period.* These include:

- intellectual disabilities
- communication disorders
- Autism Spectrum Disorder (ASD)
- Attention Deficit Hyperactivity Disorder (ADHD).

Again, this does not mean we are destined to suffer from these disorders; however, we are more likely to do so if we have been exposed to many ACEs.

If you have neurodevelopmental disorders, you may struggle with healthy coping strategies; you might exhibit behavioural issues or potentially face cognitive impairments, such as memory loss or difficulty understanding. These challenges can arise if you have experienced trauma as a child. ***They are not your fault.***

Poor coping strategies may have led to drug use, suicidality, unplanned pregnancy, mental illnesses, or risky sexual behaviour during adolescence. This emotional dysregulation can persist into adulthood. Recognising that your childhood has impacted the development of your brain is the first step toward reprogramming it for better health.

Why Childhood Trauma Impacts the Brain

Our brains do not fully develop until the age of 25. It is important to remember that the prefrontal cortex is the last area of the brain to mature, and it plays a crucial role in helping us solve problems and make rational decisions. Any negative experiences we encounter during childhood affect the development of neural pathways in the brain. These pathways multiply rapidly in children, with millions of neural connections formed every second.

At birth, our brain is only 25% the size of an adult brain, and by the end of our first year, it has doubled in weight. By age 5, it has tripled in size. Because our brains develop rapidly during these early years, toxic stress weakens our brain development and affects our ability to adapt to changes (plasticity) throughout our lives.

Childhood trauma significantly impacts our disease risk in adulthood. Adversities faced during childhood affect our immune systems, which regulate inflammation levels within the body and, in turn, influence our health in adulthood. Inflammation can lead to illness.

Childhood physical neglect and abuse also increase the likelihood of violent behaviour in adulthood, including intimate partner violence. If you witnessed intimate partner violence during your childhood, you are at risk of becoming a perpetrator or victim in adulthood.

> **Childhood physical neglect and abuse increase the likelihood of violent behaviour in adulthood.**

It's Not Your Fault—But It's Time to Heal

If you have suffered from childhood trauma in any form, you are not responsible for it. However, recognising the impact of childhood trauma is our responsibility as adults. If we endure the pain of family abuse or dysfunction, ignoring or burying our feelings merely distracts us from it, and our bodies can remind us at any time. As the poet Nicole Lyons eloquently wrote:

'The deepest pain I ever felt was denying my own feelings to make everyone else comfortable.'

Our emotions are real, and we are meant to feel them. Erasing painful memories creates space for positive experiences. We can seek help and support from professionals, family, and friends; however, the only person who can heal us is ourselves. As overwhelming and distressing as this often is, we must lance and scrape our wounds clean to mend them.

If you are struggling to raise children due to unresolved trauma and lack the necessary support systems or emotional skills, please seek help; there is no shame in asking for support. Raising children is challenging. If you have not fully healed from past traumas, you may struggle to develop healthy relationships with your children and partner.

We need to understand and break the cycles of toxic stress within our families to improve the health of our children and future generations. Intergenerational trauma can persist until the pain is addressed and alleviated. Remember, this is not a life sentence—you can heal. Part of the healing process involves recognising that we are not responsible for what we endured as children, and unless the trauma is acknowledged and treated, it may continue to impact our lives.

If you are unsure where to start addressing childhood trauma, begin with a general practitioner (GP). GPs can recommend support groups, psychologists, counsellors, and community agencies to assist you on your path to healing. Organisations such as Beyond Blue or Lifeline provide practical, compassionate advice without judgement. The phone numbers for these and other support groups are listed at the end of the book. You can heal.

Summary:

- Trauma suffered during childhood can significantly impact mental and physical health, influencing the development of diseases during adulthood.
- Adverse childhood experiences (ACEs) describe childhood exposure to physical, sexual, and emotional abuse, emotional maltreatment, and household dysfunction.
- Negative experiences during childhood impact the development of neural pathways in the brain. Children who experience extreme stress in the early years develop disruptions in their stress-response systems, which can create long-term health issues.
- There are visible differences seen on MRI scans of the brains of children who have experienced ACEs. The damage can be seen.
- Childhood adversities affect the immune system, which controls levels of inflammation in the body, influencing genetic and epigenetic patterns passed to successive generations.
- Childhood trauma significantly impacts disease risk in adulthood, and intervention at an early age to identify at-risk children can promote healing and recovery.

Chapter 11

From Awareness to Empowerment: Navigating Toxic Personalities

'From all this we may learn that there are two races of men in this world, but only these two — the "race" of the decent man and the "race" of the indecent man. Both are found everywhere; they penetrate into all groups of society. No group consists entirely of decent or indecent people. In this sense, no group is of "pure race" — and therefore one occasionally found a decent fellow among the camp guards.'
— Frankl (2004)

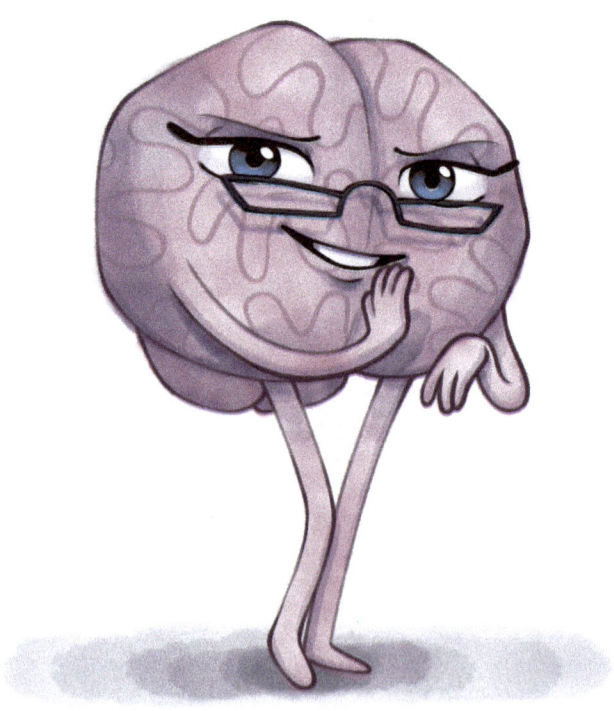

Most of us have encountered toxic personalities throughout our lives. They are often found in workplaces or families—that is, among people you would not choose to associate with, but can't always avoid. These are individuals who generate a sense of dread or sickness in the pit of your stomach, even just thinking about them. They are the people you feel compelled to protect yourself from; perhaps you find yourself crossing the street to evade them or making excuses, even lying, to maintain your distance.

They are individuals who drain you emotionally, constantly embroiled in drama and problems (who want you to listen to their rants but don't want your advice), those who gossip about others, or those who disrespect and disregard your feelings. Nothing is ever their fault because they always perceive themselves as the 'victim' and, therefore, will never apologise. If these comments have sparked the image of a particular person in your mind, then you know exactly the type I'm referring to.

Toxic personalities can be emotionally damaging, especially if you are unaware of the manipulative games being played or feel powerless to deal with them. Their toxic behaviours may be overt and unmistakable or subtle and sly. They can manifest as humiliating comments in public or abuse inflicted in private. Either way, it constitutes psychological maltreatment, which can lead to physical harm.

I recall an appointment with a psychologist many years ago. I walked into her room and sat down, unsure of what to say except that I felt ashamed to be there. I had a good husband and three healthy children, and we lived comfortably in a lovely home. It was only after I answered the many probing questions she posed that she threw her hands in the air and said, 'This is psychological abuse. Why are you surprised that you feel so bad?' I had no idea. Until that point, I couldn't recognise the manipulative behaviour that was destroying my soul and draining the essence of who I was. I couldn't see the abuse for what it was.

Receiving conduct from someone who exaggerates mistakes, humiliates, discredits, or attempts to shame and invalidate you can erode self-confidence and cause intense emotional distress. These behaviours are forms of psychological manipulation, and they can be soul-destroying. Learning to recognise emotional manipulation and toxic behaviour is empowering.

Abusers show little consideration for those they hurt. They seek to control people and situations for their own benefit. If challenged, they will vigorously justify their position, resorting to insults, criticism, and lies, and may even fabricate an alternative version of events to defend their stance. Some will sidestep the topic and refuse to participate in any discussion, employing silent treatment, disdain, and condescension to evade any conversation that threatens them.

Recognising the mind games at play is the first step in building resilience and learning how to deal with toxic personalities. We can choose not to ' play the game ' when we 'see' and understand the tactics employed.

> Learning to recognise emotional manipulation and toxic behaviour is empowering.

Toxic Tactics and Traits

Sabotaging Special Events

Sabotaging special events, such as Christmas dinners or birthday parties, is a common tactic employed by abusive family members or acquaintances. This includes behaviours like drunkenness, sarcasm, snide or cruel comments, and even violence. It can become so routine that you dread attending these gatherings. Sometimes, this behaviour is accepted as normal, excused, overlooked, shrugged off, or dismissed—such as thinking that's just the way Mum is; he never means it; or she's having a bad day! You must tread carefully to avoid even the slightest disagreement in hopes of preventing a conflict—or worse. This makes attending these events exhausting and stressful.

All families experience minor conflicts or disagreements among members, but it's not an issue as long as comments and actions remain respectful. People can agree to disagree when their beliefs differ, but if someone's behaviour involves bullying, gaslighting, violence, sexual predation, or drunken outbursts, it's not mere disagreement; it's emotional abuse.

Those who are generous in spirit, empathetic, or young often become targets for toxic personality types. Techniques for establishing rapport frequently begin with self-disclosure, where the person shares something personal and elicits a reciprocal response. These interactions often occur much earlier in a relationship than anticipated. They can include flattery, compliments, and accusations of bad behaviour.

Once someone becomes involved with a toxic person, emotional manipulation begins. Initially, this 'love-bombing' may seem positive and uplifting. However, the skilled manipulator responds to any perceived disrespect or offence with relational aggression, which can involve threats, damaging one's reputation, sulking, silent treatment, and ostracism. This behaviour often leaves victims feeling confused and deeply hurt. It's common for these manipulators to attempt to isolate their victims from family and friends socially.

Because the manipulator is skilled at portraying a false nature to those around them, they can often gain the support of others in the victim's circle of friends, family, and acquaintances, who become entangled in the lies. This further isolates the victim, who then tries even harder to please their abuser.

Often, an abuser will wait until they are alone with their victim or out of earshot of others before making a cruel or upsetting comment. Some experienced manipulators can deliver a taunt that might sound inoffensive when repeated to a third party. This is what makes it so difficult for some victims to recognise the abuse. Contempt is typically present in the delivery.

It may seem non-combatant or inoffensive to others. If challenged, an abuser often changes tack and says, 'I was only joking'. Comments like this are belittling. You may be accused of being oversensitive. Apologies from abusers are either non-existent or delivered as scathing condemnations: 'I'm sorry, but I didn't realise you would take it that way!' There will always be a 'but' followed by an excuse or an accusation, never a sincere apology. It's also worth noting that an apology without changed behaviour is not a sincere apology; it is manipulation.

> Those who are generous of spirit, who are empaths, or young, tend to be the targets for toxic personality types.

The abuse may lead to a victim experiencing acute shame and self-loathing, along with a desire to isolate from the world. Once the perpetrator has accomplished their aim and gained whatever they wished to achieve from the relationship, they will move on to their next victim. This behaviour reflects control and power, coupled with a callous disregard for those they use, which describes personality types characterised by antagonism, selfishness, and exploitative behaviour aimed at satisfying their own needs. These relationships are physically and emotionally draining.

Deception

Abusers tend to behave poorly around those they feel safe with. They hide their behaviour from individuals they wish to impress or from those who they know will not tolerate the games they play. Some make excuses for poor conduct—"I was drunk, you made me angry, it's my illness that makes me do it," etc. It's interesting to watch these individuals around people they want to impress; generally, they become charming and gracious.

Abusive behaviour can be switched on or off depending on the circumstances. What we learn from this is that if a person can control their abusive behaviour based on the company they keep, their excuses that they 'lost control' are proven false.

> **Abusers rely on silence and shifting blame onto the victim.**

Tackling Workplace Toxicity

Someone who creates an atmosphere of fear amongst staff, with everyone cautiously trying to keep them happy, is psychologically abusing their colleagues. Once again, this is about control. It's not about doing what's best for the organisation; it's the misuse of power to cause division and fear.

Studies on toxic behaviour in the workplace have identified that those who work for organisations with leaders who degrade, falsely blame, harass, or act aggressively towards staff experience significant psychological distress. Individuals with toxic personalities can appear to be high performers within organisations, often rewarded with progressively higher leadership roles.

> *They seek to obtain favours by flattering others and pretending to like them, they show a willingness to exploit others, they consider themselves as superior, and they feel entitled to privileges (Ashton, 2007 #457).*

This does not bode well for those who work alongside them. These behaviours are not confined to leaders within workplaces; however, there is typically a power imbalance between the abuser and the abused. Again, it is essential to recognise the tactics and learn how best to deal with them.

Total Control and Manipulation

Emotional manipulation serves to control the behaviour, relationships, or emotions of others, distorting situations to benefit the abuser directly. Manipulators wield control subtly, employing emotional abuse to achieve their desires. Once you experience abusive manipulation, recognising it becomes easier; however, instilling doubt in you is a key aspect of the abuse.

Manipulation often exists on a spectrum. Occasionally, employing a mild form of manipulation to simplify our lives or benefit us does not indicate that it is part of our character. We all tend to create situations that work best for us. A manipulator fears loss of face and loss of control, and any challenge to their authority may provoke retaliation; a toxic parent may withdraw attention or refuse to engage with their child. A manipulative co-worker may discredit or sabotage another's work.

Demeaning comments, intentional sabotage of plans, criticism intended to harm, and threats to expose weaknesses to others are common tactics employed by manipulative personalities.

Gaslighting

Gas Light by Patrick Hamilton (1938) tells the story of a husband sowing seeds of doubt in his wife's mind, making her question her own sanity. The term gaslighting was derived from this play and its later film adaptations (1940, 1944) and now refers to a form of emotional abuse based on lies and manipulation.

Gaslighting involves lying, belittling, and disorienting a victim so thoroughly that they begin to doubt their judgement. Masters of this manipulation may even stage bizarre incidents and then deny that they occurred.

Projection

Projection is a powerful weapon used by manipulators. This defence mechanism involves abusers accusing their victims of the very behaviours they display. They refuse to accept blame, even when it is evident that they are at fault.

Typical responses include accusations such as:

'You made me behave this way.'
'If you had only done what you were told, I wouldn't have reacted like that.'

When an abuser is challenged by boundaries being set or their rules ignored, they often respond with an attack. They may react with rage that is wholly inappropriate for the circumstances. There's even a name for this—narcissistic rage.

Recognising a narcissist and maintaining clear, concise boundaries while staying calm is the best way to handle them. They are notorious for blaming others whenever they feel confronted. It helps to disconnect from arguments and remain assertive yet emotionally detached. Stand your ground, and don't get caught up in arguments regardless of any provocation.

There can be no reasoning with a person who refuses to acknowledge their bad behaviour but instead becomes angry about how their conduct is perceived. This is an unhealthy and abnormal response to conflict.

If you grew up in a home with abusive, neglectful, or emotionally unavailable parents—or if expressing an opinion different from controlling family members led to confrontational arguments—you may struggle as an adult to express your feelings or opinions with confidence.

You can also discourage contentious issues within your family or friendships by changing the subject or downplaying them to avoid conflict.

Contentious issues can be discussed reasonably and calmly within an emotionally mature family or workplace. Conversations are conducted with respect. However, this is not the case in abusive or emotionally immature groups.

Toxic sibling relationships can develop in dysfunctional families, with adult children harbouring resentment and anger towards their siblings. Contact with these family members may become so distressing that recovery time is needed after even brief communication. Discussing past hurts may be impossible without these conversations escalating into heated arguments.

In such situations, it is often best to minimise contact, excusing yourself from family gatherings if necessary. Refusing to engage with toxic people is an act of self-care. Disengaging from family members can be very sad, but it is a wise and courageous choice when harmful or deceptive behaviour persists.

We tend to repeat learned behaviours until we discover new, more constructive ones. If we lack the confidence to manage our emotions during disagreements or differences of opinion, it can feel safer to withdraw from the conversation or avoid expressing how we feel. Unfortunately, this tacit acceptance can lead to disappointment or shame regarding our inability to be authentic. Weighing which option is safest for you is an individual choice.

How we respond to conflict can reveal our vulnerability and lack of resilience. Being able to disagree calmly is a skill that must be learned. It requires strong social skills, often instilled by healthy role models. If we were not fortunate enough to gain this from our upbringing, we can teach ourselves as part of our own healing process.

Dependent Personality Disorder

Another form of toxic behaviour is that of someone with dependent personality disorder (DPD). The *Diagnostic and Statistical Manual of Mental Disorders* (DSM-5) states that the diagnostic criteria of those with this disorder have *a pervasive and excessive need to be taken care of that leads to submissive and clinging behaviour and fears of separation beginning by early adulthood and present in a variety of contexts…*

People with DPD struggle with being alone. They fear they cannot care for themselves or function without assistance. Their need for support from others is excessive, leading them to adopt extreme measures to meet these needs, such as volunteering for undesirable tasks or being completely passive and meek in the relationship. Physical distance from others may lead to frequent phone calls or messages as a means of seeking constant validation and advice.

Engaging with this personality type can be draining. These individuals often lack self-confidence and struggle with even the most mundane decisions, such as what to wear and what to eat, as well as other everyday choices. They often struggle to complete tasks independently, feeling incapable and inadequate. If their relationships deteriorate, they often feel compelled to seek out another one urgently, sometimes becoming more submissive and compliant to fulfil their emotional attachment needs.

Extricating yourself from relationships or limiting interaction with individuals who have DPD can be challenging due to their intense fear of abandonment. Suggesting they seek treatment from a doctor or therapist is supportive but will only benefit them if they are willing to develop self-dependence and self-coping strategies. If they are not willing, you may need to seek assistance for yourself. Recognising and freeing yourself from unhealthy relationships is not selfish.

Acknowledging Abuse

Maltreatment can leave us feeling emotionally unbalanced, leading us to doubt our sanity. Mind games erode our self-confidence and cause us to question our own perceptions. We may think:

> *Perhaps I am just overly sensitive.*
> *Maybe I don't work well with others.*
> *Perhaps I don't explain myself well.*

Challenging bad behaviour can be complex and may cause retaliation, so it is prudent to plan to keep yourself safe. Acknowledging to yourself that what you are experiencing is abuse is the first step to protecting yourself.

When we buy into the abuser's story that our feelings are wrong and there must be something deficient or defective within us, it leaves us vulnerable to further abuse. Feeling trapped in an abusive relationship, where you have no sense of autonomy, leads to low self-esteem and self-doubt. The erosion of self-confidence, self-belief, and the perception that things won't improve results in pessimism becoming a vicious self-fulfilling prophecy. Recognising that abusive behaviour is unacceptable and that we deserve better interrupts that cycle.

Avoiding Conflict

Trying to cover up our emotional pain drains enormous amounts of energy and can lead to unhealthy behaviour, such as becoming a people pleaser, to avoid further conflict. We lose the essence of who we are as we carefully tiptoe around toxic, controlling personalities.

This loss may lead us to anger quickly. Our alert systems become hypervigilant, causing us to snap at those we feel safe with—typically those we love. People-pleasing and anger serve as defences to protect us from further hurt. When we have been deeply wounded, it can be challenging to maintain our composure during conflicts. Our stress levels rise, making it difficult to make rational decisions. We become victims, often at the hands of someone who claims to love us. This is frequently where depression begins.

Setting Boundaries: Your Shield Against Toxicity

When we cannot avoid a toxic personality, the best way to protect ourselves from the psychological trauma it inflicts is to set clear boundaries. Boundaries protect our autonomy while showing respect for others. They promote clear communication, encourage us to take responsibility for our behaviour, and remind us that we are accountable for our own lives and choices. Firm boundaries involve refusing to feel responsible for someone else's feelings and recognising our right to protect our emotional state.

Many of us were taught as children that we must consider the needs of others, but we were rarely allowed to value ourselves. This may make it difficult to set boundaries as adults. The good news is that you can learn effective strategies to protect your comfort levels.

Be aware, however, that to an abuser, even the tiniest boundary can be seen as a threat. Challenging bad behaviour is difficult, but the alternative is continuing to live a life controlled and coerced by others. Establishing boundaries to shield ourselves from further emotional pain will likely lead to an initial escalation of toxic behaviour.

Many people feel uncomfortable confronting conflict. Abusers often display self-confidence and intolerance for weaknesses. Their demeanour typically divides their loyalties between those who benefit them and those they regard as either unimportant or a threat.

Those they value may be reluctant to acknowledge how toxic the abuser is to others, or they may genuinely be unaware. If the abuser is a productive member of an organisation, for example, bringing in business or achieving targets, their behaviour might be overlooked. Even when the abuse is obvious, many individuals hesitate to take a stand against such strong personalities, particularly if they are not directly affected.

This refusal to condemn bad behaviour generally leads to an intensification of that behaviour. Unchallenged abuse is a tacit acceptance of psychological maltreatment.

In her book, *Trauma and Recovery*, Judith Herman, M.D., writes:

'It is very tempting to take the side of the perpetrator. All the perpetrator asks is that the bystander do nothing. He appeals to the universal desire to see, hear, and speak no evil. The victim, on the contrary, asks the bystander to share the burden of pain. The victim demands action, engagement, and remembering.'

Setting healthy boundaries can be challenging if you are in the acute stages of dealing with trauma or have been conditioned to believe that you have no right to establish them. Boundaries include having the right to say 'no' to anything you don't want to do, declining to offer support if you currently feel unable to provide it, setting time limits, deciding whether to participate in a conversation or event that feels uncomfortable for you, and needing time alone.

Essentially, boundaries involve addressing your needs and letting go of the guilt that others may impose upon you. If you struggle to establish boundaries, speaking with a psychologist or another professional counsellor can be helpful. We all have personal boundaries, and we are entitled to have them.

When Abuse is Hidden

'He's going to kill me.'

I still remember my friend crying these words as she lay curled on the floor in the foetal position, shaking with fear. Her terror was palpable that day at our workplace, as she had finally revealed the psychological manipulation and abuse inflicted upon her and her three children for years by her husband.

What had our friend done that was so wrong to reduce her to this state of utter despair? She had told his secrets. His abusive behaviour was now known to others. This was her crime.

Our kind and well-meaning boss grabbed her car keys and handbag and headed out the door to confront our friend's husband over what she had just heard. As our boss left the office, our friend began to rock back and forth, wailing—a loud keening sound—as she shook, rocked, and wept in fear. Her fear for her safety and that of her children was deeply distressing. We comforted her as best we could.

He was the abuser. She had been conditioned to hide his abuse. When she could no longer do so, and her torment could no longer be suppressed, her suffering poured out. Abusers rely on silence. Her 'transgression' shone the spotlight on his conduct. His insincerity was now known—he wasn't the 'good guy', the 'caring husband', or the 'great Dad'. He was a controlling, coercive manipulator whose façade had just been shattered. He exploded in rage that evening. Fortunately, he did not physically harm his wife and children. However, his behaviour upon being exposed reflects that of many who mistreat others. Domestic abusers rely upon this abuse being hidden.

In her book, See What You Made Me Do, Jess Hill focuses on the conduct of perpetrators, the justice system that seems to enable them, and the numerous adversities and obstacles their victims face. She describes how coercive control is likely to begin and progress, how victims can lose all sense of self and feel powerless, and how families tiptoe around their abuser to avoid 'upsetting' them. I believe this book should be read by everyone in the justice system, starting with police officers who encounter domestic abuse situations daily.

Understanding Personality

When considering what constitutes an 'abnormal' or 'toxic' personality type, we must first identify what 'normal' is. It's an ambiguous concept that varies greatly depending on our age, culture, life experiences, and time in history. Much of what we may find normal or acceptable today could have been considered mortifying fifty years ago. Fashion is undoubtedly an example of this. What's considered 'normal' behaviour varies immensely between cultures. Western cultures differ from Eastern cultures; for instance, even individual countries within these regions have distinct societal expectations. Consequently, 'normal' is difficult to define.

Psychologists have established guidelines to help identify deviations from what is considered normal behaviour, typically based on societal expectations. These benchmarks require continual adjustment and modification as societal norms evolve.

There are many models and definitions for describing individual characteristics, but a useful framework is the HEXACO model of personality dimensions, which includes:

- H—Honesty, Humility: fair, honest, loyal, sincere, unassuming versus boastful, deceitful, greedy, hypocritical, pompous, pretentious, sly
- E—Emotionality: brave, independent, self-assured, stable, tough versus anxious, emotional, fearful, oversensitive, sentimental, vulnerable
- X—Extraversion: active, cheerful, extraverted, lively, outgoing, sociable, talkative versus introverted, passive, quiet, reserved, shy, withdrawn
- A—Agreeableness: agreeable, gentle, lenient, mild, patient, tolerant versus choleric, ill-tempered, quarrelsome, stubborn
- C—Conscientiousness: careful, diligent, disciplined, organised, precise, thorough versus absent-minded, irresponsible, lazy, negligent, reckless, sloppy
- O—Openness to Experience: creative, innovative, intellectual, ironic, unconventional versus conventional, shallow, unimaginative.

Personalities emerge from the combination of these traits and are shaped by both genetic factors and environmental differences. Someone who scores highly in agreeableness and honesty is likely to be a far more nurturing and trustworthy individual than one who is deceitful, sly, or quarrelsome.

It is advantageous to learn how to recognise—and, where possible, avoid—those with undesirable traits. Unfortunately, we cannot always choose those closest to us—our family members, colleagues, or superiors at work.

If you have not been exposed to someone with a toxic personality, it can be difficult to recognise patterns of behaviour that may, on the surface, seem agreeable but are motivated by underlying self-centeredness and self-interest. These individuals may appear to function normally and seem friendly and obliging outwardly. However, they are skilled in deceit, show little regard for others, and have few inhibitions as they manipulate people and situations for personal gain. Here, we enter the realm of the dark triad of personality— narcissism, Machiavellianism, and psychopathy.

The dark triad of personality types describes individuals characterised by manipulation, callousness, and selfishness at their core. These types disregard social norms and can be untrustworthy, uncaring, manipulative, and controlling. Studies of these personality types indicate that malignant traits are generally responsible for family discord, toxic workplace environments, relationship strains, distress, and criminal activity. Each of the three types possesses unique attributes.

Narcissists have an over-inflated sense of magnificence and pretentiousness. They believe they are superior to others, are egocentric, and self-serving. Despite little proof or justification, they boast of their abilities and achievements. They are most entitled and are compelled to have power over others. Their relationships with others tend to be superficial, and they often exploit others for personal gain. They seek praise and attention and can be vengeful and hostile if challenged.

Family members may recognise that they have narcissistic abusers amongst them who create conflict and dysfunction but tend to lie to outsiders and deny any accusations of family discord. They refuse to admit dysfunction within the family unit and may unite to counter any suggestions that they are flawed. They want to present themselves to the world as being the 'perfect' family.

Those who display Machiavellian traits are skilful at manipulating and manoeuvring people and circumstances to benefit from them. They are astute, cunning, deceitful, and calculating opportunists. They are usually knowledgeable individuals with keen insight, often admired for their achievements, but often show little or no regard for anyone hurt or disadvantaged by their conduct. They are emotionally manipulative and are skilled at playing two people off against each other. They can be exceptionally adept in marketing and business, complementing those they wish to impress and particularly good at making others feel guilty. They tend to be quite cynical.

Psychopathic personalities, by contrast, are often impulsive, undisciplined, and opportunistic. They often lack empathy for others and frequently disregard rules. They are high risk-takers. Violence is more likely within this personality type, as are bullying, sadism, deviant behaviour, and criminal activity. Psychopaths may appear to function normally but have few inhibitions and lack internal moral regulation.

Navigating Family Dynamics

The Australian Counselling Directory describes an unhealthy family dysfunction (first described by family therapist Salvador Minuchin) as enmeshment. Enmeshment within a family is a form of control exerted by parents who strongly wish to influence their children's beliefs and behaviours and who find it unbearable if their children deviate from these strict boundaries, even when they have reached adulthood.

It is essential to realise that enmeshment differs from closeness. Families may be close but still recognise and respect each other's individuality.

In enmeshed families, parents are often inappropriately reliant on their children, confiding in them as if they are friends and involving themselves excessively in their children's lives. Children in these families grow up without clear emotional boundaries. They are expected to prioritise the family's well-being over their own needs and ambitions, facing strong opposition if they challenge 'the rules'.

This is a form of emotional manipulation. Children are expected to provide emotional support for their parents and are often shamed if they prioritise their own needs. Parents may view a child's independence as a betrayal. Moving far away, choosing a different career, or seeking less contact can all trigger accusations of disloyalty.

Children from enmeshed families often develop into people pleasers, avoid conflict, and struggle to assert their independence. They may feel responsible for solving others' problems, share private relationship information with their parents, and maintain emotional dependence well into adulthood.

Breaking free from an enmeshed family and achieving independence—physically, emotionally, spiritually, and intellectually—can be immensely challenging. Yet personal dreams and goals are not selfish or shameful.

Having the strength to break enmeshment bonds requires first knowing what your boundaries need to be and then setting them. Generally, situations in which you feel powerless or unsupported demand strong boundaries. Learn to say 'no' without an explanation.

If you are an adult and the path you have chosen is one that you genuinely want to follow, do not settle for the expectations of others—unless your choices are illegal or profoundly immoral.

Young adults developing autonomy may face challenging confrontations within manipulative families. For instance, they may be told they must cancel plans to attend a family event, accompanied by guilt-tripping comments such as:

'Granny will be so upset if you don't come.'
'You're letting everyone down.'
'You just don't want to be part of the family anymore.'

This is psychological manipulation—a mind game designed to guilt you into compliance. What *you* want will not matter.

Those who use emotional blackmail have little respect for equality in relationships. Their aim is control. Difficulties can arise if you depend on your family financially, but your feelings matter too. It can be empowering to assert yourself by honestly expressing why you are reluctant to attend harmful events, such as:

'I don't want to come because there's always conflict, drunken behaviour, and nasty comments made about my appearance.'

Defying toxic expectations is challenging but essential. Neglecting your needs to keep others comfortable is ultimately distressing and unhealthy. This does not mean you must be intentionally objectionable or hurtful. However, expressing your feelings should be respected, especially when abuse is involved.

From Adversity to Empowerment

There are many aspects of life we cannot control, but how we respond to others and situations is within our power. This is where our strength lies.

'Calm is a superpower.'

Remaining calm and not reacting to negativity or difficult conversations is incredibly liberating. It may take practice to maintain calmness and control over your emotions, but it is reassuring to know that we are not subject to how others may treat us.

Recognising that the opinions of others are not your concern is a form of self-preservation and self-respect. We don't have to comply with what others may expect of us. We all have values. Learn what you sincerely believe in, and don't compromise your beliefs to satisfy the needs of others. It is okay if your beliefs differ from those around you, but you must understand why your values are something you trust and stand for. Don't just follow the popular causes or those who shout the loudest. Understanding yourself is crucial to developing a growth mindset that is flexible, considered, and informed.

And know that you will make mistakes. None of us is perfect. Accept that making mistakes is okay, provided we learn from them. There's no shame in saying, *I was wrong*. It is honest, and you will earn respect. We do not know what we do not know, and acknowledging our limitations and misunderstandings is a way of being kind to ourselves. Recognising we are all fallible and admitting our errors frees others to do the same. Humility is an admirable trait.

In his best-selling book, *Man's Search for Meaning*, Dr. Viktor E. Frankl theorised that the primary purpose in life is to find meaning in our lives. He wrote this book over nine consecutive days following the liberation of the concentration camp where he had been confined. Dr Frankl was an Austrian neurologist, philosopher, and psychiatrist. He and his family were transported to a concentration camp in 1942. His pregnant wife, father, mother, and brother did not survive the camps. He was imprisoned in four camps over the course of three years.

Frankl's observations of the degradation and brutality in the camps, the daily challenges to survive, the famine, and the illnesses faced behind the barbed wire are thought-provoking. Despite grieving the loss of his family and enduring horrific abuse, he noted that those who had a reason to survive and had led meaningful lives, inspiring hope in them to return, were the most resilient of the inmates. Those who shared rations and tried to help others in suffering were the individuals Frankl concluded were most likely to survive. He encouraged people to reflect on positive memories and detach from the horrors they were experiencing. He believed that meaning is derived from love, purposeful work, and courage in the face of adversity. His determination to survive, his sense of humour during the bleakest times, his willingness to help others, and his desire to continue his work after the war all contributed to his survival.

Frankl noted that the inhumane conditions of the camps revealed the best in some people and the worst in others. He observed that some guards displayed compassion, while some inmates, particularly the capo (prisoners with special privileges), were brutal. Of course, many of the millions who were rounded up and sent to these horrendous camps had no opportunity to be resilient or find meaning in their lives. These were the individuals directed toward the gas chambers upon arrival—those who had no chance to survive, regardless of whether they had a purpose in their lives.

Critics of Frankl's book and his view that meaning can be found through suffering argue that he downplayed the horror of the Holocaust by suggesting it was survivable, as long as prisoners had a purpose in their lives. It is also suggested that Frankl utilised his experiences in the camps to promote his therapies. Others, however, describe Man's Search for Meaning as intense and reflective, offering hope to readers.

Frankl developed Logotherapy, also known as 'therapy through meaning,' which posits that finding meaning in life is the primary motivational requirement in humans. He stated that life is meaningful even during the most trying and challenging times, and we each have a choice in how we respond to the situations we face. It emphasises the future and how we can change ourselves if we cannot change the circumstances we find ourselves in. He believed that focusing less on oneself and more on others reduced anxiety and created a sense of purpose.

Finding meaning in our lives can help us manage our day-to-day anxieties. We don't need grand and meaningful goals to strive for, nor should we compare our achievements to those of others. We must allow ourselves to be who we are and discover ways to bring joy and purpose to our lives. Whether through hobbies, work, philanthropy, or simply appreciating the beauty of nature, we must resist the urge to see ourselves as less than others. Nobody is 'just' anything. Each of us has a role to play. We must understand who we are, what we want, and how to achieve both. We are not obligated to live according to the demands of others (see Chapter 17).

We may have been unaware of how we were drawn into our first relationship with a toxic person—now, it is our responsibility to address it.

'Everything can be taken from a man but one thing: the last of the human freedoms—to choose one's attitude in any given set of circumstances, to choose one's way.'
— *Viktor E. Frankl, Man's Search for Meaning*

Summary:

- Toxic personalities can be emotionally damaging if you are unaware of the manipulative games being played or are powerless to deal with them. Their behaviour is psychological maltreatment, and it causes physical damage.
- Toxic personality types exaggerate mistakes, humiliate, discredit, shame, and invalidate. They erode self-confidence and cause intense emotional distress.
- Abusers have little concern or consideration for those they hurt. They aim to control people and situations to benefit themselves.
- Recognising the mind games played by those with toxic personalities is the first step in developing resilience. When we can see the mind games being played, we can choose not to engage.
- Sabotaging special events is a common tactic.
- Abusive personality types can be charming in public or around those they wish to impress.
- Abusers rely on silence and shifting the blame onto the victim.
- Toxic behaviours in the workforce often involve power imbalances between the abuser and the abused.
- Manipulation is a tactic designed to control and coerce. Masters of manipulation can make us doubt ourselves.
- Gaslighting is a term used to describe a form of emotional abuse using lies and manipulation. Lying, belittling, and disorientating can result in doubting your judgment.
- When we buy into an abuser's story that what we are feeling is wrong and we must be defective or deficient, it

leaves us vulnerable to further abuse. When we understand that their behaviour is not okay and that we deserve better, the cycle of abuse is interrupted.
- Abuse can cause depression.
- Setting clear boundaries can protect us from abuse.
- Those who are generous of spirit, who are empaths, or who are young tend to be the targets of toxic personality types.
- Projection is another powerful weapon used by manipulators. It is where we are accused of the very behaviour used by the abuser, who refuses to accept any blame, even when it is obvious they are in the wrong.
- When considering whether behaviour is normal or abnormal, we must first define what normal is. Psychologists developed guidelines to help identify deviations from what is regarded as normal behaviour.
- Combinations of personality traits, genetic influences, and environmental differences shape personalities.
- The dark triad of personality includes narcissism, Machiavellianism, and psychopaths. Manipulation, selfishness, and callousness are at their core.
- Enmeshment is a term that describes family dysfunction, in which parents exert control over their children to influence their beliefs and behaviours strongly. The parents find it unbearable if their children deviate from their strict boundaries. The children grow up without autonomy and remain emotionally dependent on their parents.
- Learning to set boundaries, remain calm, and control our emotions is liberating.

Ticking bomb

Silent, submissive, peacekeeper, sad.
'Where is your anger?' she asked.
I didn't say.
It was nestled somewhere between fear and exhaustion.
It wasn't apathy—
That would come later.
My anger was my subtle, simmering, secret.
A torrid sludge of unchallenged
Sneers, and scorns, and poisonous slurs
Piled atop the previous.
Layers of pain,
Seething softly,
Dissolving my spirit,
Primed.

Chapter 12

From Despair to Repair: Stories of Healing

Psychological trauma can take many forms. It can be insidious and deliberate, such as in Andrea's story, where she shares her experience of coercive control within an abusive marriage; or it can occur through a sudden, life-changing event, such as Bonnie's experience with the unexpected and accidental death of her dear son. Both women suffered immensely. Trauma changed them. They both graciously agreed to share their stories.

A warning that their stories may trigger distress in some individuals. Andrea shares accounts of the terror she and her children felt, and Bonnie describes the deep grief she experienced as a mother whose child died. The stories are raw and challenging. I share them to demonstrate resilience and offer encouragement to others who are suffering similar traumas.

Andrea's Story

After the kids and I left our family home, I remember one night the three kids, my sister, and I were sitting on my bed in our rental house, and he was on the phone to us, and he was screaming abuse, and I thought he was going to kill us all. I said to my sister, someone is going to die before this is over! He was furious because I had taken control, and he was losing control. I had not told him where we had gone. He found out where we lived through his dodgy copper mate.

I left my abusive husband after 14 years of marriage. I gathered our three children and moved out of our home. I have spent the last seven years protecting my children from him. I won in court, but this is not over, because he has not won. He will not stop until he has won. The kids and I will never be safe. He will still be plotting, and the law does not fucking matter. If he wants to get to those children, he will get to those children.

I met C when I was 20 years old. I had moved out of home when I was 17. There were two men I was interested in, and I chose the one I thought would be thoughtful, financially stable, and would care for me. I chose wrong. We moved in together. C was a hard worker, and he was always very attentive. He cared for me so much that I was never allowed to catch public transport. He insisted on always driving me to and from work. I always felt so cared for. He must love me so much.

I now see that that attentiveness was, in fact, control. He was never going to be my life partner. I was happy to be with him then, but it would only be a short-term relationship. I was planning my life, working hard, saving money, and I had just enrolled to go to university when I discovered I was pregnant. I had gone to the doctor because I was feeling so ill. Pregnancy had never crossed my mind. This was not in my life plan. I could not get the words out when I rang C to tell him what the doctor had diagnosed. But he guessed. 'Are you pregnant?' Why would he think that? To this day, I believe he orchestrated me falling pregnant. I do not know how, but he knew I was getting ready to move on.

I felt like my life was over. I was going to have a baby. I had just enrolled in a teaching degree. I was trapped and became deeply depressed. I quit work and stayed at home with the blinds drawn. I sat in the dark and would not answer my phone to anyone but C. It never occurred to me to have an abortion, despite my not wanting to marry C. This was now my lot. We bought a house, and we had our first son. During this time, C was caring and loving. He was still working hard, and I was caring for our baby. We married when I was 24 and had our second son a few years later. We had planned this pregnancy, and I believed we were happily married. I adored my children but still hoped to follow my dreams and attend university one day.

We were planning to have a third child when I discovered that C had been cheating on me and having multiple affairs. I was shattered. I decided I would not have any more children with him and was planning on how I would deal with his infidelity when I discovered I was already pregnant. At this point in my life, I realised I did have options. I was not sure if I wanted this child when my marriage was so unstable. I needed time to consider what I should do, and I asked C to keep my pregnancy a secret until I had decided. He told everyone—family, friends, even the neighbours! Once again, I felt trapped.

C was still cheating on me when our daughter was born. Things started to get worse after her birth. The children were my world, and C no longer was. Our friends thought he was a great dad and husband. He could be very charming, giving me money and saying, 'You go and have a shopping trip with your sister, and I'll look after the children.' Nobody realised this was the only money I had access to. I had no access to our bank accounts. He oversaw the money. When I said I would get a bank card, he assured me he would contact the bank and organise it. It never arrived. Neither did any bank statements. We owned a business at this point in our lives, and I had been looking after the bookkeeping for a while. He would never keep receipts, though, and we would argue over this. Eventually, C said he would pay someone to do the bookkeeping. I believed him. I had no idea we had any money concerns. When our electricity was cut off, I blamed the postman for not delivering the bill. C would tell me not to worry about it—he would sort it out! And he always did. He would ring the bank, and it would be sorted.

It was not until our daughter was three (and I still did not have a bank card) that I decided to call the bank myself and see what the problem was. C had always told me never to contact the bank. This day, I did. I discovered we were only a couple of weeks away from losing our home. We were in desperate financial trouble. Our mortgage had not been paid. There was no money.

We borrowed some money from C's parents, and it was at this time I decided I would take control of our finances because he was obviously incapable. I did not understand what had happened. I had had no idea we were in any trouble. He had always told me everything was fine.

He was embarrassed initially, and then the condemnation began. Everything was my fault—his affairs, our money problems, it was all my fault!

I cannot remember how I found out, but I discovered that C had gone to the Post Office and put a forward on all our mail so it would not be delivered to our home but would go straight to his business—every piece of mail, birthday cards, bills, bank statements, everything.

Occasionally, he would bring some mail home and drop it in our letterbox so I would not suspect anything was amiss.

One day, determined to confront him about the missing mail, I drove to our business. I had never been allowed in the shop. C would come out to the car, put his hands on the door, and speak to me through the window.

On this day, I asked about the mail.

'Yes, it's inside,' he said, 'I'll bring it home tonight.'

Somehow, I managed to get out of the car and go inside.

'It's upstairs in a box somewhere,' he said.

'That's ok, I'll go and get it,' I replied.

I walked up the steps to the mezzanine floor. C had made the steps—steel frame with wooden steps, no handrails. He followed me up. He kept saying he would bring it home that night. I turned to him and said I was there now and would not leave without it.

That was when he became dangerous.

I remember him grabbing me by the arms and putting his feet on my toes. He had steel-tipped boots. I remember looking down at them.

He stood on my toes and held me backwards over the stairs, at an angle that would have made me fall had he let go.

He said, You are not taking that box.

I said, I am not leaving here without it.

And somehow, I got that box.

I do not remember how.

I drove to a friend's place to pick up my children, and she looked at me and said, 'What on earth has happened to you?'

I sat on the edge of her bathtub, and I was shaking uncontrollably—I was so scared.

It took me five hours to go through all the mail. Five hours!

He came home and challenged me. 'Why are you doing this? What does it matter now?'

I told him I needed to know what was happening because we were about to lose our house.

He had not paid any taxes for eight years. We owed hundreds of thousands of dollars.

(Later, I discovered he had not been working, and we still had to pay the wages of the other mechanic who worked for us.)

And suddenly he became embarrassed and ashamed and said, 'Oh, you're so strong, and I'm sorry, I don't know what happened!'

And I believed him.

Once again, I thought he's a good man; he just hasn't been raised with the resources to cope, and I can save him! I do not understand why I chose to believe that—because have no doubt that he would have pushed me down those stairs had I not been so determined and furious.

I had been manipulated and controlled by him for so many years that I could not see what was happening right under my nose.

He played all sorts of mind games with me, pretending he was going to kill himself because he was so ashamed of what he had done.

He orchestrated his disappearance one day. He disappeared for hours and would not answer his phone.

I arrived home after picking up the children from school. His car was there, and the front door was wide open.

I told the children to stay in the car as I was sure he had committed suicide.

He was not in the house.

He had gone for a long walk and finally contacted me to come and pick him up.

All of it was carefully construed to have me sick with worry so I would not leave him. He pretended to be a broken man, and so the cycle continued.

This happened in 2011.

In 2014, his shop 'burned down'. It was deemed an accident. We received a large insurance payout.

He was not working now. He would tell me he was going away on fishing trips with his mates, leaving me home to look after our children.

One day, I learned that these so-called fishing trips were more lies.

He was in a relationship with another woman and had been for years.

She used to visit him at our business—another reason I was never allowed to be at the shop.

Someone who had been a friend of mine. A mum from school. Our children played together.

My heart was broken.

This time, I told him to leave.

I learned that he had been telling our mutual friends that I was crazy, always angry, and mentally unstable.

He would tell them I would scream at him, and he was the poor man trying to keep his family happy and together.

So many believed him.

Of course, I was unstable; I had a lying, cheating husband, no money, and was about to lose our home.

We had three children to care for.

How were we going to cope?

I never knew when to believe him. He lied about everything.

He left to live at his parents' house and would send me messages every evening with photos from inside their home, telling me how much he loved me and that we would sort this out and be a family again.

More lies.

A few months later, two 'friends' told me he had rented a home in the neighbouring suburb and had fully furnished it! He had not been at his parents' house at all. He paid hundreds of dollars a week in rent for a home I knew nothing about. His girlfriend was a frequent visitor.

This was my breaking point.

I told him the children and I were leaving to live in a rental home. I got rental assistance and would do all I could for our children.

I made him tell the children that he had chosen to rent a house and live there.

Once we left and he realised his facade of being the 'perfect' dad and husband was crumbling, he began to threaten me. I was frightened of him.

As well as the incident on the stairs at the shop, there had been two episodes of him choking me, once when I had a tiny baby in my arms. He threatened to take the children from me and said everyone knew I was a mad fucking bitch.

My nightmare was not over.

We lived in constant fear of him.

To appease him, I agreed that the children could see him. Our oldest son had one visit with him and decided he would not revisit his father.

The younger children would stay overnight with him each weekend. They hated going, but I was afraid if C ever decided to take me to court over the children, it would be best if I had tried to encourage them to have a relationship with their father.

I had been told that if I were seen to be promoting a relationship between them, there would be no more asked of me!

C arrived at my home to pick up the two youngest children one day. Our youngest son went to the car, but our daughter refused. She would not leave the house. I was at work at the time. I had no choice but to work.

Our oldest son would not let C enter the house. He locked the door.

C stood outside pounding on the door and screaming for our daughter to get in the car. The children were terrified. Our oldest son threatened to call the police. C drove off with our middle child in his car. I did not know where they were. I went to the police station when I found out what had happened. I sat there for hours that night but did not speak to an officer. Nobody had the time to talk to me. C broke me again that night. I thought our son would be killed or C would take him away. He brought my boy home the next day.

I hated making my children visit their father. They refused to stay more than one night a week. Every weekend, I worried they would not come home. I was sick with worry that they would be killed. The children told me that C would drive drunk with them in the car, taking back roads to avoid being caught. He kept threatening to take the children from me, so I kept sending them to him to try and stop him from demanding greater access to them. He was so manipulative and had convinced so many people that he was being wronged, and I was just being vindictive. I lost so many friends. They chose to believe him. I was the mad mum.

Working three jobs was not sufficient to provide for us. I decided I needed to study and qualify for better-paid work. I chose to follow my dream and go to university.

I had tried to start a university degree several times over the last few years, but each time, C would convince me it was not the right time. There would always be a reason for me not to go. I enrolled in teaching, but it only lasted six months. Teaching was no longer a profession I felt I could manage. I chose podiatry. It took me four and a half years of full-time study and working one part-time job while raising three children as a single mum.

One of the biggest lessons I learned then was realising that it is okay to ask for help. I could not do this on my own. For years, I had never asked for help. I would never tell anyone how bad things were with C. I did not want anyone to know that we were in trouble. I was ashamed.

Fortunately, I have wonderful family and friends. They helped me enormously. The soccer club that all three children played for waived the fees, so my kids did not miss out on the game they loved. Teachers supported the children when I shared the distress we were experiencing. I finally understood that none of this was my doing. This was no longer a secret I had to keep. This was his doing.

C took me to court in 2019 to demand more access to our children. We had gone to mediation before this, but the children refused to see him anymore. He would phone the children, and they would not want to speak with him. I do not believe he wanted to see them or even loves them! He wanted them around so others could see him as the 'good dad'.

He hired a lawyer, and I had to appear in court to fight for the well-being of my children. I could not afford a lawyer, so I had to represent myself.

I stood in front of the judge, shaking and trying to explain the coercive control—all the little things that had happened over the years. The pattern of abuse, as well as the violence. Trying to explain the fear the children and I have of their father. But how do you define a thousand little abuses? The constant abuse.

Courts need specific dates, times, and events! I do not know the answer, but judges need to stop berating and belittling women because their stories may not seem plausible to someone who has never lived with coercive control. The whole system is broken when *you* are broken, and you must stand before a judge. It is so intimidating. The power imbalance is immense, and no one can help you. You are on your own. And he's sitting there with his lawyer and watching you. I used to have faith in the court process. I thought that the children and I would be listened to, but the system is not set up to believe victims. My children have learned that even if you tell the truth, you will not be believed by the police or courts. Even if you are being victimised, it doesn't matter; you won't be believed. They trust few people now.

I think back on why I made the decisions I did and why I fought so hard to continue our marriage when all the signs were there telling me to leave. I realise that I had been raised by a traumatised mother whose husband abandoned her when I was a baby. She did her best for me, but little help was available when she needed support. I don't think she has ever dealt with the pain and the shame associated with having a husband leave her.

I believe my trauma started from birth. I was born three years after my parents had a baby who died. I don't think my mother has ever recovered from losing this child. She was not given the tools nor the opportunity to deal with the loss of her child. On top of that, my father's behaviour was erratic and abusive.

I was born a month premature and then needed surgery for double hernia repairs at six weeks of age. Instead of my birth being a joyous occasion, it seemed to trigger more grief.

My father abandoned us! I wasn't good enough for him to stay.

I grew up trying to please people. To keep others happy. I had low self-esteem most of my life. Who would ever want me when even my father didn't? I tried hard to keep my family together but didn't want my husband to abandon me, either.

I share my story in the hope that other women might recognise a similar pattern of gaslighting and manipulation in their lives. I don't offer advice because each woman is on a separate journey and has a different story. No one could have told me I should leave C before I was ready to do it. He had told me many times I could never cope as a single mother, and I believed him. He said we wouldn't survive without him. I didn't think I could do it until I did it. I did it by working three jobs, studying for five years, and asking for help when needed.

My priority is to fix my children now that I have fixed myself.

What has helped me most over the last number of years are good people, good women. I can count the number of good men I know on one hand. I am not anti-men; I am anti-arsehole-men.

Women need to help each other. Just look at someone else and see yourself in them for a moment. We are all fighting something.

Once you find those good women, never let them go. They are worth a hundred men.

And there's shit women too!

And they'll never get it because they are too busy competing with each other.

The two women I am closest to are poles apart, but both have lived trauma.

You must have lived it and felt the fear and the emptiness, so you can understand the feeling of the floor disappearing from beneath your feet and falling. And you never know when it's going to end and you are going to hit the ground.

When you do, there's almost relief because now there's only one way to go, and that's up. Sometimes, the walls you must climb are slippery, and you need to reach out for someone to help you.

I'm still scared of C.

And coercive control laws must change.

Whenever I went to the police, I wasn't believed.

And my children weren't believed even though it took them enormous courage to tell the truth about their father.

Nobody's listening to the children. Start listening to them. And believe them when they tell you what they are feeling.

Stop telling them what they should be doing, and shut up and listen to them! If what they say seems irrational and they are telling you this is how they feel, their feelings must be considered. Just because what they have experienced may not tick a particular box on paper does not make their experiences any less real. They need to be believed.

Psychologists helped me realise that I wasn't mad.

They helped me understand the manipulation and gaslighting behaviour that had me doubting my sanity. Things that seemed ludicrous when I tried to explain them. Medication helped, as did reading about narcissism. Talking with other women about their experiences has helped me understand more.

I still work hard to keep my children safe; they know I love them and will always protect them, and if I say we have to go now, they know we have to go. The time for us to get help has passed. The only reason the kids and I are still here is because *I* didn't fail. I have finally been granted custody of my children, but I know he is still out there, and we are not safe yet. I want other women to be believed and to be protected. Nobody should have to hide abuse.

Bonnie's Story

My trauma has been the loss of my two sons.

I lost Josh to a car accident 15 years ago.

I lost Ben before this.

He chose to discontinue our relationship after I left my unhappy marriage.

There is an emptiness within me.

Losing Ben is, in some ways, more painful.

I accept that Josh has died. My grief for his loss will never cease, although the heartbreak is slowly abating.

Grief for a son who is still alive is ongoing.

My husband and I had been married for 18 years. After our marriage broke, I left home, and my son Josh came to live with me. Ben stayed with his father and did not speak with me for many years.

He blamed me for ending the marriage. His life had changed, and he was unable to reconcile the loss of our family unit.

He developed depression and began using marijuana to ease the despair he suffered.

Over time, he developed schizophrenia.

I was deeply concerned.

When Ben was arrested for growing marijuana on his father's property, I wrote to the magistrate whom Ben was to appear before.

I knew he needed help for his illness, and I explained this, hoping the judge would order a mental health assessment. My request backfired as the magistrate sent Ben to prison. I realised afterwards that Ben being in prison would secure him a mental health assessment.

This did little to assuage my guilt at the time.

Fortunately, Ben was assessed quickly and ended up only spending a couple of days in jail before being sent to a psychiatric unit. I still feel responsible for the time he spent in prison, but I was grateful he was at last receiving care for his mental illness.

Ben spent nearly six months in hospital, and during his stay, we slowly began to rebuild our relationship. When he was discharged, he came to live with me and Josh. He was doing well for almost a year until I was woken in the early morning hours by the click of the gate latch and a knock at the door.

Two police officers were at my door and broke the news that my 18-year-old son Josh had been killed in a car accident. My shock was such that my initial concern (after asking the officers if they were absolutely certain it was my boy) was the welfare of the officers whose job it was to have to deliver such tragic news to families following a death.

I didn't cry.

The policewoman offered to make me a cup of tea. I accepted and told her that she should add sugar to it because I was certain I was in severe shock, and this seemed appropriate at the time.

The officers asked if there was anybody I could ring to come and be with me. I said, yes—my friend Jill. I recall phoning her and feeling apologetic for waking her to say, 'Josh has been killed, and I need you to come over'! I felt terrible for inconveniencing her!

Jill immediately responded and was beside me as I rang my family and friends.

I felt compelled to be the one to phone, although I knew Jill would have readily accepted this role. This was my job, my responsibility. I needed to do it.

My family fell apart. My ex-husband, mother, and father were inconsolable. I remember my mother lying across my couch and wailing and screaming in anguish. My father had always been strong, but even he was enveloped in despair.

The agony within me was immense.

It was a pain deep inside my chest.

My heart was broken.

It was a severe physical pain, and it was locked inside me. I couldn't let it out.

I had to put my grief aside, roll up my sleeves, and do what needed doing.

I organised Josh's funeral, took care of all arrangements, and supported everyone around me. I had to be the strong one. Everyone else was collapsing around me.

After Josh's funeral, my ex-husband called Ben to move back in with him. 'I only have one son now, and I need you to be here', he told Ben.

Ben moved out, and I was left with my grief.

The pain within me remained, and finally, I visited my doctor, who started me on antidepressants.

I stayed on this medication for about six months.

I still could not cry.

My grief was writhing inside me, and this continued for three to four years.

My pain was deeply buried, but it was soon to emerge in the form of skin rashes, dandruff, and other physical ailments. My grief was surfacing. My ability to make even the smallest of decisions was impacted. I recall driving up to a roundabout and being unable to judge when I could enter it. This had once been second nature to me. My limbs were heavy. Everything was an effort.

I can't recall who suggested I see a lady trained in neuro-linguistic programming (NLP), but I made an appointment, and on my very first visit, she asked me to walk along the street back and forth while she examined my gait. I couldn't walk properly. My feet and legs felt leaden. She could discern the burden within me, and after a few appointments, she asked me to go home, lie on my lounge and do nothing but just 'be.' Be present in the moment and do nothing else. I lay down and allowed myself to do so. Within a short time, the room started spinning. I felt dizzy. When I went to bed that night, I dreamt I was losing great clumps of blood. I woke, got up, and then vomited. Then I cried. I had allowed my grief to surface. It boiled up within me and was finally released. My therapist permitted me to unload my burden.

My healing had begun.

I have always been resilient and have never felt I had a mental illness. My therapist was able to discern that my need to take responsibility for myself might be traced to an incident when I was a girl of about twelve years of age.

I had been teaching my brother to ride a bike. He overbalanced, and as I reached to grab the bike, my inner thigh was cut deeply by the bike's mudguard.

My father had planned a fishing trip that day. He loved fishing. He looked at my gaping wound and said, 'It will be ok. We'll just put a bandage on it.'

My dad was not one to fuss. I recall looking at my mum and waiting for her to respond. She said nothing.

My dad had spoken, and from this point on, I realised that I would have to look after myself.

Mum suffered severe anxiety and depression, though it was many years before I understood this. She could not give more and wasn't strong enough to speak out. My father was a good man but was not too involved with his children. The wound healed, but to this day, I still carry a large keloid scar on my thigh.

My relationship with Ben deteriorated after he moved back to live with his father. I had to arrange for him to be sectioned (compulsory committed to a psychiatric hospital) a couple of times, once because he was pouring kerosene into his ears to stop the voices he was hearing.

His father was still too deeply enmeshed in grief to seek help for Ben. He and Ben still blame me for all our family's problems.

And my ex-husband has little regard for mental illness.

It's up to me to care for Ben from afar, although he will not accept me back into his life.

When Josh died, everyone who was important to me crumbled. I had no choice but to be strong.

I tried to cope as best I could.

Whenever I felt distressed at other times in my life, I lifted myself out of my despair by listening to happy music, wearing lovely clothes and makeup to help me feel good, and surrounding myself with positive, uplifting people. This was not enough when Josh died. I knew I needed help. The medication saw me through the worst time, and my NLP therapist was instrumental in releasing my guilt a few years later.

I occasionally have triggers that cause me to overreact at times, but I can now cope.

I feel that my empathy has lessened in response to hearing bad news. Even learning that a family has lost their home to a fire (which I understand is devastating to them), I find myself thinking, 'Well, at least you haven't lost a child.'

My father developed cancer in his later years and once told me that he felt that he had not dealt with his grief sufficiently, and his grief transformed into cancer. At his funeral, my mother was able to face his death, having already endured the immense pain of losing a grandson. My brother suffers from terrible depression, but he, too, has had success with NLP therapy.

For years, I felt guilty about laughing, but now I want to live my best life with my new husband. I was once a people-pleaser and still am to some degree, but now I can stand up for myself and say what I need.

I love my work and get a lot of joy from helping people, but it is not my life. I always put in extra effort, but I make sure I have a good work-life balance.

As well as my full-time work, I am a marriage celebrant, which brings me great pleasure, as does gardening.

I have learned that I can survive.

I am most fortunate to have a wonderful husband I can rely on. He gives me much support. But I know that my healing had to come from within me because you can't fix anyone until you fix yourself. In saying that, I can still hear the click of the gate.

Andrea and Bonnie's stories differ; however, both believe their lives have been shaped by intergenerational trauma.

Andrea mentioned that her mother was unable to express the emotions stemming from her traumas or to reflect on them. She also suspects that her mum's religion may have influenced this reluctance to express her feelings—suggesting that depression was 'not allowed' and that faith in God meant 'giving your problems to Him alone'. Additionally, having depression could somehow imply that one's faith was 'weak'.

Andrea also believes the influence of her father's narcissism directly contributed to her inability to express her own emotions and share her trauma with others.

Bonnie believes her mother's depression and anxiety shaped her into a person who takes control and constantly tries to fix problems to keep others happy. She thinks her sister and brother were affected differently, experiencing their own struggles with anxiety and depression.

Trauma is universal, and earlier generations lacked the understanding of how it impacts our health. We now recognise that emotional pain must be addressed.

Loss and grief are normal experiences, but the emotions that accompany them should not be suppressed. Unless the pain is acknowledged, emotional wounds will not heal.

The batons of untreated despair are handed down to future generations.

This is especially relevant to generations of Indigenous peoples around the world whose families and cultures were destroyed through colonisation, as well as to survivors of the mass trauma experienced by millions during the Holocaust.

We can alleviate the pain of trauma when we understand how it is transmitted through successive generations until it can be unpacked and addressed.

Until recently, it was not understood how traumatic experiences from previous generations can affect our identity today.

Life can be harsh and unforgiving.

We can find peace by acknowledging pain and developing emotional intelligence. We can relinquish the compulsion to please others, accept that any resulting conflict is not our burden, and refuse to play small to keep others comfortable.

We can protect ourselves with emotional boundaries and learn to 'see' controlling or manipulative behaviour patterns. Once you see it, you can't unsee it. Setting healthy boundaries builds resilience, which allows us to be empathetic and vulnerable without fear of losing ourselves to our emotions.

Boundaries serve as our shields. When they are firmly established, we learn to express our truths. Not loudly or aggressively, but quietly, with courage and steadfastness. We regain our self-confidence and will discover our 'tribe' of like-minded individuals. We become the people we were meant to be.

If you've read this book from the beginning (thank you), you hopefully now understand how psychological stress damages our brains and bodies. In the next few chapters, we will examine how to mend the damage done and minimise further suffering. Many simple yet effective measures are worth exploring. If you are in the acute stages of a mental illness, consider discussing these suggestions with your health professional or a trusted friend before starting. We begin with the healing power of nature.

Chapter 13

The Healing Power of Nature

'I went to the woods because I wished to live deliberately, to front only the essential facts of life, and see if I could not learn what it had to teach, and not, when I came to die, discover that I had not lived.'

— *Thoreau (1854)*

If someone tells you that spending more time in nature could reduce your stress levels, you might think they are mad. The stress you may feel could be too complex and overwhelming to even contemplate that such a simple undertaking could remedy or alleviate some of your symptoms.

However, this simple and cost-effective solution helps alleviate some debilitating symptoms, and science has proven it.

Forest Bathing

In 1982, the Japanese Minister of Agriculture, Forestry, and Fisheries, Tomohide Akiyama, conceived Shinrin-yoku or taking in the forest.

Commonly referred to as forest bathing, a stroll through a forest can greatly enhance overall health and well-being. Studies reveal results supporting immune function recovery, deeply restorative relaxation of the mind and body, and increased happiness.

Research on forest bathing in several countries, including Japan, the Republic of Korea, the United Kingdom, China, the USA, Denmark, Lithuania, and Canada, supports improvements in an individual's mental and physical relaxation.

Benefits include:

- pain relief (both physical and emotional)
- symptom reduction in depression and anxiety
- decreased blood pressure and heart rate
- lower levels of the stress hormone cortisol in saliva.

All these benefits can prevent and heal diseases.

Spending excessive time indoors can disrupt the circadian rhythm, the body's internal clock that regulates sleep-wake cycles, hormone production, and overall physiological balance. This is detrimental to overall wellness.

The lack of natural light can also disrupt circadian rhythms, leading to sleep disturbances that further impact mood and mental clarity.

Natural light exposure, particularly morning sunlight, helps synchronise this rhythm by signalling the brain when to wake up and wind down. However, staying indoors—especially in environments with artificial lighting—can interfere with this process in several ways:

- Natural light, especially blue light from the sun, regulates melatonin production. If there isn't enough exposure to daylight, the release of melatonin might be delayed, making it more difficult to fall asleep at night and wake up feeling refreshed in the morning.
- Indoor environments often expose us to artificial lighting. Blue light from screens, for example, can suppress melatonin production and confuse our brains into thinking it is still daytime. This can lead to difficulty falling asleep and a reduction in sleep quality.
- Spending time in dimly lit indoor spaces during the day can signal to the brain that it is evening, which may make us feel sluggish and fatigued far too early. This can lead to irregular sleep patterns, which may result in insomnia or daytime drowsiness.
- When our circadian rhythm is out of sync, it can impact our sleep, mood, metabolism, and how well our brains work. Plus, not getting enough light can lead to higher chances of experiencing depression, anxiety, and even seasonal affective disorder (SAD).

To maintain a healthy circadian rhythm, it is essential to seek exposure to natural light during the day, especially in the morning, limit exposure to blue light in the evening, and adhere to a consistent sleep schedule.

Key Studies

The Association of Therapeutic Effects of Forests was established in 2004 to conduct studies in this field. In 2005–2006, field experiments were carried out in 24 forests and urban areas across Japan. In each experiment, some participants walked through urban environments, while the same number walked through forests. All subjects had baseline measurements of salivary cortisol, blood pressure, pulse rate, and heart rate variability recorded.

The studies showed that those exposed to forests had lower cortisol levels, pulse rates, and blood pressure, as well as increased parasympathetic nerve activity (which helps the body relax) and decreased sympathetic nerve activity (associated with fight, flight, freeze, or fawn responses).

In contrast, those who walked through urban settings did not exhibit this reduction in stress measurements.

Additionally, there was no difference in exercise levels between the two environments.

Alongside physical measurements, participants completed the Profile of Mood States (POMS), which assesses tension and anxiety, anger and hostility, fatigue, confusion, and vigour. Those who walked through the forests in all 24 experiments exhibited lower scores in their POMS assessments for all categories except vigour or energy, which was higher.

The studies indicate that forests can reduce psychological tension, depression, anger, fatigue, and confusion in humans while simultaneously increasing vigour. It was concluded that forests contribute to relaxation and restoration for people.

Nature and Mental Health

The Japanese Society of Forest Medicine was established in 2007 to promote research in forest medicine that studies the therapeutic benefits of forests on human health. Research demonstrates that even short periods in nature are beneficial for conditions such as insomnia and alcohol abuse, promoting relaxation and calmness.

South Korea has been establishing a network of Healing Forests across the country.

Approximately 85% of South Koreans reside in urban environments, where many individuals experience digital addiction, high stress levels, and depression.

Forest bathing in these Healing Forests is becoming an integral part of work and school programmes throughout South

Korea, helping people heal various ailments. Data analyses show significant reductions in stress levels and negative moods.

Although more studies are needed to fully understand the complexities of ill health and nature's healing powers, the findings suggest that nature has a positive effect on us. Chungbuk University in South Korea now offers a 'Forest Healing' degree to facilitate the creation of these healing programmes.

Mental health issues rise when individuals are disconnected from the natural world.

Escalations in mental disorders, such as depression, alcohol abuse, substance abuse, crime, and family breakdowns are related to this disconnect. Exposure to nature improves cognitive functioning, decreases attention deficit disorder (ADD), promotes self-awareness, addresses delinquent behaviour, and increases self-confidence, self-esteem, and social relationships. There is now a positive shift towards including reconnection with nature as an adjunct treatment for mental illnesses.

> *'Qualitative research indicates that benefits from nature contact may include physical relaxation, mental restoration, positive emotions towards self and place, social connectedness, and experiences of tranquillity and peace.'*
>
> *— Warber, 2015*

The Benefits of Nature

Exploring the natural world of forests, beaches, fields, and farmlands allows your mind to experience awe and wonder. The natural world stimulates the senses, particularly sight and smell, while also calming the brain by reducing symptoms of stress.

Exposure to nature can aid in the prevention and treatment of mental illnesses, not only by reducing environmental factors such as air pollution, noise, and general busyness, but also by simply being among green spaces (forests, parks, gardens, landscaping around buildings) and blue spaces (oceans, rivers, ponds, fountains). Time spent in these blue and green spaces enhances physical activity, calms your mind, and decreases ruminating over problems. Science is confirming that being in nature is beneficial for your well-being. It is also a highly cost-effective remedy for alleviating symptoms of stress.

Time spent sitting by a creek, watching it flow, or going to the beach to smell the salt air and hear the waves crash—a sound that drowns out all other noises—allows your nervous system to return to a quiet state. It can also awaken a sense of awe, which is humbling and grounding. Awe heightens our gratitude and enhances our perception of our place in time—the vastness, the symmetry, and the exquisite design. It gives us goosebumps and helps regulate the nervous system by lowering cortisol levels and reducing ruminating over problems, calming stress and anxiety in the process.

Awe also increases our feel-good neurotransmitters, such as dopamine and serotonin. Both contribute to our emotional well-being, can relieve pain, boost emotional resilience, and even improve our immune systems. It encourages mindfulness and curiosity, opening our minds to new perspectives.

Connecting with nature is profoundly restorative. The sounds of birds, the wind rustling through branches, flowing water, the rich aroma of earth and flowers, fresh scents of foliage, the grandeur of towering trees, and the mindfulness evoked by absorbing majestic views enhance our health and foster feelings of gratitude.

> Being in nature can awaken a sense of awe.
> Awe is humbling and grounding.

The Modern Disconnect

As a society, we spend significantly more time indoors than our parents and grandparents did when they were children.

For many of these generations, outdoor play was more common than staying indoors.

Children also tended to play in natural areas because there was less urbanisation than today and, of course, little or no digital technology was available.

Children led more active lives, and the combination of increased physical exercise in natural environments, along with greater interaction with other children, had positive benefits.

More than half of the world's population now resides in cities. Agriculture and extensive food production mean that most of us don't need to grow our own food. We no longer go into backyard vegetable plots or tend to fruit trees daily. The rise in inner-city living has resulted in fewer backyards, with many people now living in apartments. With the convenience of online shopping, purchasing even out-of-season fruits and vegetables is effortless for many of us. Ordering online is easy.

Yet, those of us who garden regularly appreciate the psychological benefits of getting into the garden and digging in the earth. Not only is there satisfaction in harvesting home-grown food, but gardening slows busy minds, reduces anxiety, and calms our souls. It's deeply gratifying to watch our food grow and then harvest it.

Science is proving what our bodies instinctively know.

> **Nature heals.**

While providing global connectivity, electronic gadgets have disconnected us as a society from nature.

Mobile phones, TVs, computers, and other electrical devices are not only addictive but also promote a sedentary lifestyle.

Our minds are constantly ignited and stimulated when we use them, leaving little time for our brains to quieten and be still.

Despite extraordinary technological advances, societies seem to have an ever-widening disconnect. There also appears to be a sceptical disregard for anything not manufactured—ridicule that we could find health benefits simply by walking among trees or along a beach and treating illnesses exclusively, rather than encouraging and pursuing wellness and renewing instead of preserving.

If we cannot use technology to help us achieve a solution, could it truly benefit us?

The answer is yes.

As societies become more urbanised, we must seek out green and blue spaces to promote wellness. By 2050, it is estimated that 70% of the global population will live in cities. Our environments play significant roles in the prevalence of mental illness. Living in a city can increase the risk of developing anxiety by 20% and depression by almost 40%. Cities need green and blue spaces. Planning and creating such spaces is fundamental for attaining good physical and mental health.

Where To From Here—and Why?

Therapeutic recreation is now regarded as part of healthcare programmes for recovery from mental illness.

In 2016, the Centres for Disease Control in the US reported that one in seven children has a mental, behavioural, or developmental disorder, including attention-deficit/hyperactivity disorder (ADHD), depression, anxiety, conduct issues, or learning complications.

Studies reveal that children exposed to natural surroundings:

- display significantly improved behaviour
- experience cognitive development gains
- show stress reduction
- report increases in life satisfaction, mindfulness, self-efficacy, and happiness.

Engaging in ecotherapy— connecting with nature and the earth and its systems —improves physical health, increases connectedness with others, enhances our ability to disregard external burdens, and, when combined with professional therapy, aids in recovery from depression and PTSD.

Spending as little as 30 minutes surrounded by trees can lead to lower blood pressure and heart rates. Access to and exposure to the natural world promote psychological benefits by reducing stress and anxiety, restoring calmness to our busy minds, improving memory, and soothing mental fatigue. Disconnecting from nature can significantly impact mental health, leading to increased stress, anxiety, depression, and even cognitive decline. Nature offers a sense of calm, aiding in emotional regulation, lowering blood pressure, and reducing the production of stress hormones, such as cortisol. Spending most of our time indoors or in artificial environments can heighten mental fatigue, leading to difficulty concentrating and a decline in overall well-being.

Nature encourages mindfulness and fosters a connection to something greater than ourselves, which can be grounding and comforting. This connection lessens isolation and reduces feelings of being overwhelmed by daily pressures. Moreover, spending time in natural settings has been linked to increased creativity, improved problem-solving skills, and a greater sense of purpose. When people are deprived of these benefits, they may struggle with motivation, emotional balance, and overall mental resilience. Nature heals. Put down your phone and walk amongst the trees. Notice how you feel.

> *'When we get closer to nature- untouched wilderness or a backyard tree-we do our overstressed brains a favour.'*
> *— Williams (2016 #318)*

Summary:
- Exploring the natural world of forests, beaches, fields, and farmlands allows our minds to experience awe and wonderment.
- The natural world stimulates our senses, particularly sight and smell, but it calms the brain by reducing symptoms of stress.
- As a society, we spend far more time indoors than our parents and their parents did when they were children.
- Therapeutic recreation is now considered part of healthcare programmes addressing mental illness recovery.

- Children have significantly improved behaviour, cognitive development, and stress reduction when exposed to natural surroundings. They experience increases in life satisfaction, mindfulness, self-efficacy, and happiness.
- Despite extraordinary technological advances, societies seem to have an ever-widening disconnect. Using electronic devices stimulates our brains, and switching off electronic devices allows our brains to calm down.
- Forest bathing is simply wandering through a forest and awakening our senses to the natural world. Research into forest bathing from many countries supports improvements in mental and physical relaxation.
- Benefits of forest bathing include reduced physical and emotional pain, symptom reduction in depression and anxiety, decreased blood pressure and heart rates, and lower stress hormone cortisol levels. All these benefits have the potential to prevent and heal diseases.
- Forest bathing in Healing Forests in South Korea is becoming part of work and school programmes.
- Nature therapy is proving to be a beneficial adjunct treatment for mental illnesses.

Chapter 14

Movement Matters

'When we exercise, stem cells in the hippocampus, a region of the brain that plays an important role in learning and memory, divide and turn into new neurons, which leads to improvement in memory.'

— Walker, (Reference #132)

Movement is medicine for both the body and the brain. Believe it or not, our bodies thrive on movement. It strengthens bones and muscles while helping to lubricate our joints. Additionally, it improves balance, which reduces the risk of falls, especially as we age, and enhances brain health.

We know that exercise benefits our physical health. It's also proving exceptionally effective as both a stand-alone treatment and an adjunct therapy alongside medications for treating mental illnesses.

A Few Interesting Facts Regarding Exercise

Evaluating the benefits of exercise in individuals isn't easy due to our unique genetic makeup and life experiences. There is also no precise calculation for abnormality or altered physiological markers in depression. Each of us has a distinct set of symptoms. Our perception of a particular symptom's impact can depend on its severity and how our personality influences it.

Physical ailments, including chronic diseases and neurological disorders, also play a role. We each have unique neurobiological differences and dysregulations.

Why Movement Matters

Exercise and movement strengthen the body while often calming the mind.

Exercise:

- strengthens our hearts and improves circulation
- helps regulate blood sugar levels, which reduces our risk of developing Type 2 diabetes
- promotes good balance
- improves oxygenation to vital organs in the body
- promotes better sleep
- improves cognitive function, memory, and brain health as there is increased blood flow to our brains
- boosts self-esteem and resilience
- helps to maintain bone strength and joint mobility
- boosts our immune systems, which, in turn, reduces our risk of developing chronic illnesses.

Exercise does not have to be extreme.

Even mild to moderate regular movement and exercise have positive impacts. As little as one hour of exercise each week can boost wellness. This could include running, walking, skating, cycling, swimming, lifting weights, or practising yoga. Alternatively, you might prefer team sports. Movement is medicine.

Mental Health Benefits

Many of us either don't like exercising or see it as just another chore to fit into our already busy lives. It's important to note, however, that several studies have found significant improvements in mood and depressive symptoms after physical activity. Additionally, it has been observed that exercise can reverse the symptoms of some depression, usually mild depression.

Another benefit of exercise is that it can enhance the effectiveness of certain antidepressant medications while also reducing some unpleasant side effects. This is great news and may help motivate us to incorporate some form of movement into our daily lives.

Exercise is now suggested as the first line of treatment for mild-to-moderate depression. A recent study (September 2022) indicates there is no difference between using exercise or medication for those with non-severe depression (defined as someone with major depressive disorder who has mild-to-moderate symptoms). It was determined that exercise provides a similar benefit to taking antidepressant medication.

This is an important finding, particularly for those who have an aversion to taking antidepressant medication. Accepting the need for medication may be a difficult hurdle for someone newly diagnosed with depression. The stigma around mental illness is still quite strong and accepting that you might need treatment for what is still considered by some to be a 'just get over it' sort of illness may preclude you from accepting medication. However, understanding that exercise programmes are an alternative first step in treatment and may prevent the disorder from worsening provides us with options.

The same study investigated whether a combination of exercise and antidepressants, compared to either treatment alone, would be more effective for adults with mild-to-moderate depressive symptoms. The benefits of combining exercise and medication were similar to those of using just one treatment. Each treatment, including the combination of exercise and medication, provided more benefits than those participating in the study who were in the control/placebo group (i.e., those who received no treatment).

Some evidence suggests that combining exercise with medication can also lessen some of the medication's side effects. This is a significant finding, as side effects can be problematic for some individuals. Reducing side effects may enhance recovery rates and encourage adherence to the medication.

If depression is causing you emotional pain, either exercise, medication, or a combination of both could help relieve the severity of your symptoms. The combination of exercise and medication offers many benefits. If your doctor recommends medication and you decide to follow this advice, consider starting an exercise programme as soon as you begin the treatment. It doesn't have to be extreme. It's important to note that most antidepressant medications take at least four weeks for any clinical effect to occur. Exercising during this time may help minimise debilitating symptoms and side effects while waiting for the treatment to take effect.

Exercise not only proves successful in treating depression; it has also been shown to effectively slow or improve deficiencies in neurodegenerative disorders such as:

- mild cognitive impairment
- dementia
- Parkinson's disease
- it is also effective in psychiatric conditions such as schizophrenia.

Findings from at least nine major studies support the theory that exercise is also beneficial for alleviating the symptoms of anxiety.

We know that anxiety disorders significantly burden personal lives and the economy, contributing to absenteeism at work. The prevalence of anxiety disorders can drain healthcare resources and is also responsible for many unidentified medical symptoms. These studies show that even small amounts of exercise effectively reduce symptoms of anxiety. This alleviates suffering, helps address insomnia, and enhances overall health and well-being. If we suffer from anxiety, we should consider regular exercise as a treatment to alleviate the debilitating symptoms.

And remember, the exercise doesn't have to be intense. If possible, it can be as simple as a half-hour daily walk or as often as we can manage it. We might also consider swimming, walking (or jogging) outdoors or on a treadmill, cycling, martial arts, yoga, or a sport like tennis or golf.

> Exercise is effective in slowing or improving deficiencies in neurodegenerative disorders such as mild cognitive impairment, dementia, Parkinson's disease, and psychiatric conditions such as schizophrenia.

Movement, especially regular exercise, can significantly alleviate symptoms of PTSD. It enhances sleep quality, reduces stress, boosts energy levels, and promotes overall well-being. Long-term benefits encompass the development of strength and endurance while decreasing the risk of chronic diseases.

A National Comorbidity Survey in the United States conducted from 1990 to 1992, involving 5877 individuals aged 15 to 54 years, found that regularly active adults had a 25 to 38% reduced risk of experiencing current major depression compared to those who were not regularly active. Increased physical activity was associated with fewer depressive symptoms and a decreased risk of developing major depressive disorder (MDD).

Research revealed that 150 minutes of moderate-to-vigorous physical activity each week seems effective in treating mild to moderate depression.

Different exercise intensities and longer exercise programmes show the most significant benefits. There's considerable evidence validating that being physically active and having high cardiovascular fitness protects against depression. If we can be more physically active, the severity of the symptoms is significantly reduced. MDD is associated with poor cardiovascular and metabolic outcomes, and a sedentary lifestyle may intensify these illnesses—another good reason to be physically active.

A separate study, the Trøndelag Health Study (The HUNT Study), which began in 1984 in Norway, followed a 'healthy' group of 33,908 adults selected based on having no symptoms of mental illness or limiting physical illnesses, and was followed for the next 11 years. Data was collected from them at the start of the study and included information about exercise habits as well as baseline levels of anxiety and depression. The study revealed that as little as one hour of exercise per week was associated with reduced incidences of future depression, though not anxiety. It also predicted that 12% of future cases of depression could have been prevented had the participants engaged in at least one hour of physical activity per week. The level of exercise intensity was irrelevant; even low levels were predicted to reduce the incidence. We don't need to run marathons or sweat our way through a tough session at the gym to improve our health.

Exercise improves executive functioning (organising thoughts, focusing, controlling emotions, recalling information). Cognitive (thinking, reasoning, remembering) impairment has been recognised as a significant symptom of major depressive disorder (MDD), and research shows positive results indicating that exercise enhances mood and cognitive symptoms. Aerobic exercise has been demonstrated to improve attention, mental processing speed (how quickly we can process information), executive function, memory, verbal fluency, and global cognition (developing complex skills).

The Science Behind It

It has been suggested that exercise influences depression by normalising stress responses—fight, flight, freeze, and fawn. This stress response causes cortisol levels in the blood to rise. If our stress levels are high, we produce more of the stress hormone cortisol. Remember that many people experiencing depressive or anxiety symptoms have stress response systems that are unbalanced and not functioning properly. Their cortisol levels do not return to normal even when their stress is reduced. Exercise helps to lower these levels, thereby minimising symptoms.

Exercise influences BDNF levels. Brain-derived neurotrophic factors are essential for maintaining healthy brain cells, making increased levels beneficial. BDNF production significantly rises following exercise, including acute exercise, repeated exercise sessions, and long-term exercise programmes. Research indicates that BDNF levels are lower in individuals with major depressive disorder compared to those who do not suffer from it. Increasing BDNF production can help reduce symptoms of depression, providing another compelling reason to exercise.

Many studies have shown that BDNF is necessary for some antidepressants to be effective. This is an important finding. If medication helps reduce symptoms of depression, its impact is likely to be more significant if exercise is included. It makes sense to try to increase BDNF levels to maximise the benefits from medication.

Serotonin, dopamine, and norepinephrine levels increase after exercise, which may contribute to antidepressant effects. It makes sense that the higher the levels of these wonderful feel-good neurotransmitters buzzing around in our bodies, the better we will feel.

Overcoming Barriers to Exercise

One of the main barriers to exercise for people suffering from mental illnesses is that exhaustion is one of the symptoms. Even getting out of bed can be challenging during the worst episodes. Finding the motivation to exercise is difficult when energy levels are low. If we are at this acute stage of the illness, we may need to wait until our energy levels improve. Now is not the time to add worrying about not exercising to how we feel.

Remember: any movement is positive.

Stretching, bed/chair yoga, and moving limbs up and down while lying in bed may not dramatically affect physical fitness, but they enhance blood flow to the brain and keep joints lubricated. If we cannot get out of bed, we can try doing a slow, mental body scan. Breathe deeply and slowly, moving joints one by one, starting at our toes and working our way up the body. Try lifting limbs, stretching, and flexing them. Any movement is beneficial.

Other physical barriers to exercise include headaches or gut discomfort. Nausea and diarrhoea are common side effects of mental illnesses. There is little inclination to engage in much movement if we are feeling sick. Another issue is that exercise stimulates adrenaline release, which may be triggering for us if we experience severe anxiety and/or panic attacks. An increase in adrenaline levels within the bloodstream can mimic anxiety symptoms. Slower and gentler exercises are best to counter these physical barriers. Options include yoga, tai chi, and walking. We will explore the many positive benefits of yoga in the next chapter.

If walking alone is not safe, consider that many local councils and community groups offer free initiatives such as:

- walking groups
- yoga in the park
- Park-to-Park Runs
- boot camps
- canoeing groups
- tai chi sessions
- bushwalking groups
- gardening societies.

> **Movement and exercise can reduce symptoms of anxiety, depression, and PTSD.**

Emotional barriers include a lack of motivation, which is prevalent in mental illness.

Starting an exercise program is not just difficult; remaining consistent with regular exercise is also hard.

Everything can feel overwhelming when dealing with depression, anxiety, or PTSD. Exercise may appear to be just another task to complete! Feelings of apathy and sadness can be discouraging, and improvements in mood and health do not occur quickly. We do not see immediate results, which can be disheartening, leading us to give up before we notice any benefits.

Agoraphobia can be a significant barrier to overcome. Being unable to leave home limits our choices for activities; however, many free exercise videos, such as yoga, aerobics, stretching, or dancing, are available online. Lifting canned goods can serve as simple weights if our goal is to improve strength and muscle tone. Any movement is beneficial.

Don't Delay—Start Today

If you have not exercised for quite a while, it may be wise to speak with your doctor before commencing activities. Doctors can determine if you are well enough to begin an exercise regimen, advise on possible side effects from medications you may be taking, and check your blood pressure and heart function. Hopefully, most will recognise the barriers faced by those suffering from mental illnesses when discussing the initiation of physical activity and encourage activities to motivate us.

Incorporating more movement into our daily routine becomes easier if we make it a habit. If we are unsure where to begin, start with a simple walk. This can be challenging if we struggle with severe depression, anxiety, or PTSD; we may only be able to manage a few steps. That is understandable. And if that is all we can handle to start with, that is okay. Remember that any activity is a good activity. Small changes make a big impact. Start small and work your way up. If we can manage 10 steps one day, aim for 11 the next. Tomorrow might be a tough day, and we might only manage two or three steps. We must not berate ourselves. Our exercise programme has begun.

> **Any movement or exercise is beneficial. As little as one hour each week can benefit overall wellness.**

If we can manage a 30-minute walk, aim to do this a few times a week. When we feel ready for more, lengthen the walks or strive for five times a week. Small steps are the key. If we miss a day, let it go. Just try again tomorrow. As we feel better and exercise more regularly, we will likely find that our overall well-being has improved, and we have a greater sense of 'wellness'. This can take time, though. Remember that mental illnesses often take a long time to develop. They require time to treat.

We can boost our exercise routines when we feel good. Not only is this beneficial for us in the short term, but it can also reduce symptoms and potentially prevent acute episodes of depression and anxiety from developing in the future. Once we start to notice some improvement in symptoms, our motivation to exercise often increases. Surprisingly, some physical symptoms, such as headaches and nausea, diminish once exercise begins, leading to improvements in both physical and mental well-being. This should not be surprising; the mind and body are connected—what is good for one will help the other.

Many of us tend to lead sedentary lifestyles. Inactivity can generate sluggishness and lethargy, contributing to dwelling on or ruminating over past or potential problems. We also have fewer opportunities to experience new and more positive encounters. Social support from family and friends, especially having a friend to drag us along (albeit reluctantly), is beneficial for starting and maintaining an exercise regime. Exercising with a friend not only holds us accountable for showing up, but it is also more enjoyable. And if we do not enjoy the activity, we will at least have someone to complain to. If we usually catch up with a friend at a café, for example, consider getting a takeaway coffee and walking through a park while chatting. It is a simple change that may enhance our overall well-being.

Once we can begin physical activity, it is wise to select a specific time each day or every other day and commit to it. This practice helps establish the habit. We can add it to our calendar and set a reminder. We might choose a few types of exercise—swimming, walking, lifting weights, bike riding, or perhaps playing a sport. Aqua aerobics is an excellent option if we struggle with joint pain from weight-bearing exercises. Regardless of our choice, it is important to enjoy it. Exercise is often viewed as a chore, just another obligation we must fulfil. Try to make it something to anticipate.

Start slow. We are unlikely to regret exercising, even if beginning an activity is challenging. It is rare to feel worse after exercising unless we have pushed our bodies too hard. Generally, our mood lifts, and we not only gain the physical benefits of moving but also experience a sense of satisfaction and pride in caring for ourselves. The sense of accomplishment felt after completing your exercise task for the day is encouraging and motivating. Ticking anything off a to-do list is fulfilling; feeling good about ourselves while directly improving our health checks many boxes.

As we discovered in the previous chapter, the benefits of exercise are enhanced when performed in a natural setting. A daily walk, especially in nature, can significantly lift feelings of despair and sadness. These physical benefits include an increase in BDNF levels in the brain and the psychological calm that comes from being outdoors. This makes it a straightforward yet effective remedy to counteract some of the negative effects of mental disorders.

If you are fortunate enough to live by the beach, you may already appreciate the advantages of beach walking. Walking along a beach increases strength and endurance, and the activity is tranquil and stress-reducing, which tends to extend the distance covered. The sound of waves crashing on the shore drowns out negative thoughts. It becomes a white noise that promotes meditation. This is probably why it is marketed as an online tool to download and assist with falling asleep or meditating.

Bushwalking is equally relaxing. The longer we walk, the more exercise we receive, which enhances our health. Immersing ourselves in nature enables us to experience stress reduction and boost our overall well-being. We can remain present in the moment. Achieving mindfulness becomes easier when there are fewer distractions.

> **Exercise is now being suggested as the first line of treatment for mild to moderate depression.**

Studies suggest that only a modest amount of exercise is required to improve our mental health. Only one hour a week can make a difference. Knowing this is an excellent motivating factor if we struggle to move. Don't compare yourself or your abilities with anyone else. Each of us is on our own 'wellness journey'. Just keep going.

Summary:
- Exercise/movement is good for our joints, muscles, and bones. It can significantly improve some symptoms of depression, anxiety, and PTSD. It can enhance sleep quality, reduce stress, increase energy levels, and promote well-being.
- Exercise strengthens our bodies and can calm our minds.
- Exercise can be as simple as going for a walk.
- Little steps are the key to developing exercise or movement activity. If we feel unwell, we may be unable to manage more than a few steps. Any activity is good activity.

- Support from family and friends is beneficial to starting and maintaining an exercise regime.
- Small changes practised regularly can create good habits.
- Starting an exercise programme when first diagnosed with mild-moderate depression may alleviate some symptoms and prevent the disorder from worsening.
- Exercise can help regulate the HPA axis and lower cortisol levels. It can also increase BDNF levels and decrease chronic inflammation.
- Choose activities we enjoy, and if possible, set aside time to make regular exercise a habit.

Chapter 15

Namaste

'Yoga does not transform the way we see things; it transforms the person who sees.'
— B.K.S Iyengar

The Origins and Philosophy of Yoga

Yoga originated in ancient India, and Eastern cultures have practised this discipline for over 5000 years. 'Yoga' means 'yoke' or 'unite'. It incorporates physical movements and poses, breathing techniques, and meditation.

There are various forms of yoga, but they all aim to calm the mind and move the body. Yoga has gained increasing popularity worldwide. There is a general understanding that physical movements strengthen the body and increase flexibility, while meditation and breathing techniques can quiet and clear the mind. These positive outcomes have generated numerous scientific studies evaluating whether yoga should be considered an adjunct (complementary) therapy alongside conventional treatments for trauma-related conditions and mental illnesses or if it might even serve as a stand-alone remedy.

Unfortunately, some churches consider yoga dangerous because it is rooted in the Hindu religion, and the use of the Sanskrit language to describe various poses suggests that participating in yoga classes is somehow sinful. Yoga is undoubtedly associated with spirituality and the pursuit of meaning in life. It encompasses faith and compassion for oneself and others, promoting wisdom and peace. Many Western yoga practitioners teach yoga as a form of physical exercise and stretching, while recognising the spirituality associated with yoga without including religious philosophies in their classes.

In contrast, many Hindus argue that practising yoga solely as a physical exercise, without incorporating its spiritual elements, is incomplete and that secularising the practice is disrespectful to ancient and profound beliefs.

Whatever your beliefs about practising yoga may be, the decision to incorporate yoga as a healing balm for severe depression, anxiety, or PTSD is yours alone. I speak from experience when I say that conversations with God are far easier when your mind is calm and clear, rather than profoundly distressed or despairing. We must choose our path if we can. No matter how well-intentioned others may be in offering advice, they will not fully understand the depths of our suffering, and judgement is rarely helpful.

Yoga for Trauma and Mental Illness

Remember that psychological damage is damage from within. Healing, therefore, must also come from within. The mental and physical health benefits of yoga practice have become widely recognised: physical fitness, recovery from injuries, treatment of cardiovascular or metabolic diseases, and relief of symptoms of mental illnesses.

The despair we experience as trauma survivors with mental illnesses can cause a disconnect between our minds and bodies, along with feelings of hopelessness and emotional shutdown. We may feel overwhelmed. When stress seems uncontrollable, we may perceive that we have lost the ability to cope. With each new stress encountered, this learned helplessness can magnify, even if these subsequent stresses are mild. Yoga as therapy is being investigated to help break the feelings of powerlessness through active meditation.

Research shows that practising the physical poses of yoga has antidepressant and anti-anxiety effects, and that slow breathing patterns stimulate the vagal nerves (the main parts of our parasympathetic nervous system—our rest and relax system). Trauma can make our nervous systems highly reactive and constantly on high alert. The body's physical movement and the mind's engagement help relieve agitation by giving our minds something else to focus on. Noradrenaline, dopamine, and serotonin (feel-good neurotransmitters) are also increased.

Adopting yoga poses under the instruction of a yoga teacher promotes body movement while allowing the mind to relax, as it is necessary to focus on forming the correct pose and holding it. Yoga therapy positively influences hormone regulation and has been shown to enhance melatonin levels within the body, promoting improved immunity and sleep quality. Yoga directly impacts the nervous system by reducing the stimulation of the sympathetic nervous system (fight, flight, freeze, or fawn), thereby calming our bodies.

'Physical activity improves behavioural functions and the ability to cope with depressive emotions by stimulating biochemical pathways and restoring neuronal structures'
— *McCall (2013).*

> **Practising the physical poses of yoga has antidepressant and anti-anxiety effects.**

The disconnect, or numbness, we feel from having suffered trauma is a defence mechanism to protect us from experiencing mental pain. Severe forms of this disconnect constitute a condition called alexithymia, which, as we know, is described as the inability of a person to have any awareness of the emotions they are feeling. If we suffer from alexithymia, we are unable to describe our emotions and may have trouble understanding the feelings of others.

Alexithymia can also generate physical symptoms, including headaches or stomach pains, which seem to lack any real physical explanation. This often becomes evident when we visit our doctor with vague symptoms of varying severity, but we are unable to articulate what we are feeling. We simply feel unwell. This disconnect may shield us from emotional pain, but it also prevents us from experiencing sensations like happiness or joy. Yoga serves to reconnect with our emotions by focusing on breathing techniques and being present in the body, while also incorporating movements and poses.

The physical movements in yoga facilitate meditation while remaining active. Meditation is typically performed while sitting or lying in a comfortable position, focusing on breathing; however, if we suffer intense anxiety due to severe or chronic trauma, it can impede our ability to sit quietly and clear our minds. Being in a highly anxious state can cause severe agitation that may make it impossible for us to sit still and meditate. We may experience toe-tapping and jiggling legs while seated or may be unable to sit for any duration. Being in such an agitated state is distressing, often leading to irritability, confusion, and an inability to concentrate or practise meditation and mindfulness.

> *'Multiple studies have shown that mindfulness-based meditation can also help alleviate the symptoms of depression by improving attention control and regulating the HPA axis' (Desrosiers et al., 2013; Gard et al., 2014; McCall, 2013; Rp & Pl, 2005).*

Mindfulness involves being aware of our thoughts and feelings moment by moment, acknowledging and accepting these feelings without judgment. It emphasises the present rather than worrying about what has happened or what may occur in the future. Mindfulness-based stress reduction was founded by Jon Kabat-Zinn in 1979 to assist individuals suffering from chronic illnesses by alleviating anxiety, depression, and pain. Research has shown it can improve immune function and cognition. It teaches us to overcome our habitual reactions to stress and trauma, allowing us to respond with greater awareness and less reactivity. Integrating mindfulness and yoga enhances well-being and quality of life by improving perception, emotional recognition and regulation, and reducing stress. Combining breathing techniques with posture awareness and poses fosters physical and emotional relaxation.

> Yoga is active meditation.

Trauma-Informed Yoga: Creating Safe Spaces

In his book, The Body Keeps the Score, Bessel van der Kolk describes how yoga focuses on breathing and sensations from moment to moment. He discusses how yoga helps connect emotions with our bodies, noting that recognising what we feel aids in emotional regulation. This process can be unsettling if feelings of rage or fear arise, but a good teacher will recognise this and implement a gradual progression into the practice. If we have been severely traumatised, we may feel trapped in our trauma. Having a trauma-informed yoga teacher is essential to guide us through mindful poses that allow us to become open to our emotions or discomfort.

Trauma-informed teachers recognise that students may need to proceed slowly through their practice to avoid feeling vulnerable or anxious. These teachers understand that individuals who have undergone intense trauma might find it distressing to be touched, make eye contact, or close their eyes. Certain poses may be too confronting, especially for those who have experienced sexual abuse. A good teacher will notice if anyone is struggling during a class and will respond appropriately. They will also recognise that becoming aware of emotions that may arise during yoga practices can be painful. Emotional awareness allows healing to begin, although it may be painful and overwhelming. A trauma-informed yogi creates a safe space for students.

If we feel stuck in our trauma, yoga allows us to experience the physical sensations of muscle tenderness or stretching, but we know that these sensations will ease once the pose is completed. Holding yoga poses for a specific duration makes us feel the discomfort of the pose, and then the release helps us recognise that the pain we associate with trauma is in the past, and we can perceive this.

A yoga teacher may state that we need to hold a pose for a certain length of time. This practice allows us to sit with the difficulty of a pose, knowing it will only last for a predictable duration. Breathing slowly through any tension helps us understand that we can acknowledge unease, sit with it, and subsequently release it. We begin to realise that we can employ these techniques to cope with emotional pain and that we are capable of healing.

Yoga practice encompasses much more than increasing muscle strength and flexibility. This active meditation reconnects the mind and body. Combining mindfulness, breathing exercises, mind-body harmony, and meditation can enhance sleep, decrease anxiety, reduce cortisol levels, increase blood flow to muscles, and improve heart rate and blood pressure.

Haydie Osborne is a yoga instructor from Inspirit Health and Yoga in Brisbane, Queensland. She has practised yoga for over 30 years and describes herself as someone inspired to help others heal and a listener who *hears* people.

As a yoga teacher, you can generally see if people are struggling with trauma. Trauma, stress, and anxiety are held within the body, and many people dissociate from their bodies when they are dealing with trauma. They don't want to be in their bodies, particularly if they have suffered sexual abuse. They often find it hard to say what has happened to them and have difficulties saying what they are comfortable with in terms of physical contact. People shut down in their trauma and become stuck in their pain. They have low self-esteem, are self-critical, and are overwhelmed. Many have experienced having their power taken away, and shutting down emotionally is a coping technique. Yoga is a soothing practice.

Yoga in Schools and for Children

Yoga and mindfulness studies for school children improve core strength and flexibility while promoting calmness and coping skills. These practices also boost attention span and memory. One study involved a 10-week programme for children struggling with behavioural and emotional problems, including 30 children across three schools. The results were highly encouraging. All participants had displayed unhealthy coping behaviours and psychological difficulties. Kundalini yoga was the selected practice, which emphasises breathing and meditation. During the study, yoga was taught one to two times weekly during regular physical education classes.

Classroom teachers were consulted at the end of the study. The three interviewed teachers reported increased focus and concentration, noting changes in students' attitudes toward their peers. The students appeared more emotionally stable and less reactive to peer triggers. Some students became engaged in understanding and respecting their yoga practice and encouraged the involvement of family and friends.

The study results indicated that the students developed increased resilience and decreased stress. There was some question about whether the students became more aware of their emotions or if being better able to cope with their feelings allowed some negative emotions to surface; however, the positive effects of increasing resilience and decreasing stress encourage the continuation of yoga practice, making yoga programmes in schools more accepted.

Research on Yoga's Impact

Another study involving 54 individuals with major depression was conducted, where 16 participants received only antidepressant therapy, 19 underwent only yoga therapy, and the remaining 19 received a combination of both therapies. Yoga practice consisted of one hour daily for 10 days, followed by once a week for two weeks, then practice at home. Additional practice sessions were incorporated during the initial weeks of the second and third months.

At the beginning of the study, each participant completed a depression score questionnaire to assess the severity of their condition. Blood levels of cortisol and BDNF were measured, and these tests were repeated after three months of treatment. It is important to note that major depression is typically linked to high levels of cortisol and low levels of BDNF. By the end of the three-month study, serum cortisol levels decreased in 31 of the 54 participants. However, levels increased in the remaining 23 individuals, although most participants in the yoga groups exhibited reduced cortisol levels, regardless of medication usage.

A different study evaluating the benefits of Kundalini yoga was conducted on a group of 80 people with PTSD. Some group members participated in eight yoga sessions, and their symptoms were compared with those of a control group that did no yoga. Those who practised yoga experienced improvements in stress levels, sleep, anxiety, and resilience, and their PTSD scores were significantly better than those of the control group.

Although evidence suggests that yoga is a promising intervention for addressing the effects of trauma, it lacks precision regarding how it works and whether it can assist all forms of trauma. Studies have measured possible biomarkers in the body, including BDNF and oxytocin (a hormone produced in the hypothalamus that plays a role in reproduction, uterine contractions following childbirth, and lactation). Magnetic resonance imaging has detected functional changes within the brain, and the results are positive. It is beneficial as an ancillary or supplementary therapy.

A recent investigation that examined 13 literature reviews analysing 185 distinct studies on trauma treatment with yoga suggests that yoga may enhance and sustain the relief provided by more recognised treatments for trauma-related symptoms. This is because yoga is believed to alter awareness by helping to decrease repetitive negative thoughts and ruminations, encouraging flexible or adaptive thinking. This thinking allows us to recognise unforeseen situations and quickly determine the best response.

Yoga appears to quiet our HPA axis stress-response systems, which in turn helps lessen depression. Decreasing depressive symptoms allows neural plasticity (the brain's ability to change and adapt) to function properly and helps prevent damage and death to neurons. Neural plasticity becomes disrupted by depression. We know that neurons are the fundamental functioning units in our brains. They integrate and transmit signals throughout the body, responding to emotions and environmental stimuli. Stress negatively impacts neural plasticity, which subsequently affects memory formation and may lead to long-term depression. Yoga can help reduce stress through movement, breathing, and meditation and restore neural plasticity.

Choosing the Right Type of Yoga

There are many forms of yoga, including Iyengar, Kundalini, Hatha, Bikram, Vinyasa, and Ashtanga yoga. All practices utilise physical poses (asanas) to enhance strength, balance, and flexibility, in conjunction with breathing techniques (pranayama) and meditation to regulate breathing and calm the mind. Some forms are more rigorous than others, while some are more relaxing and restorative. If you have physical injuries or disabilities, it is important to consider these factors when choosing a practice.

Determining which type of yoga is best for different mental illnesses remains uncertain. However, the physical components seem to alleviate symptoms of PTSD, meditation appears to assist survivors of child abuse, and breathing techniques help reduce anxiety. There are some risks associated with beginning yoga therapy, which generally include flashbacks or triggers as the mind starts to relax. These may induce intense fear. If you are a survivor of trauma, it's important to select a yoga instructor who is trauma-aware and trained to anticipate and recognise emotional distress. Trauma-aware teachers minimise touch and focus on alleviating anxiety, providing a safe space for a slow reconnection between mind and body. Once healing has commenced, resilience follows.

Summary:

- Yoga means union, incorporating physical movements, poses, breathing techniques, and meditation.
- All forms of yoga aim to calm the mind and move the body.
- Holding yoga poses for a certain period helps us feel the discomfort of the pose and then release it. This helps us recognise that the trauma and pain we have suffered is in the past and that we can let go of it.
- Yoga is a form of active meditation that has antidepressant and anti-anxiety benefits. This active meditation reconnects the mind and body.
- The combination of mindfulness, breathing, mind-body harmony, and meditation benefits sleep, and anxiety, decreases cortisol levels, increases blood flow to muscles, and improves heart rate and blood pressure
- Slow breathing patterns stimulate the vagus nerve and increase noradrenaline, dopamine, and serotonin (our feel-good neurotransmitters). It boosts our parasympathetic nervous system (our rest and relaxation system).
- Alexithymia is the inability to be aware of what we are feeling. Trauma experiences can create a disconnect or numbness in emotions to protect us from feeling mental pain.
- Yoga programmes for children struggling with behaviour and emotional problems were completed at schools.

The programmes showed encouraging results in focus, concentration, and attitude changes towards other students. The children became more emotionally stable and less reactive to peers.
- Other studies report reductions in cortisol levels following yoga therapy programmes in individuals with major depressive disorder.
- Yoga has the potential to improve the psychological consequences of trauma. It can lead to mindfulness, which supports healing.

Chapter 16
The Power of the Pet

'...in trauma treatment groups for children and young people aged 7–17 years who had experienced sexual abuse, the inclusion of 15 minutes of unstructured canine contact at the beginning of sessions (preceded by 30 minutes in the waiting room) resulted in significant reductions in trauma symptoms.'

— Jones et al. (2019)

Introduction to Animal-Assisted Therapy

Animal-assisted therapy (AAT) focuses on the bond between humans and animals. It involves structured and intentional interactions between individuals and trained animals to help trauma survivors, promote rehabilitation in hospitals and care facilities, and provide therapy for individuals with learning disabilities and autism. Professionals such as psychologists, counsellors, physical therapists, and occupational therapists conduct this organised, goal-directed therapy, with sessions typically including activities such as grooming, petting, or playing with the animal.

Although humans and animals have interacted for thousands of years, animal-assisted therapy (AAT) was formally introduced as a therapeutic tool in the 1960s.

The capacity of animals to aid in restoring mental health is encouraging science-based studies to determine the effectiveness of human-animal relationships in treating both physical and psychological ill health. Studies into the therapeutic benefits of using animals such as horses, dogs, dolphins, cats, birds, and gerbils to address trauma in adults and children provide comfort and engagement in settings such as nursing homes (where feline-assisted therapy is popular) and in treating mental disorders, are showing promising results. Dolphin-assisted therapy, for example, is used for people with physical disabilities who are unable to walk; dolphins can provide the sensation of movement when a person holds a dolphin's fin and experiences being pulled through the water.

Canine-Assisted Therapy

Canine-assisted therapy, also known as Canine-Assisted Psychotherapy (CAP) is one of the most common forms of animal-assisted therapy. The relationship between humans and dogs has existed for thousands of years, and their bonds are evident in ancient cave paintings and historical literature. The wolf was revered by Native Americans who believed it to have mystical powers, and ancient Egyptians are reported to have kept dogs as companion animals, sometimes burying the dogs with their deceased masters.

Including dogs as therapeutic aids in mental health therapies and play therapies for traumatised children recognises these unique bonds, and the meaningful inclusion of trained animals is becoming more widely studied to establish evidence-based records. Many of these studies report meaningful, beneficial outcomes from incorporating the use of dogs during therapy sessions, with improvements in overall health, the capacity to connect with others, expression of emotions, self-esteem, and coping with stress.

Dogs excel at understanding nonverbal cues and are nonjudgemental. Their presence can be calming, especially for trauma survivors who have a deep distrust of people. Dogs provide safety and enable a traumatised individual to connect with a therapist, often leading to greater disclosure during sessions. Additionally, dogs encourage follow-up visits for treatment. Adults and children involved in CAP report increased positivity, reduced stress, fewer distress or depressive symptoms, and improved functioning.

Canine-assisted therapy is used to help reduce anxiety, depression, and PTSD in children. Studies reflect positive impacts on social skills, self-esteem, problem-solving abilities, anxiety, and mood. This therapy can assist children with autism spectrum disorder, attention-deficit disorder (ADD), learning disorders, selective mutism, and depression. When used to treat children who have experienced abuse, the dogs provide both physical and emotional comfort. If a child has suffered abuse at the hands of an adult, they are likely to have a deep distrust of people. Dogs can effectively capture a child's attention during therapy and may help lighten the mood during the sessions. Reducing a child's anxiety during treatment encourages them to return for more visits. These studies have shown decreases in blood pressure, stress levels, immune functioning, and cortisol levels.

Service dogs show promising results for military veterans with PTSD. Veterans and their family members describe how having a service dog helps manage distressing symptoms, reduces anger and depression, and minimises suicidal ideation. They report that participating in a programme to work with a service dog encourages them to leave the house and engage with others. The presence of the dog alleviates anxiety levels, as the dog can be trained to alert the veteran to potentially triggering situations.

The dogs also provide a calming presence, waking their owners if they have nightmares and comforting them during panic attacks. Dogs can also assist in situations where veterans have physical impairments, such as warning of impending seizures or helping a veteran who has visual impairments.

Dogs are used for pet therapy during hospital visits. Studies show that pain levels decrease in sick children after pet therapy visits. The dogs benefit both the children and their parents, who report satisfaction and pleasure in interacting with them. The dogs help to reduce hyperarousal levels in children with ADHD. When interacting with dogs, children are more likely to open up and communicate willingly.

Dog visits to nursing homes are beneficial, particularly for patients with dementia. Patients with dementia can struggle with behavioural issues, which may lead to antipsychotic medications being prescribed. These medications have side effects, and canine-assisted therapy demonstrates improvements in behaviour and emotional symptoms in these patients, without the associated side effects (nonpharmacologic intervention). Dog visits to nursing homes also encourage communication and interaction among residents, helping to address loneliness. Hospital visits involving geriatric patients have indicated that even a one-time visit by dogs lasting between 12 and 20 minutes can reduce anxiety levels for these patients.

Equine Therapy: Healing Through Horses

> *'Horses gently command us to be present in the here and now while encouraging us to be meditative and peaceful.'*
> *— Kane (2017)*

Horses also provide similar comfort and interaction in nursing homes and hospitals, as well as being used to complement cognitive behavioural therapy (CBT) for people suffering from PTSD, depression, and anxiety. Research shows that equine-facilitated therapy (EFT) is beneficial because it promotes new insights and perspectives on old behaviour patterns and relationships. EFT includes activities such as grooming, handling, and riding horses.

Therapists have found that clients who work with horses become more empowered. Their self-esteem and self-confidence improve, and they develop a more positive self-image. Equally important, horses are highly attuned to body language, vocalisations, and breathing; they respond effectively only when the client is calm, confident, and demonstrates leadership qualities, emphasising the significant role of trust-building in this therapy.

Equine-assisted psychotherapy (EAP) is used to assist veterans struggling to adjust to civilian life after combat, dealing with PTSD, sustaining physical injuries, or experiencing combat trauma. Studies in this field show positive results, with participants reporting high satisfaction from working with horses and significantly lowering blood pressure, cortisol, and muscle tension.

Veterans often face dissonance when returning to civilian life after combat. Many have endured physical injuries and deep emotional trauma, leading to intense ongoing suffering. Some may have been held captive or engaged in unorthodox behaviours that they find difficult to reconcile. These traumatic memories can resurface at any time and result in acute distress, violent behaviour, or feelings of disempowerment and disconnection.

The majestic nature of horses creates a sense of peace and calmness in people struggling with PTSD. Programmes developed to connect veterans with horse therapies report substantial improvements in the healing process. Participants work with the horses, grooming, rugging, and sometimes working around them, cleaning out stalls, and engaging with them. Some programmes include riding the horses. Horses are sensitive to changes in the emotions of those interacting with them and respond best when approached with calmness and confidence. Survivors of trauma must recognise their emotions instead of disconnecting from them. Being in touch with emotions and understanding why they are present helps keep the participant 'in the moment', empowering them to improve self-confidence and positive mindsets. The horses will not remain still and quiet if those tending to them cannot control their feelings. The hypervigilance often experienced by people living with PTSD settles as they breathe with, groom, or stroke the horses. Their reactions become more controlled, blood pressure decreases, and they often feel a sense of inner peace.

In her book, Equine-Assisted Counseling and Psychotherapy, Hallie Sheade discusses the history of human-equine interaction, how horses can perceive and respond to various human emotions, and the advantages of incorporating horses in counselling and psychotherapy. She highlights how being in an outdoor, natural environment benefits clients seeking healing through equine therapies— *one of the most significant advantages clients report is experiencing an overall sense of peace from being outside.* (Sheade, 2020 #429). Her book emphasises equine welfare and the practical as well as academic factors to consider when employing equine-assisted therapies.

'Having a large and powerful horse respond to commands in a calm and favourable manner can provide abuse victims with a sense of authority and validation.'
— *Signal (2013).*

Phoenix House, a sexual assault referral centre in Queensland, Australia, conducts EFT programmes for survivors of child sexual assault (CSA), including children, adolescents, and adults. There is a strong relationship between CSA and depression. Long-term issues may include anxiety, PTSD, anti-social behaviour, personality disorders, eating disorders, suicidal ideation, substance abuse, and sexualised behaviour.

Children who have been victims of CSA tend to mistrust adults. Research shows that CSA is often perpetrated by an adult known and trusted by the child. This can include immediate family members, relatives, neighbours, and others in close contact with the child. Establishing trust with a child can be difficult for a therapist, but EFT is showing positive results. These are the words of a dear friend of mine, a young woman, S, who is a survivor. S graciously shared her experiences working with horses.

Working with horses kept me out of hospital. I truly believe it helped me break the hospital/home/hospital cycle. I don't know what it was about it, but I found it therapeutic cleaning out their stalls, filling their water troughs, patting them, and gaining their trust. I was so worried because of 1) their size and 2) the fact that they were racehorses and that they were going to hurt me. But they never did, and I learnt that it was okay to be nervous if I didn't pretend I wasn't. Because that's when they get strange if you pretend you're feeling something you're not. Helping the owner out gave me a purpose, and sharing the space with horses was lovely. S. (2022)

> **The majestic nature of horses has the effect of creating a sense of peace and calmness in people who are struggling with PTSD.**

Studies exploring the healing power of horses include an experiment that involved a qualitative assessment of seven young people, aged 11–21, who interacted with horses over a two-year period. All participants showed increased confidence, empathy towards the horses, and a heightened sense of mastery over their situations.

Equine-assisted psychotherapy (EAP) was utilised in another study involving 63 children who had witnessed family violence and been diagnosed with PTSD, ADHD, and mood disturbances, including depression and adjustment disorder. The study consisted of 19 sessions, and all 63 participants demonstrated significant improvement in Global Assessment of Functioning (GAF) scores. These scores are used to assess the severity of a mental illness and may include a questionnaire, evidence from medical records, or information from a doctor, police, or court records. Although the studies indicate that clients experienced notable improvement in depressive symptoms, further research is necessary to expand and include such treatments.

Other Animal Therapies: Cats, Dolphins, and More

Cats can be excellent therapy animals. They have a calming presence that offers peaceful companionship. Cats are very sensitive to human emotions and can often sense when a person is sad or lonely. Their gentle energy is therapeutic in settings like nursing homes for the elderly and hospitals. Petting a therapy cat is soothing, lowers blood pressure, and the rhythmic sound of a cat purring helps reduce stress levels and ease anxiety, facilitating the implementation of therapies.

In addition to providing companionship for the elderly, cats also comfort those facing end-of-life care. Their presence is calming and grounding, making them ideal for helping individuals with PTSD and anxiety. Children with autism often respond positively to a therapy cat, initiating connections and sometimes communication.

Dolphin-assisted therapy is also popular. It originated in the 1970s and is believed to improve attention spans and develop social skills. It has proven effective in assisting with mental health problems and has demonstrated improvements in pain management and learning, particularly in children with cerebral palsy or neurodivergent conditions. It can be utilised by individuals with physical disabilities who cannot walk, allowing them to experience the sensation of movement as they hold onto a dolphin's fin and are pulled through the water.

Dolphins are highly intelligent, social, and playful creatures that can learn skills and follow instructions. However, therapy with dolphins is expensive and difficult to access. Limited data is available to support the effectiveness of the treatment, and ethical concerns exist regarding the captivity of dolphins and the risk of injury to participants. Further research is needed before establishing standards for this therapy.

Other animals are utilised in AAT, including alpacas, guinea pigs, ferrets, and even chickens. All serve to provide comfort and encourage communication and social skills.

AAT and Trauma Recovery

AAT is proving immensely beneficial as an adjunct or alternative treatment for survivors of PTSD, MDD, and severe anxiety. These are life-altering illnesses; sometimes, available treatments do not provide relief. If our trauma has been prolonged or severe, we may experience extreme distress, panic attacks, and suicidal thoughts, which can persist long after the trauma has abated. Medications and therapies may be insufficient or ineffective when memories of the trauma are overwhelming and ongoing. Having severe mental illness alters our perception of ourselves and the safety of the world. We may be so traumatised that we are unable to leave the house, interact with others, or feel comfortable in a crowd or in traffic. This is where interactions with a pet or therapy animal may prove invaluable.

> Animal-assisted therapy (AAT) is proving immensely beneficial as an adjunct or alternative treatment for survivors of PTSD, MDD, and severe anxiety.

Animal-assisted therapies can utilise the affinity between humans and animals to help traumatised individuals learn to manage and regulate their emotional responses to situations that may have once triggered them. Incorporating the physical touch of animals can reestablish acceptance of the sensations of interacting with others. Grooming and petting animals and building trust with them allow therapists to connect with traumatised clients. This fosters a safe and constructive relationship, which benefits healing. Using animals to build rapport between therapists and those suffering from psychological trauma is becoming more prevalent and yielding positive results. Our relationships with animals can be intensely emotional, and growing evidence shows that our connection with animals is valuable for improving our health. Companion animals, emotional support animals, and even animals we encounter daily can reduce anxiety, lower blood pressure, and elevate mood. Pets help alleviate stress, encourage physical activity, and counter issues such as loneliness or isolation.

Caring for a pet gives us a reason to get up in the morning, and exercising with a dog or horse compels us to leave the house and be physically active. Some pets can be trained to recognise distress, even intervening to prevent self-harm, anticipating emotional distress, or warning us of an impending medical emergency. They do not judge us, do not demand conversation, or ask more of us than we can give. They provide a reason to keep living.

Healing from trauma is possible, even if it often feels impossible. Movement, connecting with nature, yoga, and interaction with animals are all worth considering. Each positive change we make in our daily lives increases our resilience, although we may not recognise it at the time. Progress is often slow, but small adjustments in our lives can steer us in new directions. These changes do not need to be monumental. Repeating beneficial adjustments to our patterns and behaviours is crucial for overcoming the damage caused by our stress responses.

Summary:
- There is growing evidence that our connectedness with animals is a valuable resource to improve our health.
- Pets help alleviate our stress, encourage us to be more active, and help counter problems such as loneliness or isolation.
- Animals can help foster rapport between therapists and their patients.
- Animals provide comfort and engagement in settings such as nursing homes.
- The use of dogs during therapy sessions shows meaningful, beneficial outcomes as they are adept at comprehending non-verbal cues, are non-judgemental, and their presence can be calming. This is especially so if a survivor of trauma has a deep distrust of people.
- Equine therapy is showing positive results for those suffering from PTSD and/or depression. Horses are acutely attuned to body language, vocalisations, and

breathing and tend only to respond effectively if we are calm and confident and show leadership qualities.
- Keeping in touch with our emotions instead of disconnecting from them helps improve our self-confidence and positive mindsets.
- Animal-assisted therapies can help us learn to regulate and manage our emotional triggers.

Chapter 17

From Pain to Purpose: Transforming Suffering into Strength

Making Good Choices

Making good choices that enhance our overall health and well-being is challenging when we are faced with illnesses—whether physical or mental. It is incredibly tempting to choose what is easiest instead of what is best. We understand that we must take authority over our health—acting as our own health advocates—and we know what we ought to do. Living with mental illness often means struggling to get through each day—without panic attacks or severe depressive episodes. The challenges are real. The exhaustion and shame are palpable. All those affected can do is strive for positive improvements to manage their symptoms and hope they won't become overwhelming.

Markus Parks said in 2020 that "Mental illness is not your fault, but it is your responsibility." Finding the best ways to stay healthy is easy in theory but challenging when emotions are triggered or stress levels are high. Even one bad day can seem to undo a week of good days. Fortunately, experts in resilience are available, focusing on developing healthy habits and living happier, healthier lives. They offer simple but effective suggestions to encourage and motivate making good choices. We can learn to cultivate a more positive outlook and eliminate bad habits.

The Power of Tiny Changes

James Clear, the author of "Atomic Habits: An Easy and Proven Way to Build Good Habits and Break Bad Ones," discusses the cumulative effects of making small positive changes in everyday life that enhance our well-being. He emphasises that these changes need not be significant; simply repeating them each day cultivates habits.

This can be as simple as walking for 10 minutes a day. A 10-minute walk may not have an immediate impact on overall health, but by the end of the week, it adds up to 70 minutes. By the end of a month, it totals 210 minutes, or 3.5 hours. If 10 minutes of walking increases to 30 minutes daily, that equals 210 minutes each week and 840 minutes, or 14 hours, each month. Continue this for a year, and it will accumulate to more than 180 hours of walking. That is 180 hours of movement instead of inactivity. Small choices can lead to significant impacts. The cumulative effect of making positive life changes will enhance wellness.

Good dietary habits can start small. Replacing sugary drinks with water, even once a day, will result in seven fewer sugary drinks a week or 30 in a month. Substituting a fast-food lunch with a homemade meal using fresh, whole foods, like salads and fruit, can make a difference. For instance, decide that each

Wednesday will be a 'take-lunch-to-work day'. Make it a habit to ensure that ingredients are prepared before Wednesday morning. Small changes can lead to significant impacts when repeated.

The little things we do, day in and day out, can positively impact our well-being. Brushing our teeth and flossing twice a day serve as perfect examples. It takes only a few minutes. Nevertheless, this simple act significantly reduces tooth decay and gum disease—both of which can lead to heart disease, joint inflammation, mouth cancers, and illnesses like pneumonia and bronchitis.

Each day, when I walk my dog, I pick up rubbish discarded by passing cars or other walkers. While picking up a single can or fast-food wrapper may not significantly impact the environment, I've been walking my neighbourhood streets since 2000, and the rubbish I have collected over the past 25 years would fill a couple of trailers. This amount truly makes a difference. This is another example of how small changes can have a significant impact.

Breaking Cultural and Family Beliefs

James Clear discusses how people often adopt habits without questioning them. Many of these habits arise from the culture in which individuals were raised, and they are frequently followed simply because that is how things have always been done.

For instance, many of us are told that we must finish school, secure a job, buy a house, get married, have children, and then live our lives exactly as our parents and their parents did. While this can be a rewarding path if we choose it, this route is not set in stone. We can forge our own path and break habits that do not align with our goals.

Meeting others' expectations at the expense of our mental health is harmful. We do not have to follow generational patterns. It is perfectly acceptable to choose a path that suits us best. Of course, I speak from the perspective of a privileged white woman in a first-world country, and I recognise the risks that some (mostly women) face when pursuing their dreams and living life on their terms. I deeply empathise with those whose lives are controlled by individuals who are uncompromising and rigid in their beliefs.

For those fortunate enough to choose how they wish to live, identifying positive habits that enhance health will yield significant long-term benefits. If we feel uncertain, it's best to start small—minor changes practised consistently can have a substantial impact.

Recognise that each of us is only responsible for our behaviour and conduct—not that of others. How others act and what they believe to be right is their business, and each of us has this same right. However, be mindful that behaviours and beliefs carry consequences. Taking responsibility for our actions and beliefs involves accepting the inevitable results; therefore, our choices should be healthy ones.

Understanding Belief Systems

It is sensible to reassess decisions as we age or face new challenges. Our lives are not static; we must adjust and adapt as necessary. At times, we need to reconsider what we have always believed to be correct—our belief systems.

Belief systems are the principles we trust. They are views that shape our behaviour. Most of us adopt beliefs from our parents, especially during childhood. As we become adults, we may find that our belief systems no longer serve us or hinder who we want to be. They may prevent us from pursuing a career, travelling, or leading the life we desire. Belief systems that we have outgrown or that no longer fulfil us can be altered. If we adhere to the law and respect the rights of others, that is enough.

We should not let the expectations of others, no matter how well-intentioned, dictate the course of our lives. Our purpose is not to carry the burden of keeping everyone else happy. If that feels hard to accept, it is worth asking ourselves why.

Do we fear disapproval from others? If so, why do we need this approval? Why is the approval of another more important than our happiness? Do we fear abuse or worse? Are cultural or religious restraints insurmountable barriers? Is it dangerous for us to challenge family or community beliefs?

Living our lives to please others can create psychological stress. Understanding why we hold the beliefs we do and allowing ourselves to abandon the ideologies that no longer serve us is incredibly liberating.

> **Belief systems we have outgrown or those that are not fulfilling us can be changed.**

Building Resilience Through Self-Care

If we encounter an issue that generates emotional pain, it is often connected to something that occurred in our past—something that caused us anguish. Recognising what triggers this pain aids in healing.

Speaking with a therapist helps identify habitual behaviours that may hinder fulfilment. Once identified, these habits can be changed. Another option is to engage in self-reflection. Seven years ago, I attended a week-long silent retreat, which provided me the time and space to examine and contemplate the patterns of behaviour that had contributed to the depression and anxiety I suffered for many years. It was a time free of interruptions, external influences, and offered the opportunity to explore belief systems and relationships that negatively affected my health. Self-reflection played a significant role in my healing, as did sessions with psychiatrists and psychologists.

The other life-changing influence for me was seeking clarity and understanding through sessions with a life coach. My initial doubts about the effectiveness of life coaching in addressing mental illness—when I had known and trusted only science-based approaches—were soon put to rest. The sessions were motivating and transformative. I was fortunate that my life coach has been a dear friend of mine for over 30 years.

Kerri Speyers is a life coach at Life Choices Coaching in Brisbane. She emphasises the importance of healing our emotional wounds to liberate ourselves from shame and hurt. She says that:

Many of our problems stem from parental belief systems—we hold ourselves back from following our own paths because we are trapped in the family traditions and mindsets that often have been repeated for generations. We can live our lives as we choose; however, our belief systems usually prevent us from living our best lives. We fear recrimination, emotional blackmail, and being ostracised from our families simply because we, as individuals, want to forge our own paths. Developing resilience to counter the adverse reactions from others alleviates feelings of guilt and the belief that choosing a different path from what was expected of us has somehow let others down.

Identifying behavioural patterns that could harm our health can be challenging, especially if the behaviour has been ongoing for a long time. Seeking professional help from an objective therapist can be valuable. Therapists help sift through and identify what may be causing emotional pain. Once the traumas are recognised, healing can begin.

Healing benefits the sufferer and their loved ones, typically family. It is essential to recognise, however, that some traumas may remain impossible to fully recover from. Nevertheless, we can strive to minimise the impact that trauma has on our lives. We will likely experience relapses, but such relapses do not signify failure. They are a natural part of the healing journey, and with each relapse, we can build resilience.

Resilience restores self-confidence, self-control, self-awareness, and self-acceptance, originating from and contributing to the self. No one can give it, pass it on, or sell it to us; we must develop our own. Resilience is individual. It becomes a suit of emotional armour that allows vulnerability without fear of further hurt. It is a learned process, strengthened through regular self-care and self-compassion.

It can involve establishing personal boundaries (particularly within complex relationships), maintaining a healthy work-life balance, and integrating beneficial practices into daily life. Taking time to engage in self-care is neither selfish nor self-indulgent. It is a kindness we offer ourselves.

Self-care is an essential aspect of developing emotional resilience. Aside from the physical benefits of healthy decisions, there is the psychological sense of achievement and pride, knowing we are taking control of our health. Seek medical advice if unsure.

Insights from Experts

An expert in developing resilience is Dr. Lucy Hone, an adjunct senior fellow at the University of Canterbury in Christchurch, New Zealand, and co-director of the New Zealand Institute of Wellbeing and Resilience. In 2019, she delivered a powerful TED Talk, titled "The Three Secrets of Resilient People." It was voted one of the top TED Talks globally in 2020.

Dr. Hone has worked with many organisations in different countries to help people understand how to build resilience when faced with difficult circumstances. These include communities that have experienced natural disasters, as well as assisting the bereaved in coping with the death of loved ones. Sadly, she had to confront a devastating loss when her 12-year-old daughter, Abi, was killed in a car accident in 2014. Her TED Talk describes her transition from being a resilience expert to a grieving mother. Her world was abruptly turned upside down, and the reality of living the rest of her life without her beloved daughter became her 'new normal'. Her family of five had become a family of four.

Dr. Hone's grief is palpable when listening to her speak and reading her book on resilient grieving. However, what she shares in both is hope. She describes how she applied the knowledge she acquired over the many years she devoted to studying resilience to help herself and her family cope with the tragedy.

Dr Hone says it is possible to grieve and move forward despite enduring severe hardships and that anyone can learn coping strategies. The three main strategies she shares are:

- Acknowledgement that suffering happens to everyone—instead of thinking 'why me', think 'why not me'. Resilient people understand that bad things happen to everyone.

- Look for the good in situations, even if it is difficult to find. Focus on what can be changed and accept the things that cannot be; be grateful for the good things.
- Make decisions that will help us, not harm us—making good choices creates a sense of control of one's life.

Dr. Hone's book, "Resilient Grieving: How to Find Your Way Through Devastating Loss," is a profoundly moving and practical guide to dealing with tragedy and learning resilience. She discusses how people grieve and how grief differs for everyone—there is no right or wrong way to grieve.

She speaks of hope and discusses strategies and techniques that anyone can learn. She reveals how a person will never 'get over' losing someone they love but accepting that the loss has happened and cannot be undone is the beginning of learning to live with the loss.

Her strategies may not be embraced by everyone experiencing deep grief, but they provide insight into what worked for her and her family. This book can be referenced in many situations involving loss and discusses how to regain some semblance of control in our lives.

When life takes a devastating turn and we must face a 'new normal' way of life, Dr. Hone's loss and her studies in resilience can galvanise practical and effective techniques to adopt that may alleviate some of the heartaches. She acknowledges that no part of the grieving process is easy, and each person's journey is unique. We will all face loss. Learning how to develop resilience will be beneficial during these times and will help us process and prepare for other difficulties we may encounter.

Another expert in developing coping strategies and embracing wellness is Aaron Antonovsky. Aaron Antonovsky (1923–1994) was an Israeli-American sociologist and academic who, in 1979, first devised the word 'salutogenesis', which comes from the Latin salus, meaning health, and the Greek genesis, meaning origin. Salutogenesis describes the relationship between health, stress, and coping. Antonovsky studied how people can manage, overcome, survive, and adapt to life's stressors. He determined that life experiences shape one's sense of coherence or understanding and focus on the origins of health instead of disease—what makes and keeps people healthy.

The Macquarie Dictionary describes 'coherence' as a natural or logical connection, congruity, and consistency. Antonovsky hypothesised that having a strong sense of coherence helps individuals utilise the resources available to cope with stressors and manage tension. His focus on what makes people healthy instead of what makes them sick is based on positive psychology and positive behaviour. He wondered how stress affects our development of resilience and how social and physical environments may be designed to maximise well-being. For example, a healthy environment enhances performance, mood, and wellness.

Antonovsky believed that good health is more than just the absence of disease. He concluded that viewing life as manageable, meaningful, and positive contributes to good health and fosters thinking that promotes favourable health and salutogenesis (what causes health) instead of merely preventing disease and pathogenesis (the development of disease). He focused on actively promoting wellness and developing strategies that emphasised strength and vitality. Identifying approaches to manage tension, adapting to change, and utilising general resilience helps reduce stress and illness. Antonovsky identified three prerequisites necessary for a person to cope with stressors:

- manageability—recognising what resources are necessary and being willing to pursue them.
- comprehensibility—having the attitude that the world is understandable, consistent, meaningful, and orderly.
- meaningfulness—perceiving that life makes sense and is worth living.

He encouraged further research into programmes designed to improve and promote health in institutions. He advocated for individuals to have the resources necessary to care for their own well-being, encompassing social, mental, and physical health. He examined the environment in which people live—social, ecological, and economic.

He supported disease prevention and health promotion, encouraging people to take control of their health and understand how best to cope with the life stressors and difficulties they encounter. To achieve this, he emphasised avoiding behaviours that do not support good health and recognising that resources must be provided to cater to individual needs. Social support, integration, and fostering motivation to adopt a healthy lifestyle can help improve both physical and mental health.

One example is Antonovsky's description of research into occupations such as nursing. He determined that although nursing can be enriching and deeply satisfying, it can also lead to burnout and mental fatigue. He explained that nurses must be reflective and seek meaning. They must monitor their self-care closely and intervene if their health begins to decline.

The characteristics of a person, including their knowledge, intelligence, ability to develop coping strategies, and flexibility in decision-making, can all influence levels of resilience and a sense of coherence. Everyone has a responsibility to act as their own health advocate.

Healing Trauma, Breaking Cycles

Healthcare should be a shared responsibility between healthcare professionals and patients, and medical advice should be followed accordingly. This can be very difficult during the acute phases of trauma when our fight-or-flight, freeze, or fawn system is still on high alert or if we are severely depressed. Once these stages have eased and we can make some decisions, it is wise to choose healthy ones.

We can easily become disheartened when struggling with illness. Even minor stresses or setbacks can cause us to react disproportionately and lead us to believe that our health is spiralling out of control again. However, our healing must come from within us. When we feel better, we must take charge of our own health. There is no 'can't-be-bothered' pill. Yes, it is hard, but it is harder being sick, and it is often frightening. We do not have control over some diseases that can strike with little warning or injuries from accidents; however, we can make healthy choices in our daily lives. Make the best choices possible to promote wellness. Focus on what can be changed.

Unresolved traumas can lead us to hurt others. Hurt people hurt. We must address our pain to stop the cycle of abuse. Psychological trauma causes deep wounds. Unless these wounds are opened and healed, the poison of past traumas is difficult to erase. If the abuse has been severe or prolonged, this process will likely be long and painful.

Generational dysfunction may persist through successive generations until someone finds the strength and courage to break the cycle. Each of us has the chance to break the cycle of abuse. As adults, we can ensure that we do not pass our sufferings on to our children. We need to confront the impact of what we have endured, seek to heal our past wounds, and learn from them. Understanding that we are free to choose the life we want to live is immensely liberating. Whether these beliefs are cultural, religious, or conventional, we each have choices. We do not need to please others. We can say no (mostly).

> **Making good choices supports physical and mental health.**

It may take years to overcome adversities, but we have a new chance to heal each day. We need to surround ourselves with supportive people and disregard the opinions of those who have no interest in our welfare or who choose to invalidate our feelings. The motivational speaker Jim Rohn said that we are the average of the five people we spend the most time with. Being around positive, motivational, and caring individuals will benefit our health significantly more than spending time with negative, critical, or cruel companions. Choosing friends wisely is a form of self-care.

We must not compare our lives to others. Life is not a competition to see who has suffered the most. Bad things happen to everyone; they are often unfair and painful. How we respond to these bad things, however, is where our power lies. This is only possible with healing when the trauma endured has been firmly placed where it belongs: in the past. Even then, it can still fail despite the belief that recovery was complete. Addressing and rejecting these behavioural patterns facilitates recovery from trauma and promotes resilience.

Summary:
- We must keep trying to make good choices that benefit our health.
- Keeping healthy is challenging when emotions or stress levels are triggered.
- Experts in resilience and developing healthy habits can help us live happier, healthier lives.
- Small choices repeated regularly can have significant impacts on our lives.
- We can be trapped following habits that have been part of our culture but are now not supporting the life we choose to live. We can choose to forge our paths if it is safe for us to do so.
- We are each responsible for our own behaviour and conduct and must accept the consequences of our actions.
- We often adopt the same belief systems as our parents. Belief systems we have outgrown or no longer serve us can be changed.
- It is not our job to keep others happy. Living our lives to please others can cause psychological stress.
- Speaking with a therapist helps identify habitual behaviours hindering fulfilment. So can self-reflection.
- Bad things happen to each of us.
- We can build resilience by learning coping strategies.

- We each grieve differently.
- We must avoid bad habits that do not support good health. This can be very difficult, though, in times of severe stress or suffering. During these times, we can struggle with even the most straightforward decisions. Know that this is not a time for making big decisions. Be kind to yourself.

A Final Word

In 2006, our family dog, Ellie—a six-year-old Border Collie and Kelpie mix—ate poisonous bait that was on the footpath near our letterbox.

Ellie walked with me to check the mail. I saw her eating something and thought it might be discarded lunch scraps from one of the local children.

A few hours later, my two youngest sons and I watched her die a painful, cruel death.

Our oldest son was away on a school trip. The younger boys were 14 and 11 years old.

Although we rushed Ellie to our local vet, she could not be saved. The vet suspected strychnine poisoning.

Ellie was more than a dog to me.

She had been my support during some of my most difficult depressive episodes. We walked together every day. Even when I lacked the motivation to move, she would sit patiently, nudge me with her nose, and wait until I put on my shoes and grabbed her lead.

Her gentle presence helped anchor my well-being.

Six weeks after her death, I still had not returned to walking. I had descended into a deep depression—sickened by the callousness of her death and devastated by the loss of her calming companionship.

Finally, I asked for help and saw my general practitioner.

She immediately doubled my antidepressant dosage and asked whether I was still walking.

I told her, *No, I can't walk without my dog.*

She looked at me for a long while and then said words I have never forgotten: *It's strength of character. You know you must walk for your health. Just do it.*

Those were the words I needed.

Yes, I was grieving, but for my sake and the sake of my family, I walked that very day.

It was sad to go alone, but I realised this was a choice I needed to make.

I share this story to illustrate how those living with mental illness have increased vulnerability to what may appear to others as only mild trauma. Even when we feel we have recovered from our traumas and moved on, we remain susceptible to further traumas. These traumas need not be severe, and others may not even recognise them as traumas.

Relapse is common. Ellie's death may seem trivial to some, but for me, it emphasises how mental illness deepens our vulnerabilities. This insight reminds me of the importance of self-compassion and seeking support, lessons I hope to share with others.

The death of a dog does not compare to the horrors of war, physical attacks, or severe sexual or psychological abuse. However, it compounded the psychological trauma I had experienced for years and serves as an example of how the effects of trauma can be magnified disproportionately in those suffering from mental illnesses. Prolonged and severe mental illness diminishes the ability to cope. A minor trauma can magnify exponentially when you are close to breaking.

I recognise that the trauma I have faced is minimal compared to that encountered by many others. Over the years, one of my biggest mistakes was ignoring and dismissing bad behaviour from others and downplaying its impact on my family and me. I should have spoken out against the disrespect and manipulative games played by toxic influences in our lives.

Unfortunately, my mental illnesses were so severe at the time that I was unable to address the conflict. I felt that many other people were facing far worse situations than I was, and I tolerated far more than I should have. I have learned that minimising the hurt does not remove it; it simply buries it. Developing the resilience to speak up has taken a long time, and it has given me the strength and determination to share what I have learned. Now that I am healed, I want to help others.

Mental illness is complex and challenging to treat, but do not lose hope. Scientists and doctors are unravelling the perplexing mysteries of our brains. There is an increasing understanding of interactions within the brain and communication between the brain and the rest of the body, particularly the gut. Medication, meditation, exercise, and other therapies can alleviate the severity of some symptoms. Mental illness can be treated. Give yourself time. Never lose hope.

I wish I had discovered my voice earlier, but I now understand that healing takes time and begins when we forgive ourselves. Healing from psychological trauma is not a linear process; it is not about erasing our mistakes but embracing them as part of our growth. For me, that meant silence. Yet silence has lessons to teach. For me, silence was not a failure—it was survival. And now, I can speak.

This will do

Clarity and understanding
My reward for staying alive
Medication, my thief of joy
And safety net
I'm grateful.

Where to Seek Help (Australia)

- **In an emergency:**
  Phone **000** if you or someone else is at immediate risk of suicide or self-harm.

Mental Health Support Lines:

- **Beyond Blue:** 1300 22 4636
- **Lifeline:** 13 11 14
- **Blue Knot Foundation Helpline:** 1300 657 380
- **Butterfly Foundation's National Helpline (Eating Disorders):** 1800 33 4673
- **eheadspace (Young People 12–25 years):** 1800 650 890
- **FriendLine (for anyone feeling lonely):** 1800 424 287
- **Kids Helpline (ages 5–25 years):** 1800 55 1800
- **Head to Health (Mental health advice and support):** 1800 595 212
- **MensLine Australia (Men's mental health and relationships):** 1300 78 99 78
- **MindSpot (Online and phone therapy):** 1800 61 44 34
- **QLife (LGBTIQA+ peer support):** 1800 184 527
- **PANDA (Perinatal Anxiety and Depression Australia):** 1300 726 306
- **SANE Australia (Complex mental health support):** 1800 187 263
- **Suicide Call Back Service:** 1300 659 467
- **Open Arms — Veterans and Families Counselling:** 1800 011 046

For more services and information:
🔗 **Healthdirect – Australian Mental Health Services**

Suggested Reading

1. Asmundson, G. J. G., & Afifi, T. O. (Eds.). *Adverse Childhood Experiences.*
2. Fournier, A. K. *Animals as Anodyne.* In *Animal-Assisted Intervention.*
3. Chandler, C. K., & Otting, T. L. *Animal-Assisted Interventions for Emotional and Mental Health: Conversations with Pioneers of the Field.*
4. Rachman, S. *Anxiety.*
5. Cross, M. *Anxiety: Expert Advice from a Neurotic Shrink Who Has Lived with It All His Life.*
6. MacLean, P. *A Triune Concept of the Brain and Behaviour.*
7. Brown, B. *Braving the Wilderness.*
8. Bui, E., Charney, M. E., & Baker, A. W. (Eds.). *Clinical Handbook of Anxiety Disorders: From Theory to Practice.*
9. Bui, E. (Ed.). *Clinical Handbook of Bereavement and Grief Reactions.*
10. Cha, D. *Cognitive Impairment in Major Depressive Disorder: Clinical Relevance, Biological Substrates, and Treatment Opportunities.*
11. Pradhan, R. K., & Kumar, U. (Eds.). *Emotion, Well-Being, and Resilience: Theoretical Perspectives and Practical Applications.*
12. Goleman, D. *Emotional Intelligence: Why It Can Matter More Than IQ* (25th Anniversary Edition).
13. Neal, M. J. *How the Endocrine System Works.*
14. Fournier, A. K. *Human–Animal Interaction Analysis.* In *Animal-Assisted Intervention.*
15. McIntyre, R. S. (Ed.). *Major Depressive Disorder.*
16. Frankl, V. E. *Man's Search for Meaning: The Classic Tribute to Hope from the Holocaust.*

17. Carter, R. *Mapping the Mind*.
18. Bowins, B. *Mental Illness Defined: Continuums, Regulation, and Defense*.
19. Sayyed, R. Z., & Khan, M. (Eds.). *Microbiome-Gut-Brain Axis: Implications on Health*.
20. Ballard, E. D., Henter, I. D., & Zarate, C. A. *Neurobiology of Depression*.
21. Brukner, P., & Khan, K. (Eds.). *Physical Activity in the Prevention and Treatment of Depression*.
22. LeDoux, J., Keane, T., & Shiromani, P. (Eds.). *Post-Traumatic Stress Disorder*.
23. Bremner, D. J. (Ed.). *Posttraumatic Stress Disorder, Front Matter*.
24. Brandelli, A. (Ed.). *Probiotics*.
25. Starcevic, A. *Psychological Trauma*.
26. Smith, R. E., & Ascough, J. C. *Promoting Emotional Resilience: Cognitive-Affective Stress Management Training*.
27. Wright, S. E. *Redefining Trauma: Understanding and Coping with a Cortisoaked Brain*.
28. Hone, L. C., Ph.D. *Resilient Grieving: How to Find Your Way Through Devastating Loss*.
29. Hill, J. *See What You Made Me Do: Power, Control and Domestic Violence*.
30. Fink, G. (Ed.). *Stress: Neuroendocrinology and Neurobiology*.
31. Fink, G. (Ed.). *Stress: Physiology, Biochemistry, and Pathology*.
32. Brady, M. S. *Suffering and Virtue*.
33. van der Kolk, B., M.D. *The Body Keeps the Score: Brain, Mind, and Body in the Healing of Trauma*.
34. Carter, R. *The Brain Book: An Illustrated Guide to Its Structure, Function, and Disorders*.
35. Loveday, C. *The Brain: What It Does, How It Works & How It Affects Behaviour*.
36. Lyons, M. *The Dark Triad of Personality*.

37. Lee, K., & Ashton, M. C. *The H Factor of Personality: Why Some People Are Manipulative, Self-Entitled, Materialistic, and Exploitive—And Why It Matters for Everyone.*
38. Burke Harris, N., M.D. *The Deepest Well: Healing the Long-Term Effects of Childhood Adversity.*
39. Solomon, A. *The Noonday Demon: An Atlas of Depression.*
40. Kauffman, J. *The Shame of Death, Grief, and Trauma.*
41. Herman, J. L. *Trauma and Recovery.*
42. van der Kolk, B. A., McFarlane, A. C., & Weisaeth, L. *Traumatic Stress: The Effects of Overwhelming Experience on Mind, Body, and Society.*
43. Kim, Y. K. (Ed.). *Understanding Depression.*
44. Sapolsky, R. M. *Why Zebras Don't Get Ulcers.*

Glossary

ADD: Attention Deficit Disorder *(p. 217)*

ADHD: Attention-Deficit/Hyperactivity Disorder *(p. 250)*

agoraphobia: A fear of leaving an environment that is considered safe *(p. 47)*

Alzheimer's Disease: A neurodegenerative disease causing behavioural changes, mood swings, disorientation, loss of motivation, memory loss, and loss of bodily functions *(p. 77)*

anhedonia: The inability to feel pleasure *(p. 59)*

arthritis: Inflammation of joints *(p. 77)*

asthma: An inflammatory disease of the airways of the lungs *(p. 77)*

avoidance of social encounters due to a fear of rejection or embarrassment *(p. 47)*

BDNF: Brain-derived neurotrophic factor, an essential neurotrophin that aids development and survival during brain development, and plays an essential role in learning and memory *(pp. 69–70)*

cognitive: Of, relating to, being, or involving conscious intellectual activity (such as thinking, reasoning, or remembering) *(passim)*

coherence: Having logical and meaningful understanding *(pp. 270–272)*

corpus callosum: A collection of over two million brain cells that link the left and right hemispheres of the brain *(p. 102)*

cortisol: One of the main steroid hormones in the human body, produced by the adrenal cortex *(p. 77)*

CSA: Child sexual abuse *(p. 254)*

dorsal anterior cingulate cortex: A region within the brain stimulated during physical pain *(p. 139)*

dysthymia: Persistent depressive disorder *(p. 62)*

EFT: Equine-Facilitated Therapy *(p. 254)*

emotional dysregulation: Being unable to function in everyday life *(p. 34)*

epigenetics: Environmental and behavioural influences that can change how much information our genes express; our DNA does not change, but positive or negative experiences can affect how genetic information is passed to the next generation *(p. 76)*

fear conditioning: Feeling unsafe in a safe environment *(p. 35)*

GAF: Global Assessment of Functioning scores *(p. 255)*

generalised anxiety disorder: Worrying about many issues such as work, ill-health, financial worries, etc. *(p. 47)*

genetics: Hereditary traits in our DNA *(p. 76)*

heart diseases: Diseases involving the heart, such as coronary artery disease, cardiomyopathy, and abnormal heart rhythms *(p. 77)*

hippocampus: A structure within the brain where memories are formed and stored; new neurons can form in this region *(p. 107)*

HPA axis: Hypothalamic-pituitary-adrenal axis, one of the main stress responses in the body *(p. 77)*

hypothalamus: Brain structure linking the nervous and endocrine systems, sometimes called the Master Gland *(p. 107)*

insomnia: Difficulty sleeping *(pp. 26, 77)*

limbic system: An area in the brain comprising different structures responsible for instinctive behaviours, emotions, relationships, and behaviours *(p. 105)*

long-term potentiation: Strengthening of synapse signalling in neural pathways to retain memories *(p. 112)*

Machiavellianism: Skilled manipulators; little regard for others; manoeuvre people and circumstances to benefit themselves *(p. 183)*

MDD: Major depressive disorder (also called clinical depression), involving at least two weeks of low mood and loss of pleasure *(p. 62)*

narcissists: One of the dark triad of personality types; feel superior to others, have an over-inflated sense of self, and become hostile if challenged *(p. 182)*

neural plasticity: The brain's ability to change and adapt, particularly in learning and memory *(p. 244)*

obsessive-compulsive disorder: Repetitious behaviour to cope with unwanted thoughts or anxiety *(p. 47)*

panic disorder: Frequent panic attacks with intense fear *(p. 47)*

persistent depressive disorder: A chronic form of major depressive disorder *(p. 63)*

pituitary gland: Major gland linked to the hypothalamus, controlling hormone release from other glands; sometimes called the Master Gland *(p. 107)*

pre-frontal cortex: Front region of the frontal cortex responsible for decision-making, thought processing, and self-control *(p. 106)*

psychomotor agitation: Anxiousness and restlessness, including pacing and toe tapping *(pp. 26, 57, 77)*

psychomotor retardation: Slow thinking and slow body movements *(pp. 26, 77)*

psychopaths: Impetuous, undisciplined, high risk-takers; likely to display violence, bullying, and sadism *(p. 183)*

social anxiety disorder: Avoidance of social encounters due to a fear of rejection or embarrassment *(p. 47)*

thalamus: The major relay station in the brain; regulates consciousness, sleep, alertness, and planning *(p. 107)*

Type 2 diabetes: Also known as adult-onset diabetes; occurs primarily as a result of obesity *(p. 77)*

References

1. American Psychiatric Association. (2013a). *Anxiety disorders*. In *Diagnostic and statistical manual of mental disorders* (5th ed.).
2. American Psychiatric Association. (2013b). *Depressive disorders*. In *Diagnostic and statistical manual of mental disorders* (5th ed.).
3. Abonahas, H. H., Darwish, A. M. G., Abd El-Kareem, H. F., Abonahas, Y. H., Mansour, S. A., Korra, Y. H., Sayyed, R. Z., Abdel-Azeem, A. M., & Saied, E. M. (2022). Trust your gut: The human gut microbiome in health and disease. In R. Z. Sayyed & M. Khan (Eds.), *Microbiome-gut-brain axis: Implications on health* (pp. 37–65). Springer Singapore. https://link.springer.com/chapter/10.1007/978-981-16-1626-6_3
4. Ai, M., Wang, J., Chen, J., Wang, W., Xu, X., Gan, Y., Li, X., Gou, X., Cao, J., Lv, Z., Chen, X., Wang, H., Ma, Q., & Li, K. (2019). Plasma brain-derived neurotrophic factor (BDNF) concentration and the BDNF Val66Met polymorphism in suicide: A prospective study in patients with depressive disorder. *Pharmacogenomics and Personalized Medicine, 12*, 97–106. https://doi.org/10.2147/PGPM.S201187
5. Anavkar, A., Patel, N., Ali, A., Rajan, W., & Alim, H. (2022). Gut microbes: Influencers of human brain. In R. Z. Sayyed & M. Khan (Eds.), *Microbiome-gut-brain axis: Implications on health* (pp. 1–36). Springer Singapore. https://doi.org/10.1007/978-981-16-1626-6_1
6. Andrade, C., & Kumar Rao, N. S. (2010). How antidepressant drugs act: A primer on neuroplasticity as the eventual mediator of antidepressant efficacy. *Indian Journal of Psychiatry, 52*(4), 378–386. https://doi.org/10.4103/0019-5545.74318
7. Andrews, L. W. (2010). *Encyclopedia of depression*. ABC-CLIO. https://www.bloomsbury.com/au/encyclopedia-of-depression-9780313353673/
8. Baldauf, D., & Desimone, R. (2014). Neural mechanisms of object-based attention. *Science, 344*(6182), 424–427. https://www.science.org/doi/10.1126/science.1247003
9. Ballard, E. D., Henter, I. D., & Zarate, C. A. (2019). The classification of depression: Embracing phenotypic heterogeneity in the era of the RDoC. In J. Quevedo, A. F. Carvalho, & C. A. Zarate (Eds.), *Neurobiology of depression* (pp. 3–15). Academic Press. https://doi.org/10.1016/B978-0-12-813333-0.00001-9
10. Barone, A. (2022). Animal-assisted therapy for children with autism spectrum disorder (Doctoral dissertation). ProQuest. https://www.proquest.com/docview/2658751303

11. Bathina, S., & Das, U. N. (2015). Brain-derived neurotrophic factor and its clinical implications. *Archives of Medical Science: AMS, 11*(6), 1164–1178. https://www.ncbi.nlm.nih.gov/pmc/articles/PMC4697050/
12. Bissière, S., Plachta, N., Hoyer, D., McAllister, K. H., Olpe, H. R., Grace, A. A., & Cryan, J. F. (2008). The rostral anterior cingulate cortex modulates the efficiency of amygdala-dependent fear learning. *Biological Psychiatry, 63*(9), 821–831.
13. Boes, A. D., McCormick, L. M., Coryell, W. H., & Nopoulos, P. (2008). Rostral anterior cingulate cortex volume correlates with depressed mood in normal healthy children. *Biological Psychiatry, 63*(4), 391–397. http://www.sciencedirect.com/science/article/pii/S0006322307007305
14. Bremner, J. D. E. (2016). *Posttraumatic stress disorder* (Front matter). Wiley Online Books. https://doi.org/10.1002/9781118356142.fmatter
15. Brewin, C. R., Cloitre, M., Hyland, P., Shevlin, M., Maercker, A., Bryant, R. A., Humayun, A., Jones, L. M., Kagee, A., Rousseau, C., Somasundaram, D., Suzuki, Y., Wessely, S., Van Ommeren, M., & Reed, G. M. (2017). A review of current evidence regarding the ICD-11 proposals for diagnosing PTSD and complex PTSD. *Clinical Psychology Review, 58*, 1–15. https://www.sciencedirect.com/science/article/abs/pii/S0272735817301460
16. Briones, B. A., & Gould, E. (2019). Adult neurogenesis and stress. In G. Fink (Ed.), *Stress: Physiology, Biochemistry, and Pathology* (pp. 113–125). Academic Press. https://www.sciencedirect.com/science/article/abs/pii/B9780128131466000072
17. Brown, E. S., & Chandler, P. A. (2001). Mood and cognitive changes during systemic corticosteroid therapy. *Primary Care Companion to the Journal of Clinical Psychiatry, 3*(1), 17–21. https://pubmed.ncbi.nlm.nih.gov/15014624/
18. Bucci, M., Marques, S. S., Oh, D., & Harris, N. B. (2016). Toxic stress in children and adolescents. *Advances in Pediatrics, 63*(1), 403–428. https://www.sciencedirect.com/science/article/abs/pii/S0065310116300020
19. Bush, G., Vogt, B. A., Holmes, J., Dale, A. M., Greve, D., Jenike, M. A., & Rosen, B. R. (2002). Dorsal anterior cingulate cortex: A role in reward-based decision making. *Proceedings of the National Academy of Sciences of the United States of America, 99*(1), 523–528. https://pubmed.ncbi.nlm.nih.gov/11756669/
20. Cardinali, D. P. (2018). Third level: The hypothalamus. In *Autonomic nervous system* (pp. 159–182). Springer. https://link.springer.com/content/pdf/10.1007/978-3-319-57571-1.pdf
21. Carter, R. (1998). *Mapping the mind*. Wiedenfeld & Nicolson.
22. Carter, R. (2014). *The brain book: An illustrated guide to its structure, function, and disorders*. Dorling Kindersley Limited.
23. Castrén, E. (2014). Neurotrophins and psychiatric disorders. In G. R. Lewin & B. D. Carter (Eds.), *Neurotrophic factors* (pp. 295–317). Springer. https://www.sciencedirect.com/science/article/pii/S0006322321013044

24. Chang, L., Wei, Y., & Hashimoto, K. (2022). Brain–gut–microbiota axis in depression: A historical overview and future directions. *Brain Research Bulletin, 182*, 44–56. https://www.sciencedirect.com/science/article/pii/S0361923022000375
25. Chung, S., Son, G. H., & Kim, K. (2011). Circadian rhythm of adrenal glucocorticoid: Its regulation and clinical implications. *Biochimica et Biophysica Acta (BBA) - Molecular Basis of Disease, 1812*(5), 581–591. https://www.sciencedirect.com/science/article/pii/S0925443911000329
26. Collazzoni, A., Stratta, P., Pacitti, F., Rossi, A., Santarelli, V., Bustini, M., Talevi, D., Socci, V., & Rossi, R. (2020). Resilience as a mediator between interpersonal risk factors and hopelessness in depression. *Frontiers in Psychiatry, 11*, 10. https://www.frontiersin.org/articles/10.3389/fpsyt.2020.00010/full
27. Coria Páez, A. L., Flores Hidalgo, B. L., Morales Matamoros, O., Moreno Escobar, J. J., & Quintana Espinosa, H. (2024). Soft systems methodology in standardizing the method for applying dolphin-assisted therapies in neurodivergent patients: Case study of Delfiniti Mexico. *Systems, 12*(8), 294. https://www.mdpi.com/2079-8954/12/8/294
28. Cox, D. T. C., Shanahan, D. F., Hudson, H. L., Plummer, K. E., Siriwardena, G. M., Fuller, R. A., Anderson, K., Hancock, S., & Gaston, K. J. (2017). Doses of neighborhood nature: The benefits for mental health of living with nature. *BioScience, 67*(2), 147–155. https://academic.oup.com/bioscience/article/67/2/147/2900179
29. Cross, M. (2020). *Anxiety: Expert advice from a neurotic shrink who's lived with it all his life*. ABC Books.
30. Daffre, C., Oliver, K. I., & Pace-Schott, E. F. (2020). Neurocircuitry of anxiety disorders. In E. Bui, M. E. Charney, & A. W. Baker (Eds.), *Clinical handbook of anxiety disorders: From theory to practice* (pp. 25–44). Springer International Publishing. https://link.springer.com/chapter/10.1007/978-3-030-30687-8_2
31. Davis, T. N., Weston, R., Hrabal, J., Lively, P., & McHenry, R. (2022). Animal-assisted therapy. In J. L. Matson & P. Sturmey (Eds.), *Handbook of autism and pervasive developmental disorder: Assessment, diagnosis, and treatment* (pp. 1389–1407). Springer. https://link.springer.com/chapter/10.1007/978-3-030-88538-0_62
32. Dean, J., & Keshavan, M. (2017). The neurobiology of depression: An integrated view. *Asian Journal of Psychiatry, 27*, 101–111. https://www.sciencedirect.com/science/article/abs/pii/S1876201816303197
33. Dube, S. R. (2020). Twenty years and counting: The past, present, and future of ACEs research. In G. J. G. Asmundson & T. O. Afifi (Eds.), *Adverse childhood experiences* (pp. 1–14). Academic Press. https://www.sciencedirect.com/science/article/abs/pii/B978012816065700001X
34. Ebmeier, K. P., & Zsoldos, E. (2019). Cerebral metabolism, brain imaging, and the stress response. In G. Fink (Ed.), *Stress: Physiology, biochemistry,*

and pathology (pp. 47–61). Academic Press. https://www.sciencedirect.com/science/article/abs/pii/B9780128131466000035

35. Ellison, J. M., Colvonen, P. J., Haller, M., Norman, S. B., & Angkaw, A. C. (2019). Examining the relation between PTSD and insomnia on aggression. *Military Psychology, 31*(3), 241–250. https://www.tandfonline.com/doi/full/10.1080/08995605.2019.1598220

36. Escobar, J. J. M., Matamoros, O. M., del Villar, E. Y. A., Espinosa, H. Q., & Hernández, L. C. (2024). Employing Siamese networks as quantitative biomarkers for assessing the effect of dolphin-assisted therapy on pediatric cerebral palsy. *Brain Sciences, 14*(8), 778. https://www.proquest.com/docview/3097838509

37. Fields, R. D. (2009). *The other brain: From dementia to schizophrenia, how new discoveries about the brain are revolutionizing medicine and science.* Simon & Schuster.

38. Florowska, A., Hilal, A., & Florowski, T. (2022). Prebiotics and synbiotics. In A. Brandelli (Ed.), *Probiotics* (Chapter 2). Academic Press. https://www.sciencedirect.com/science/article/abs/pii/B978032385170100018X

39. Foster, J. A., & McVey Neufeld, K. A. (2013). Gut–brain axis: How the microbiome influences anxiety and depression. *Trends in Neurosciences, 36*(5), 305–312. https://www.sciencedirect.com/science/article/abs/pii/S0166223613000088

40. Foster, J. A., Rinaman, L., & Cryan, J. F. (2017). Stress and the gut-brain axis: Regulation by the microbiome. *Neurobiology of Stress, 7*, 124–136. https://www.sciencedirect.com/science/article/pii/S2352289516300509

41. Frankl, V. E. (2004). *Man's search for meaning: The classic tribute to hope from the Holocaust.* Rider.

42. Gagliardi, A., Totino, V., Cacciotti, F., Iebba, V., Neroni, B., Bonfiglio, G., Trancassini, M., Passariello, C., Pantanella, F., & Schippa, S. (2018). Rebuilding the gut microbiota ecosystem. *International Journal of Environmental Research and Public Health, 15*(8), 1679. https://pmc.ncbi.nlm.nih.gov/articles/PMC6121872/

43. Gayathri, D., Prashantkumar, C. S., & Vasudha, M. (2022). Current insights on the modulation of gut microbiome and its effect on human health. In R. Z. Sayyed & M. Khan (Eds.), *Microbiome-gut-brain axis: Implications on health* (pp. 67–96). Springer Singapore. https://link.springer.com/chapter/10.1007/978-981-16-1626-6_2

44. Gilbert, P., & Procter, S. (2006). Compassionate mind training for people with high shame and self-criticism: Overview and pilot study of a group therapy approach. *Clinical Psychology & Psychotherapy, 13*(6), 353–379. https://onlinelibrary.wiley.com/doi/10.1002/cpp.507

45. Greer, T. L., Furman, J. L., & Trivedi, M. H. (2017). Evaluation of the benefits of exercise on cognition in major depressive disorder. *General Hospital Psychiatry, 49*, 19–25. https://www.sciencedirect.com/science/article/abs/pii/S0163834317301020

46. Hafford, W. (2014). *Wild minds: Adventure therapy, ecopsychology, and the rewilding of humanity* (Doctoral dissertation). Antioch University. https://etd.ohiolink.edu/apexprod/r/1501/10?clear=10&p10_accession_num=antioch1414664206
47. Hamer, H. M., Jonkers, D., Venema, K., Vanhoutvin, S., Troost, F. J., & Brummer, R. J. (2008). Review article: The role of butyrate on colonic function. *Alimentary Pharmacology & Therapeutics, 27*(2), 104–119. https://onlinelibrary.wiley.com/doi/10.1111/j.1365-2036.2007.03562.x
48. Hansen, M. M., Jones, R., & Tocchini, K. (2017). Shinrin-yoku (forest bathing) and nature therapy: A state-of-the-art review. *International Journal of Environmental Research and Public Health, 14*(8), 851. https://pmc.ncbi.nlm.nih.gov/articles/PMC5580555/
49. Harvey, S. B., Øverland, S., Hatch, S. L., Wessely, S., Mykletun, A., & Hotopf, M. (2017). Exercise and the prevention of depression: Results of the HUNT cohort study. *American Journal of Psychiatry, 175*(1), 28–36. https://psychiatryonline.org/doi/10.1176/appi.ajp.2017.16111223
50. Hayen, C. J. (2017). *Canine-assisted psychotherapy: Finding the way back to our animal soul* (Doctoral dissertation). Pacifica Graduate Institute. https://www.proquest.com/docview/1972657993
51. Herman, J. L. (1997). *Trauma and recovery*. BasicBooks.
52. Herring, M. P. (2018). Exercise for the management of anxiety and stress-related disorders. In B. Stubbs & S. Rosenbaum (Eds.), *Exercise-based interventions for mental illness* (pp. 11–24). Academic Press. https://www.sciencedirect.com/science/article/abs/pii/B9780128126059000022
53. Hill, J. (2019). *See what you made me do: Power, control and domestic violence*. Black Inc.
54. Hong, P. Y., & Lishner, D. A. (2016). General invalidation and trauma-specific invalidation as predictors of personality and subclinical psychopathology. *Personality and Individual Differences, 89*, 211–216. https://www.sciencedirect.com/science/article/abs/pii/S0191886915006509
55. Huang, T. T., Lai, J. B., Du, Y. L., Xu, Y., Ruan, L. M., & Hu, S. H. (2019). Current understanding of gut microbiota in mood disorders: An update of human studies. *Frontiers in Genetics, 10*, 98. https://pmc.ncbi.nlm.nih.gov/articles/PMC6389720/
56. Ittermann, T., Völzke, H., Baumeister, S. E., Appel, K., & Grabe, H. J. (2015). Diagnosed thyroid disorders are associated with depression and anxiety. *Social Psychiatry and Psychiatric Epidemiology, 50*(9), 1417–1425. https://link.springer.com/article/10.1007/s00127-015-1043-0
57. Jackson, P. L., Brunet, E., Meltzoff, A. N., & Decety, J. (2006). Empathy examined through the neural mechanisms involved in imagining how I feel versus how you feel pain. *Neuropsychologia, 44*(5), 752–761. https://www.sciencedirect.com/science/article/abs/pii/S0028393205002666
58. Jaggar, M., Fanibunda, S. E., Ghosh, S., Duman, R. S., & Vaidya, V. A. (2019). The neurotrophic hypothesis of depression revisited: New insights

and therapeutic implications. In J. Quevedo, A. F. Carvalho, & C. A. Zarate (Eds.), *Neurobiology of depression* (pp. 105–124). Academic Press. https://www.sciencedirect.com/science/article/abs/pii/B9780128133330000068

59. Jawahar, M. C., Toben, C. G., & Baune, B. T. (2019). Gene-environment interactions and epigenetic mechanisms in depression. In J. Quevedo, A. F. Carvalho, & C. A. Zarate (Eds.), *Neurobiology of depression* (pp. 39–56). Academic Press. https://www.sciencedirect.com/science/article/abs/pii/B9780128133330000032

60. Jiang, H., Ling, Z., Zhang, Y., Mao, H., Ma, Z., Yin, Y., Wang, W., Tang, W., Tan, Z., Shi, J., Li, L., & Ruan, B. (2015). Altered fecal microbiota composition in patients with major depressive disorder. *Brain, Behavior, and Immunity, 48*, 186–194. https://www.sciencedirect.com/science/article/pii/S0889159115001105

61. Jindani, F., Turner, N., & Khalsa, S. B. S. (2015). A yoga intervention for posttraumatic stress: A preliminary randomized control trial. *Evidence-Based Complementary and Alternative Medicine, 2015*, Article 351746. https://onlinelibrary.wiley.com/loi/4747

62. Gabrieli, J. D. E., Poldrack, R. A., & Desmond, J. E. (1998). The role of the left prefrontal cortex in language and memory. *Proceedings of the National Academy of Sciences of the United States of America, 95*(3), 906–913. https://www.researchgate.net/publication/13782970_The_role_of_the_prefrontal_cortex_in_language_and_memory

63. Jones, M. G., Rice, S. M., & Cotton, S. M. (2019). Incorporating animal-assisted therapy in mental health treatments for adolescents: A systematic review of canine-assisted psychotherapy. *PLOS ONE, 14*(1), e0210761. https://journals.plos.org/plosone/article?id=10.1371/journal.pone.0210761

64. Juruena, M. F., Cleare, A. J., & Young, A. H. (2018). The role of early life stress in HPA axis and depression. In Y. K. Kim (Ed.), *Understanding depression: Volume 1. Biomedical and neurobiological background* (pp. 39–52). Springer Singapore. https://link.springer.com/chapter/10.1007/978-981-10-6580-4_5

65. Kane, E. (2017). Beasts of emotional burden. *DVM360, 48*, 36–38. https://www.dvm360.com/view/beasts-emotional-burden

66. Kauffman, J. (2010). *The shame of death, grief, and trauma*. Taylor & Francis Group. https://ebookcentral.proquest.com/lib/uql/detail.action?docID=646564

67. Keane, T. M., Marshall, R. D., & Sloan, D. M. (2009). Post-traumatic stress disorder: Definition, prevalence, and risk factors. In J. Ledoux, T. M. Keane, & P. Shiromani (Eds.), *Post-traumatic stress disorder* (pp. 1–14). Humana Press. https://doi.org/10.1007/978-1-60327-329-9_1

68. Kim, N., Yun, M., Oh, Y. J., & Choi, H. J. (2018). Mind-altering with the gut: Modulation of the gut-brain axis with probiotics. *Journal of Microbiology, 56*(3), 172–182. https://link.springer.com/article/10.1007/s12275-018-8032-4

69. Kim, S., Thibodeau, R., & Jorgensen, R. S. (2011). Shame, guilt, and depressive symptoms: A meta-analytic review. *Psychological Bulletin, 137*(1), 68–96. https://psycnet.apa.org/doi/10.1037/a0021466
70. Kinser, P. A., Goehler, L. E., & Taylor, A. G. (2012). How might yoga help depression? A neurobiological perspective. *Explore, 8*(2), 118–126. https://www.sciencedirect.com/science/article/abs/pii/S1550830711003429
71. Krause, E. D., Mendelson, T., & Lynch, T. R. (2003). Childhood emotional invalidation and adult psychological distress: The mediating role of emotional inhibition. *Child Abuse & Neglect, 27*(2), 199–213. https://www.sciencedirect.com/science/article/abs/pii/S0145213402005367
72. Krumholz, C. (2016). *Therapeutic benefits of canine-assisted therapy* (Doctoral dissertation). Alliant International University.
73. Lavin, C., Melis, C., Mikulan, E., Gelormini, C., Huepe, D., & Ibáñez, A. (2013). The anterior cingulate cortex: An integrative hub for human socially-driven interactions. *Frontiers in Neuroscience, 7*, Article 64. https://www.frontiersin.org/articles/10.3389/fnins.2013.00064/full
74. LeDoux, J. (2012). Rethinking the emotional brain. *Neuron, 73*(4), 653–676. https://www.sciencedirect.com/science/article/pii/S0896627312001298
75. LeDoux, J. E. (1993). Emotional memory systems in the brain. *Behavioural Brain Research, 58*(1–2), 69–79. https://www.sciencedirect.com/science/article/abs/pii/0166432893900914
76. Lee, K., & Ashton, M. C. (2012). *The H factor of personality: Why some people are manipulative, self-entitled, materialistic, and exploitive—and why it matters for everyone*. Wilfrid Laurier University Press. https://muse.jhu.edu/book/47623
77. Lee, K., & Ashton, M. C. (2020). HEXACO model of personality. In P. A. Hanton & G. T. Tennen (Eds.), *The Wiley encyclopedia of personality and individual differences* (pp. 249–256). Wiley. https://onlinelibrary.wiley.com/doi/10.1002/9781119547143.ch42
78. Lewis, H. B. (1971). Shame and guilt in neurosis. *Psychoanalytic Review, 58*(3), 419–438. https://www.proquest.com/docview/1310161519
79. Lin, E. T. S. (2020). Gene-environment interactions and role of epigenetics in anxiety disorders. In Y. K. Kim (Ed.), *Anxiety disorders* (pp. 71–85). Springer. https://doi.org/10.1007/978-981-32-9705-0_6
80. Liu, H., Ren, H., Remme, R. P., Nong, H., & Sui, C. (2021). The effect of urban nature exposure on mental health—A case study of Guangzhou. *Journal of Cleaner Production, 304*, Article 127100. https://www.sciencedirect.com/science/article/pii/S0959652621013196
81. Liu, W., Ge, T., Leng, Y., Pan, Z., Fan, J., Yang, W., & Cui, R. (2017). The role of neural plasticity in depression: From hippocampus to prefrontal cortex. *Neural Plasticity, 2017*, Article 6871089. https://onlinelibrary.wiley.com/doi/full/10.1155/2017/6871089
82. Liu, Y., Wang, H., Gui, S., Zeng, B., Pu, J., Zheng, P., Zeng, L., Luo, Y., Wu, Y., Zhou, C., Song, J., Ji, P., Wei, H., & Xie, P. (2021). Proteomics

analysis of the gut–brain axis in a gut microbiota-dysbiosis model of depression. *Translational Psychiatry, 11*(1), 568. https://www.nature.com/articles/s41398-021-01689-w
83. Loveday, C. (2016). *The brain: What it does, how it works & how it affects behaviour*. Carlton Publishing Group.
84. Lu, B., Nagappan, G., & Lu, Y. (2014). BDNF and synaptic plasticity, cognitive function, and dysfunction. In G. R. Lewin & B. D. Carter (Eds.), *Neurotrophic factors* (pp. 223–250). Springer. https://link.springer.com/chapter/10.1007/978-3-642-45106-5_9
85. Lyons, M. (2019). Introduction to the Dark Triad. In M. Lyons (Ed.), *The Dark Triad of Personality* (pp. 1–18). Academic Press. https://www.sciencedirect.com/science/article/abs/pii/B9780128142912000012
86. MacLean, P. (2019). *A triune concept of the brain and behaviour*. University of Toronto Press. https://muse.jhu.edu/book/108319
87. Macy, R. J., Jones, E., Graham, L. M., & Roach, L. (2015). Yoga for trauma and related mental health problems: A meta-review with clinical and service recommendations. *Trauma, Violence, & Abuse, 19*(1), 35–57. https://www.jstor.org/stable/27010960
88. Marin, M.-F., Raymond, C., & Lupien, S. J. (2019). Memory and stress. In G. Fink (Ed.), *Stress: Physiology, biochemistry, and pathology* (pp. 137–157). Academic Press. https://www.sciencedirect.com/science/article/abs/pii/B9780128131466000060
89. McCormick, R. (2017). Does access to green space impact the mental well-being of children: A systematic review. *Journal of Pediatric Nursing, 37*, 3–7. https://www.sciencedirect.com/science/article/pii/S0882596317301859
90. McEwen, B. S. (2019). Resilience of the brain and body. In G. Fink (Ed.), *Stress: Physiology, biochemistry, and pathology* (pp. 25–46). Academic Press. https://www.sciencedirect.com/science/article/abs/pii/B9780128131466000023
91. McEwen, B. S., Bowles, N. P., Gray, J. D., Hill, M. N., Hunter, R. G., Karatsoreos, I. N., & Nasca, C. (2015). Mechanisms of stress in the brain. *Nature Neuroscience, 18*(10), 1353–1363. https://www.nature.com/articles/nn.4086
92. McEwen, B. S., Gray, J., & Nasca, C. (2015). Recognizing resilience: Learning from the effects of stress on the brain. *Neurobiology of Stress, 1*, 1–11. https://pmc.ncbi.nlm.nih.gov/articles/PMC4260341/
93. Meyer, J., & Schuch, F. B. (2018). Exercise for the prevention and treatment of depression. In B. Stubbs & S. Rosenbaum (Eds.), *Exercise-based interventions for mental illness* (pp. 5–20). Academic Press. https://www.sciencedirect.com/science/article/abs/pii/B9780128126059000010
94. Mittelmark, M. B., & Bauer, G. F. (2017). The meanings of salutogenesis. In M. B. Mittelmark et al. (Eds.), *The handbook of salutogenesis* (pp. 7–13). Springer. https://link.springer.com/chapter/10.1007/978-3-319-04600-6_2

References

95. Moretto, U., & Palagini, L. (2019). Sleep in major depression. In H. C. Dringenberg (Ed.), *Handbook of behavioral neuroscience* (Vol. 28, pp. 683–696). Academic Press. https://www.sciencedirect.com/science/article/abs/pii/B9780128137437000463
96. Muir, J., & Bagot, R. C. (2019). Optogenetics: Illuminating the neural circuits of depression. In J. Quevedo, A. F. Carvalho, & C. A. Zarate (Eds.), *Neurobiology of depression* (pp. 267–278). Academic Press. https://www.sciencedirect.com/science/article/abs/pii/B9780128133330000147
97. Murata, C., & Kondo, K. (2020). Depression. In K. Kondo (Ed.), *Social determinants of health in non-communicable diseases: Case studies from Japan* (pp. 119–135). Springer. https://link.springer.com/book/10.1007/978-981-15-1831-7
98. Musazzi, L., Treccani, G., Mallei, A., & Popoli, M. (2013). The action of antidepressants on the glutamate system: Regulation of glutamate release and glutamate receptors. *Biological Psychiatry, 73*(12), 1180–1188. https://www.sciencedirect.com/science/article/pii/S0006322312009900
99. Myers, Z. (2020). Our nature in/of the city. In Z. Myers (Ed.), *Wildness and wellbeing: Nature, neuroscience, and urban design* (pp. 1–20). Springer. https://link.springer.com/chapter/10.1007/978-981-32-9923-8_1
100. Naveen, G. H., Varambally, S., Thirthalli, J., Rao, M., Christopher, R., & Gangadhar, B. N. (2016). Serum cortisol and BDNF in patients with major depression—effect of yoga. *International Review of Psychiatry, 28*(3), 273–278. https://www.tandfonline.com/doi/full/10.1080/09540261.2016.1175419
101. Park, B. J., Tsunetsugu, Y., Kasetani, T., Kagawa, T., & Miyazaki, Y. (2009). The physiological effects of Shinrin-Yoku (taking in the forest atmosphere or forest bathing): Evidence from field experiments in 24 forests across Japan. *Environmental Health and Preventive Medicine, 15*(1), 18–26. https://link.springer.com/article/10.1007/s12199-009-0086-9
102. Park, S. C., & Kim, Y. K. (2021). Challenges and strategies for current classifications of depressive disorders: Proposal for future diagnostic standards. In Y. K. Kim (Ed.), *Major depressive disorder: Rethinking and understanding recent discoveries* (pp. 93–111). Springer. https://link.springer.com/chapter/10.1007/978-981-33-6044-0_7
103. Parker, G. (2019). The role of environmental and psychosocial factors in depression. In J. Quevedo, A. F. Carvalho, & C. A. Zarate (Eds.), *Neurobiology of depression* (pp. 19–36). Academic Press. https://www.sciencedirect.com/science/article/pii/B9780128133330000020
104. Perkins, A. (2019). Toxic stress in children. *Nursing Made Incredibly Easy, 17*(2), 42–49. https://oce.ovid.com/article/00152258-201903000-00008/HTML
105. Picton, C., Fernandez, R., Moxham, L., & Patterson, C. (2019). Experiences of outdoor nature-based therapeutic recreation programs for persons with

a mental illness: A qualitative systematic review protocol. *JBI Database of Systematic Reviews and Implementation Reports, 17*(12), 2517–2524. https://oce.ovid.com/article/01938924-201912000-00009/HTML

106. Plöger, S., Stumpff, F., Penner, G. B., Schulzke, J. D., Gäbel, G., Martens, H., Shen, Z., Günzel, D., & Aschenbach, J. R. (2012). Microbial butyrate and its role for barrier function in the gastrointestinal tract. *Annals of the New York Academy of Sciences, 1258*(1), 52–59. https://nyaspubs.onlinelibrary.wiley.com/doi/full/10.1111/j.1749-6632.2012.06553.x

107. Poojara, L., Acharya, D. K., Patel, J., & Rawal, R. M. (2022). Gut-brain axis: Role of the gut microbiome on human health. In R. Z. Sayyed & M. Khan (Eds.), *Microbiome-gut-brain axis: Implications on health* (pp. 175–198). Springer. https://link.springer.com/chapter/10.1007/978-981-16-1626-6_8

108. Ports, K. A., Ford, D. C., Merrick, M. T., & Guinn, A. S. (2020). ACEs: Definitions, measurement, and prevalence. In G. J. G. Asmundson & T. O. Afifi (Eds.), *Adverse childhood experiences* (pp. 15–29). Academic Press. https://www.sciencedirect.com/science/article/pii/B9780128160657000021

109. Queensland Brain Institute. (n.d.). Queensland Brain Institute. Retrieved February 5, 2020, from https://qbi.uq.edu.au/

110. Rachman, S. J. (2020). *Anxiety* (4th ed.). Psychology Press. https://www.taylorfrancis.com/books/mono/10.4324/9780429458958/anxiety-stanley-rachman

111. Réus, G. Z., Generoso, J. S., Rodrigues, A. L. S., & Quevedo, J. (2019). Intracellular signaling pathways implicated in the pathophysiology of depression. In J. Quevedo, A. F. Carvalho, & C. A. Zarate (Eds.), *Neurobiology of Depression* (pp. 147–163). Academic Press. https://www.sciencedirect.com/science/article/pii/B978012813333000010X

112. Rhee, S. H., Pothoulakis, C., & Mayer, E. A. (2009). Principles and clinical implications of the brain–gut–enteric microbiota axis. *Nature Reviews Gastroenterology & Hepatology, 6*(5), 306–314. https://www.nature.com/articles/nrgastro.2009.35

113. Rudzki, L., & Maes, M. (2020). The microbiota–gut–immune–glia (MGIG) axis in major depression. *Molecular Neurobiology, 57*(10), 4269–4295. https://link.springer.com/article/10.1007/s12035-020-01961-y

114. Saladin, K. (2020). *Human Anatomy* (3rd international ed.). McGraw-Hill. https://ebookcentral.proquest.com/lib/uql/detail.action?docID=6212611

115. Samtiya, M., Dhewa, T., & Puniya, A. K. (2022). Probiotic mechanism to modulate the gut-brain axis (GBA). In R. Z. Sayyed & M. Khan (Eds.), *Microbiome–Gut–Brain Axis: Implications on Health* (pp. 199–220). Springer. https://link.springer.com/chapter/10.1007/978-981-16-1626-6_10

116. Sapolsky, R. (2015a). Anxiety, hostility, repression, and reward. In *Stress and Your Body* [Video lecture]. Kanopy Streaming. https://www.kanopy.com/en/product/148095?vp=uq

117. Sapolsky, R. (2015b). Stress and the biology of depression. In *Stress and Your Body* [Video lecture]. Kanopy Streaming. https://www.kanopy.com/en/product/148091?vp=uq
118. Sapolsky, R. (2015c). Stress and the psychology of depression. In *Stress and Your Body* [Video lecture]. Kanopy Streaming. https://www.kanopy.com/en/product/148093?vp=uq
119. Sapolsky, R. (2015d). Stress, judgment, and impulse control. In *Stress and Your Body* [Video lecture]. Kanopy Streaming. https://www.kanopy.com/en/product/148081?vp=uq
120. Sapolsky, R. M. (2001). Depression, antidepressants, and the shrinking hippocampus. *Proceedings of the National Academy of Sciences of the United States of America, 98*(22), 12320–12322. https://www.jstor.org/stable/3056897
121. Sarkissian, M., Trent, N. L., Huchting, K., & Singh Khalsa, S. B. (2018). Effects of a Kundalini yoga program on elementary and middle school students' stress, affect, and resilience. *Journal of Developmental & Behavioral Pediatrics, 39*(3), 210–216. https://oce.ovid.com/article/00004703-201804000-00004/HTML
122. Sevinc, G., Gurvit, H., & Spreng, R. N. (2017). Salience network engagement with the detection of morally laden information. *Social Cognitive and Affective Neuroscience, 12*(7), 1118–1127. https://academic.oup.com/scan/article/12/7/1118/3064491
123. Shalev, A. Y., & Bremner, D. J. (2016). *Posttraumatic stress disorder: From neurobiology to clinical presentation*. Wiley Online Library. https://onlinelibrary.wiley.com/doi/book/10.1002/9781118356142
124. Sheffler, J. L., Stanley, I., & Sachs-Ericsson, N. (2020). ACEs and mental health outcomes. In G. J. G. Asmundson & T. O. Afifi (Eds.), *Adverse Childhood Experiences* (pp. 51–66). Academic Press. https://www.sciencedirect.com/science/article/pii/B9780128160657000045
125. Shen, L. (2018). The evolution of shame and guilt. *PLOS ONE, 13*(7), e0199448. https://journals.plos.org/plosone/article?id=10.1371/journal.pone.0199448
126. Signal, T., Taylor, N., Botros, H., Prentice, K., & Lazarus, K. (2013). Whispering to horses: Childhood sexual abuse, depression and the efficacy of equine facilitated therapy. *Sexual Abuse in Australia and New Zealand, 5*(1), 24–32. https://search.informit.org/doi/abs/10.3316/informit.395058812631232
127. Simpson, C. A., Diaz-Arteche, C., Eliby, D., Schwartz, O. S., Simmons, J. G., & Cowan, C. S. M. (2021). The gut microbiota in anxiety and depression—A systematic review. *Clinical Psychology Review, 83*, 101943. https://www.sciencedirect.com/science/article/pii/S0272735820301318
128. Simpson, C. A., Schwartz, O. S., & Simmons, J. G. (2020). The human gut microbiota and depression: Widely reviewed, yet poorly understood.

Journal of Affective Disorders, 274, 73–75. https://www.sciencedirect.com/science/article/pii/S0165032720307588

129. Sivashov, N. (2018). *The wonders of nature: Healing the soul through the natural world* (Master's thesis). Pacifica Graduate Institute. https://www.proquest.com/docview/2036824883

130. Song, J. L. (2011). *Thalamus: Anatomy, functions and disorders.* Hauppauge, NY: Nova Science Publishers. ISBN: 9781613241523

131. Spencer, R. L., & Bland, S. T. (2019). Hippocampus and hippocampal neurons. In G. Fink (Ed.), *Stress: Physiology, Biochemistry, and Pathology* (pp. 85–104). Academic Press. https://www.sciencedirect.com/science/article/pii/B9780128131466000059

132. Spohn, S. N., & Young, V. B. (2018). Gastrointestinal microbial ecology with perspectives on health and disease. In H. M. Said (Ed.), *Physiology of the Gastrointestinal Tract* (6th ed., pp. 795–808). Academic Press. https://www.sciencedirect.com/science/article/pii/B9780128099544000323

133. Stefanaki, C., Mastorakos, G., & Chrousos, G. P. (2021). Gut microbiome and mental stress-related disorders: The interplay of classic and microbial endocrinology. In M. Gazouli & G. Theodoropoulos (Eds.), *Gut Microbiome-Related Diseases and Therapies* (pp. 99–122). Springer. https://link.springer.com/chapter/10.1007/978-3-030-59642-2_7

134. Stiemsma, L. T., Nakamura, R. E., Nguyen, J. G., & Michels, K. B. (2020). Does consumption of fermented foods modify the human gut microbiota? *The Journal of Nutrition, 150*(8), 1680–1692. https://www.sciencedirect.com/science/article/pii/S0022316622022210

135. Stubbs, B., & Schuch, F. B. (2019). Physical activity and exercise as a treatment of depression: Evidence and neurobiological mechanism. In J. Quevedo, A. F. Carvalho, & C. A. Zarate (Eds.), *Neurobiology of Depression* (pp. 413–424). Academic Press. https://www.sciencedirect.com/science/article/pii/B9780128133330000263

136. Sullivan, G. (2014). Shame. In T. Teo (Ed.), *Encyclopedia of Critical Psychology* (pp. 1701–1704). Springer. https://link.springer.com/referenceworkentry/10.1007/978-1-4614-5583-7_283

137. Taft, C. T., Creech, S. K., & Murphy, C. M. (2017). Anger and aggression in PTSD. *Current Opinion in Psychology, 14,* 67–71. https://www.sciencedirect.com/science/article/pii/S2352250X16302147

138. Taillieu, T. L., Davila, I. G., & Struck, S. (2020). ACEs and violence in adulthood. In G. J. G. Asmundson & T. O. Afifi (Eds.), *Adverse Childhood Experiences* (pp. 119–133). Academic Press. https://www.sciencedirect.com/science/article/pii/B9780128160657000070

139. Taupin, P. (2008). *Hippocampus: Neurotransmission and plasticity in the nervous system.* Nova Science Publishers. https://ebookcentral.proquest.com/lib/uql/detail.action?docID=3018020

140. Thoreau, H. D. (1854). *Walden; or, Life in the Woods.* Boston: Ticknor and Fields.

141. Van Der Kolk, B. A., McFarlane, A. C., & Weisaeth, L. (1996). *Traumatic stress: The effects of overwhelming experience on mind, body, and society*. Guilford Publications. https://ebookcentral.proquest.com/lib/uql/detail.action?docID=330594
142. Van Der Kolk, B. (2015). *The Body Keeps the Score: Brain, Mind, and Body in the Healing of Trauma*. Penguin Books.
143. Vig, K. D., Paluszek, M. M., & Asmundson, G. J. G. (2020). ACEs and physical health outcomes. In G. J. G. Asmundson & T. O. Afifi (Eds.), *Adverse Childhood Experiences* (pp. 95–117). Academic Press. https://www.sciencedirect.com/science/article/pii/B9780128160657000057
144. Warber, S. L., Dehudy, A. A., Bialko, M. F., Marselle, M. R., & Irvine, K. N. (2015). Addressing nature-deficit disorder: A mixed methods pilot study of young adults attending a wilderness camp. *Evidence-Based Complementary and Alternative Medicine, 2015*, 1–8. https://www.proquest.com/docview/1751964954
145. Ward, R., Brady, A., Jazdzewski, R., & Yalch, M. (2021). Stress, resilience, and coping. In R. K. Pradhan & U. Kumar (Eds.), *Emotion, Well-Being, and Resilience: Theoretical Perspectives and Practical Applications* (pp. 17–34). Apple Academic Press. https://www.taylorfrancis.com/chapters/edit/10.1201/9781003057802-2/stress-resilience-coping-rachel-ward-abbie-brady-rebekah-jazdzewski-matthew-yalch
146. Wekerle, C., Hébert, M., Daigneault, I., Fortin-Langelier, E., & Smith, S. (2020). ACEs, sexual violence, and sexual health. In G. J. G. Asmundson & T. O. Afifi (Eds.), *Adverse Childhood Experiences* (pp. 135–152). Academic Press. https://www.sciencedirect.com/science/article/pii/B9780128160657000069
147. Williams, F. (2016). *This Is Your Brain on Nature*. National Geographic Partners.
148. Won, E., Ham, B. J., & Kim, Y. K. (2018). Imaging genetics studies on susceptibility genes for major depressive disorder: Present and future. In Y. K. Kim (Ed.), *Understanding Depression* (pp. 191–214). Springer.
149. Yang, Y., & Raine, A. (2009). Prefrontal structural and functional brain imaging findings in antisocial, violent, and psychopathic individuals: A meta-analysis. *Psychiatry Research: Neuroimaging, 174*(2), 81–88. https://www.sciencedirect.com/science/article/pii/S0925492709000882
150. Young, E. (2012). Gut instincts: The secrets of your second brain. *New Scientist, 216*(2892), 38–42.

Index

A

Aaron Antonovsky 231
accelerated aging 56
Adrenaline 25, 72
Adverse childhood experiences 27, 67, 127, 134, 137, 251, 258
Adverse Childhood Experiences 54, 126, 127, 243, 259, 260, 261
alexithymia 29, 204
amygdala 19, 20, 26, 41, 44, 45, 64, 72, 85, 87, 88, 92, 250
amygdalae 73, 76, 87, 88, 89
Andrew Solomon 50
anhedonia 47, 48, 60, 114, 246
Animal-Assisted Therapy 212
antidepressant medications 59, 190, 191
anxiety 5, 6, 7, 8, 17, 18, 19, 20, 21, 22, 23, 25, 27, 29, 30, 31, 35, 36, 38, 39, 40, 41, 42, 43, 44, 45, 46, 49, 52, 54, 55, 56, 61, 68, 85, 87, 88, 89, 90, 96, 99, 100, 101, 103, 105, 106, 107, 112, 113, 121, 123, 124, 128, 129, 130, 133, 157, 174, 176, 179, 180, 181, 183, 184, 185, 186, 187, 191, 192, 193, 194, 195, 196, 197, 199, 202, 203, 204, 205, 206, 208, 210, 214, 215, 216, 218, 220, 221, 228, 247, 248, 251, 252, 253, 255, 258, 259
asthma 20, 23, 55, 62, 131, 246
attention-deficit/hyperactivity disorder 185
autonomic nervous system 69, 72, 97

B

BDNF 55, 56, 61, 91, 194, 198, 200, 208, 246, 249, 256, 257
Bessel van der Kolk 205

brain 5, 6, 8, 9, 18, 19, 20, 21, 22, 23, 25, 26, 27, 28, 29, 31, 32, 33, 35, 37, 39, 41, 44, 45, 46, 48, 49, 51, 55, 56, 57, 61, 62, 64, 65, 67, 68, 69, 70, 72, 73, 75, 76, 77, 78, 79, 80, 81, 82, 83, 84, 85, 86, 87, 88, 89, 90, 91, 92, 96, 97, 98, 99, 102, 103, 105, 106, 109, 112, 113, 115, 120, 121, 122, 123, 127, 130, 131, 132, 134, 135, 137, 179, 180, 182, 186, 188, 189, 194, 195, 198, 209, 239, 246, 247, 248, 249, 250, 251, 252, 254, 255, 256, 258, 261
Brain-derived neurotrophic factor 55, 246, 250
brainstem 78, 79, 84, 85, 86, 87, 88, 89
Brené Brown 115, 116, 125
butyrate 101, 102, 107, 253, 258

C

Canine-Assisted Psychotherapy 213
cerebral cortex 83, 86
cognitive behavioural therapy 37, 216
Compassionate Mind Training 119
cortisol 25, 55, 61, 62, 73, 74, 76, 87, 88, 89, 91, 99, 112, 115, 179, 181, 183, 186, 187, 194, 200, 206, 208, 210, 211, 214, 216, 246, 257

D

dementia 191, 192, 215, 252
depression 5, 6, 7, 8, 10, 17, 18, 19, 20, 21, 22, 23, 25, 27, 31, 35, 39, 43, 46, 47, 48, 49, 50, 51, 52, 53, 54, 55, 56, 57, 58, 59, 60, 61, 68, 84, 85, 88, 89, 90, 96, 99, 100, 103, 104, 105, 106, 107, 112, 113, 114, 115, 120, 121, 122, 123, 124, 125, 127, 129, 130, 132, 133, 148, 159, 172, 174, 175,

176, 179, 180, 181, 182, 185, 186, 187, 189, 190, 191, 192, 193, 194, 196, 197, 199, 200, 202, 204, 205, 208, 209, 214, 216, 218, 219, 222, 228, 237, 248, 249, 251, 252, 253, 254, 255, 256, 257, 258, 259, 260
Diagnostic and Statistical Manual of Mental Disorders 7, 18, 50, 134, 146
DNA 60, 129, 130, 247
dopamine 57, 58, 59, 61, 80, 85, 183, 194, 203, 210
Dr. Lucy Hone 230
Dr. Mark Cross 44
Dr. Nadine Burke 131
Dr. Robert Sapolsky 7
Dr. Viktor E. Frankl 156
dysbiosis 96, 98, 99, 100, 103, 105, 106, 256

E

emotional abuse 66, 127, 128, 137, 141, 143, 144, 158
emotional blackmail 155, 229
endocrine system 69, 70, 73, 76
Enmeshment 153, 159
enteric nervous system 97, 105, 106
Equine-Facilitated Therapy 247
exercise 45, 56, 59, 69, 81, 130, 131, 181, 184, 188, 189, 190, 191, 192, 193, 194, 195, 196, 197, 198, 199, 200, 202, 239, 252, 260

F

feline-assisted therapy 213
fight, flight, or freeze 68
forest bathing 179, 187, 253, 257
frontal cortex 61, 84, 89, 92, 93, 248

G

gaslighting 28, 141, 144, 170, 171
glial cells 84, 90
glutamate 58, 60, 80, 257

gratitude 123, 125, 183
grief 3, 8, 9, 49, 54, 101, 116, 121, 161, 170, 172, 173, 174, 175, 176, 230, 231, 254
gut-brain axis 96, 98, 105, 106, 249, 252, 254, 258

H

Hallie Sheade 217
Haydie Osborne 206, 263
heart disease 9, 18, 20, 23, 59, 104, 105, 131, 134, 226
HEXACO 151, 255
high blood pressure 20, 23, 98
hippocampus 19, 20, 26, 41, 45, 81, 85, 86, 87, 90, 92, 188, 247, 255, 259
homeostasis 64, 70, 75, 78, 96
hormones 20, 25, 26, 45, 54, 64, 73, 76, 86, 88, 89, 92, 121, 128, 186, 246
HPA (hypothalamic-pituitary-adrenal) Axis 74
Huntington's disease 56
hypervigilance 20, 41, 42, 46, 52, 64, 87, 115, 217
hypothalamus 19, 41, 69, 70, 72, 73, 74, 75, 76, 85, 86, 92, 208, 247, 248, 250

I

inflammation 62, 99, 100, 102, 104, 106, 107, 133, 135, 137, 200, 226
insomnia 5, 31, 39, 41, 46, 180, 181, 192, 247, 252
invalidation 28, 64, 108, 111, 113, 119, 253, 255

J

James Clear 225, 226
Jess Hill 118, 150
Jim Rohn 234
Judith Herman 149

K

Kerri Speyers 228
Kundalini 207, 208, 209, 259
Kundalini yoga 207, 208, 259

L

limbic system 19, 23, 26, 44, 48, 61, 69, 75, 78, 79, 84, 85, 86, 88, 89, 92, 121, 127, 247
Logotherapy 157

M

Machiavellianism 152, 159, 248
major depressive disorder 6, 28, 37, 48, 50, 53, 56, 60, 61, 190, 192, 193, 194, 211, 248, 252, 254, 261
manipulation 9, 111, 140, 141, 142, 143, 144, 150, 152, 154, 155, 158, 170, 171
Markus Parks 225
microbiome 97, 98, 99, 105, 106, 249, 252, 258, 260
microbiota 96, 97, 98, 99, 100, 101, 103, 105, 106, 107, 251, 252, 253, 254, 256, 258, 259, 260
mindfulness 45, 56, 59, 82, 183, 185, 186, 187, 199, 204, 205, 206, 207, 210, 211
MRI 19, 51, 77, 84, 132, 137
multiple sclerosis 9, 20, 55, 56, 91, 98, 131, 133
myelin 83, 84, 90, 91

N

narcissism 152, 159, 171, 176
nature 8, 33, 121, 125, 141, 157, 174, 177, 179, 181, 182, 183, 184, 185, 186, 198, 199, 217, 218, 222, 251, 253, 255, 256, 257, 258, 260, 261
neocortex 78, 79, 88, 89, 92
nervous system 30, 33, 45, 69, 70, 71, 72, 75, 84, 86, 92, 97, 105, 106, 134, 183, 203, 210, 250, 260
Neurodevelopmental disorders 134
neurogenesis 81, 87, 90, 250
neurons 55, 56, 70, 72, 77, 80, 81, 83, 84, 87, 91, 92, 96, 97, 105, 188, 209, 247, 260
neuroplasticity 61, 81, 82, 249
neurotransmitters 57, 58, 59, 61, 79, 80, 85, 183, 194, 203, 210
NLP (neuro-linguistic programming) 174, 175
noradrenaline 25, 57, 58, 59, 60, 61, 72, 74, 76, 80, 85, 87, 88, 210

O

obesity 56, 100, 104, 128, 248
oligodendrocytes 84, 90

P

parasympathetic nervous system 33, 72, 203, 210
Parkinson's disease 35, 56, 98, 103, 191, 192
PET (positron emission tomography) 77
pituitary gland 69, 76, 85, 86, 92, 248
post-traumatic stress disorder 5, 6, 17, 23, 88
prebiotics 102, 103, 107
pre-frontal cortex 61, 248
probiotics 102, 103, 107, 254
Professor Avshalom Caspi 53
Professor Paul Raymond Gilbert 119
Projection 144, 159
psychological trauma 6, 7, 9, 21, 43, 63, 66, 67, 82, 87, 105, 109, 111, 113, 116, 148, 221, 238, 239
psychomotor retardation 48, 248
psychopathy 152
psychotherapy 34, 56, 216, 217, 219, 253, 254

Q

Queensland Brain Institute 71, 80, 258

R

resilience 6, 7, 8, 9, 21, 29, 32, 36, 65, 66, 67, 82, 91, 101, 108, 111, 115, 116, 118, 119, 120, 121, 122, 123, 124, 125, 140, 146, 158, 161, 177, 183, 186, 189, 207, 208, 210, 222, 225, 229, 230, 231, 232, 233, 235, 238, 256, 259, 261

S

salutogenesis 231, 232, 256
(sympathetic–adrenal–medulla system) 72, 73, 74, 76
schizophrenia 17, 23, 56, 61, 98, 128, 130, 172, 191, 192, 252
serotonin 53, 57, 58, 59, 60, 61, 80, 85, 183, 203, 210
shame 5, 8, 20, 21, 25, 29, 30, 32, 35, 37, 42, 49, 64, 88, 101, 108, 109, 111, 113, 114, 115, 116, 117, 119, 120, 124, 125, 128, 136, 139, 142, 146, 156, 158, 169, 225, 228, 252, 254, 259

Shinrin-yoku 179, 253
stress response 25, 26, 64, 67, 69, 70, 72, 74, 75, 76, 89, 115, 127, 130, 132, 134, 194, 251
suicide 9, 59, 114, 127, 129, 165, 242, 249
sympathetic nervous system 72, 75, 203
synapse 58, 80, 247
synbiotics 103, 252

T

thalamus 69, 79, 85, 86, 88, 92, 248
thyroid 54, 253
Tomohide Akiyama 179
toxic personalities 28, 118, 139, 140, 143, 158
treatment-resistant depression 57, 59
Trøndelag Health Study 193
type 2 diabetes 20

Y

yoga 45, 56, 190, 192, 195, 196, 201, 202, 203, 204, 205, 206, 207, 208, 209, 210, 211, 222, 254, 255, 257, 259, 264

Acknowledgements

To all my family and friends who encouraged and supported me in writing this book, thank you:

To my husband, Ross, for standing by my side for four decades, even while carrying your own pain. Our journey has faced many challenges, but we share the path and will continue to walk it together. Your love and support have made this book possible.

To my amazing sons, Stuart, Brad, and Matt, you are the lights in my darkest moments, my strength when I had little, and joy when I felt despair. I tried to shield you from harm, and I hope my love for you has broken the trauma we faced. To your wonderful partners, Fitz, Jess, and Harriet, thank you for loving my boys.

To my parents, Reg and June Pike, thanks for always being the soft place for me to land, and for your unconditional love. And to my siblings, Julie and John, and your spouses, Kerry and Liesl, and all your children, thank you for the gift of family.

To Drew, Philippa, Iain, Monique, Jane, and Kevin, and my wonderful nieces and nephews, may our shared pain heal, and reconciliation become our goal.

To Andrea, my funny, courageous, dedicated, loving and generous friend, may the years ahead bring you peace and happiness. Thank you for your fierce loyalty and unwavering support.

To Bonnie, a beacon of light and goodness in an often-cruel world. Your kindness and generosity are second-to-none. So glad you have Ben back in your life.

To Estelle, for your loyalty, love, and support, and for reading chapters and offering endless advice when I felt discouraged, despite your own challenges with finalising your PhD. Our tea times are precious to me. Special thanks to Cat and Gert for allowing me to be a part of Oliver's life. And to Oliver, for being such a joy.

To Haydie Osborne, thank you for generously offering your time and knowledge to speak with me about trauma-related yoga. And for your kindness.

To Janet, my quiet and gentle friend, who exemplifies courage in the face of adversity. You inspire me with your positivity and ease—a safe and kind friend.

To Jolanta, my artistic, creative, and inspiring friend, who fills me with joy and encourages connection with others through art. Your work is exquisite.

To Judy, my childhood friend, who has been a steadfast, courageous, and loyal confidante, and has helped me through some of my darkest times. Life is wonderful with you and your loving family.

To Karen, one of the most positive women I know. Despite battling breast cancer 3 times, you lift the spirits of all those around you. Thanks for the laughter and tears we have shared.

To Kathy S, one of the kindest, warmest, most generous women I know. Thanks for your friendship over many years.

To Kathy W, who lights up any room with your joyfulness, and exemplifies kindness, generosity, inclusiveness, and fun. It's wonderful to have you in my life.

To Ken, my childhood friend, it was great to reconnect with you after so many years and to fall into the easy banter and friendship we always shared. Thanks for your ongoing support and for believing in me.

To Kerri, my life-saver, who opened her arms and her heart to me when I broke. Thanks for being the stitches that mended my soul. And for your enduring friendship.

To Kylie, for your inspiration and brilliant conversation, and for encouraging me to read chapters while walking on your treadmill during our gym sessions. I love your candour and your brilliance.

To Nathalie, who came to stay for 3 nights, and stayed for 3 months. We love you and hope to see you and your beautiful family when you visit Australia.

To Philippa, who showed me that I was not crazy, for your support and kindness.

To Rachel, your illustrations for my book are extraordinary and have captured the emotions I hoped to portray. You are not only talented but also a beautiful soul.

To Robyn, for the many hours we spent drinking tea while you worked through my chapters, offering advice and guidance, and encouraging me that my book was worth writing. Your friendship and support have been a godsend.

To Stevie, you are the proof that survival is possible, and life can be wonderful, thanks to your quiet determination, immense courage, and gentle strength. Your quirky sense of humour is contagious, and your love is immense. Keep shining, my gorgeous friend.

To Russ Wright, for generously giving of your time and explaining the wonderful benefits of virtual reality.

To my many other friends and kind neighbours who don't hurt others and who make the world a better place, thank you.

And finally, to the dogs in my life who have given me love and devotion: Ellie, Susie, Jess, Leo, Ruby, Toby, Ginny, and Miki.